AT SEA UNDER
IMPRESSMENT

ALSO BY JEAN CHOATE

*Disputed Ground: Farm Groups That Opposed
the New Deal Agricultural Program*
(McFarland, 2002)

AT SEA UNDER IMPRESSMENT

*Accounts of Involuntary Service
Aboard Navy and Pirate
Vessels, 1700–1820*

Edited by Jean Choate

McFarland & Company, Inc., Publishers
Jefferson, North Carolina, and London

Selections from *The Nagle Journal* by John C. Dann © 1988 by
John C. Dann, used by permission of Grove/Atlantic, Inc.

Selections from *James Durand, an Able Seaman of 1812*, by James R.
Durand, edited by George Sprague Brooks (New Haven, CT:
Yale University Press, 1926), used by permission.

LIBRARY OF CONGRESS CATALOGUING-IN-PUBLICATION DATA

At sea under impressment : accounts of involuntary service aboard
  navy and pirate vessels, 1700–1820 / edited by Jean Choate.
      p.   cm.
  Includes bibliographical references and index.

  ISBN 978-0-7864-4374-1
  softcover : 50# alkaline paper ∞

  1. Sailors — United States — Biography. 2. Sailors — Great
Britain — Biography. 3. Impressment — History — 18th century.
4. Impressment — History — 19th century. 5. United States —
History, Naval — 18th century. 6. United States — History,
Naval — 19th century. 7. Great Britain — History, Naval — 18th
century.   8. Great Britain — History, Naval — 19th century.
9. Pirates — History. 10. Seafaring life — History.   I. Choate,
Jean.
  HD8039.S42U6125   2010
  387.5092'241— dc22   2010013728

British Library cataloguing data are available

©2010 Jean Choate. All rights reserved

*No part of this book may be reproduced or transmitted in any form
or by any means, electronic or mechanical, including photocopying
or recording, or by any information storage and retrieval system,
without permission in writing from the publisher.*

Front cover: *Nelson's Flagships at Anchor*, by Nicholas Pocock
(National Maritime Museum, Greenwich, London)

Manufactured in the United States of America

McFarland & Company, Inc., Publishers
  Box 611, Jefferson, North Carolina 28640
       www.mcfarlandpub.com

Contents

Preface 1
Introduction 3

Part I: Impressed

1 — John Newton 17
2 — Joshua Davis 44
3 — Joshua Penny 50
4 — Pirates! 80
5 — John Stradley 92
6 — Jacob Nagle 97
7 — Joseph Bates 104
8 — Dartmoor Prison 126
9 — Stephen Cabot 139
10 — James R. Durand 148
11 — Thomas Urquhart 161

Part II: Afterward

12 — William Molyneux Afterward 169
13 — John Newton Afterward 171
14 — Joseph Bates Afterward 174

Contents

15 — Jacob Nagle Afterward 181
16 — Joshua Penny Afterward 184

Conclusion 198
Chapter Notes 203
Bibliography 209
Index 211

Preface

I would like to dedicate this book to my ancestor William Molyneux, who was impressed by the British. Although he had no experience as a seaman (he was a weaver from a small village inland), he was taken against his will in the early 1790s. With no chance to say good-bye to his family, he was marched in a group to Liverpool, where he was eventually placed onboard ship. He served on a British warship until the ship anchored in Chesapeake Bay.

One night while the ship was at anchor, William had his chance. Determined to make an escape, he slipped away and swam for his freedom. He reached land and found that he had come to Pennsylvania. He avoided Philadelphia because he feared that he might be caught and returned to the ship by press gangs that operated in the city. So he joined a group going up the Susquehanna River.

Farther up the river, he served for a time in a surveying crew and recognized the great potential of the Appalachian mountains of Pennsylvania. One of the first to settle in Sullivan County, he built a cabin, cleared land to farm and started a sawmill. Two years later he returned to England to find that his wife and infant son had died. He brought his other children back to America, narrowly escaping a second attempt at impressment. This impressment experience changed his life and the lives of his descendents.

Apparently, William never wrote an account of his impressment experiences or if he did, it has disappeared. But others did write accounts, many of which are collected here. Every attempt has been made to present the accounts as written. Corrections were made only superficially; double quotes were changed to single where context demanded it, for example.

Preface

I wish to thank the librarians and archivists at the Massachusetts Historical Society, Charleston Historical Society, Savannah Historical Society and the National Maritime Museum in London for their assistance in searching out and making available these impressment accounts. I also wish to thank Heather Tibbets Brown and Duressa Pujat the College of Coastal Georgia in Brunswick, Georgia, for their assistance with many library requests. And most of all I wish to thank my husband, Woody Choate, whose help and encouragement were two of the most important things in my life.

Introduction

Impressment of sailors and able-bodied landsmen in time of war was an old English practice. The process went like this: the King signed a letter calling for the forced service of sailors into his navy. Then, naval officers were placed in command of a press gang. Often the officer was assigned an area to operate in and then given orders to find men for his gang. The men who served on the press gang were usually strong, unemployed men who did not mind participating in a fight. One newspaper of the time described a member of a press gang as a "profligate and abandoned wretch, perpetually lounging about the streets and incessantly vomiting out oaths and horrid curses."[1] The purpose was generally to find men with shipboard experience, but in times of emergency landsmen were also taken. They were caught by the press gang and held on land or in a ship close by until they were transported to a naval vessel that needed additions to its crew. The impressed men had no choice in the matter and often had no way of getting word back to their friends or families as to their fate.

The practice greatly increased when the British became involved in wars with France during Napoleon's reign. The British navy had nearly 1,000 ships, and manning them required approximately 150,000 officers and men. After years of war, the British were desperate for more men and sought them through impressments of their merchant sailors, landsmen, and, increasingly, of sailors of other nations, including the United States.

Complicating the matter was the fact that U.S. citizens also spoke English and thus captains of English ships could often claim that they were indeed British citizens. Even though Americans might carry protections in the form of certificates of citizenship, in many instances, these were disregarded. Some historians have estimated that there were 300

Introduction

Americans in the 1,000 men onboard Admiral Nelson's flagship, HMS *Victory*, at Trafalgar.[2] N.A.M. Roger estimates that between one-third and two-thirds of a ship's crew were impressed men.[3]

Americans had long resented the British claim of the right of impressment. In 1747, fifty British sailors deserted the HMS *Lark* while it was docked in Boston. The *Lark*'s captain ordered the area around the docks to be searched. If the deserters were not found, the crew was instructed to find and impress Americans to take their place. But a crowd of Boston men gathered to rescue the impressed men. In 1769, John Adams defended four American sailors accused of killing a British officer who had boarded an American ship intent on impressing them into the British navy. Adams was able to secure their acquittal on the grounds that they were acting in self-defense.[4] Apparently, these were not the first or only times Americans had shown their resentment of impressments before the American Revolution.[5]

Following the Revolution, in 1798, a British officer boarded the USS *Baltimore* off the coast of Havana and impressed fifty-five seamen. The American president at the time, John Adams, was greatly disturbed when he learned of the incident. He dismissed Isaac Phillips, the captain of the American ship from which the impressed men had been taken, from the United States Navy without a trial or even a hearing.[6]

The U.S. secretary of state, Thomas Pickering, then wrote a note to the British minister, Robert Liston: "[I]mpossible, Sir, for the American Government to imagine that this outrage can be the consequence of any orders from His Britannic Majesty; and equally impossible for the United States quietly to bear the repetition of insults and injuries, of this kind: The President of the United States has therefore directed that all attempts to commit them be resisted." The note proceeds to state that orders had been issued to U.S. naval officers to resist British efforts at impressment.[7]

A month after Captain Phillips' dismissal from the U.S. Navy, another ship, the USS *Ganges*, was boarded by a British officer with the intention of retrieving any British deserters and examining the protections of American sailors. However, the captain of the ship, Captain Tingley, replied, "A Public Ship carries no protection but her flag. I do not expect to succeed in a contest with you, but I will die at my quarters before a man shall be taken from the ship." The crew, it is reported, gave three cheers and hurried to quarters in preparation for a fight. In consequence, the report of the incident states, the British officers, "hearing of our determination chose rather to leave ... than to fight for dead men."[8]

The return of Jonathan Robbins in 1799 to the British engendered strong emotions. Even when it was proved that he was a British subject whose real name was Thomas Nash, his subsequent execution as a mutineer angered Americans.

In 1806, negotiations between the U.S. ministers Monroe and Pinkney and the British commissioners Lord Auckland and Lord Holland were begun concerning many matters, including the British practice of impressments. When the four first met, the Americans followed their own instructions and demanded the abandonment of impressments not only on the ocean but also on shore; in return they said that the United States would undertake to return British sailors to the British authorities. The question of impressments on land did not receive much attention because the British had stopped impressing men in American ports by this time. No one seems to have questioned the practice of impressments in British ports and the subject of impressments in neutral ports was still undecided. When Lord Holland reported to Lord Grenville concerning the discussions he did not mention ports. He said that the "main points are not impressing seamen on the high seas and the question of a continuous or interrupted voyage."[9]

In the first progress report submitted to Lord Howick, the new foreign secretary, these points are also mentioned: "Impressing: Our present practice is to impress British seamen on board American ships within our own jurisdiction and upon the high Seas, but not within the jurisdiction of the United States, or of any neutral port." Unfortunately, the last part of the statement was not true, since British ships had occasionally impressed Americans in neutral ports. But possibly the practice of some captains of the navy did not represent the official policy of the British government.

The document continues:

> They are also ready to adopt regulations in our favor for the recovery of our Seamen within the limits of their own jurisdiction, and to give us the full benefit of the laws which Congress has enacted for the prevention and punishment of deserters in their own Navy. But they insist in our giving up the practice of impressing Seamen on board American vessels on the high Seas, where they contend we have no municipal jurisdiction, and where the exercise of this power leads to acts of outrage and violence, which have

raised a clamour against us throughout all America. It must be confessed that this is a question of equal difficulty and importance. If it were admitted that our Sea faring people might transport themselves with impunity to the American Service, our homeward bound fleets would return being manned by foreigners at the commencement of every War, and our Navy might be confined to Port for want of hands. On the other hand it is the evident Duty of the United States to protect their lawful Trade from interruption and outrage, and their citizens from being compelled to fight the battles of a foreign Power.[10]

Around this time, the British commissioners decided to ask the British Admiralty two questions: One, how many British seamen were serving aboard American ships, and two, how many American seamen were serving aboard British ships? The British Lords of the Admiralty answered that they could not find the answer to how many British seamen were on American ships from any documents they had in Great Britain. As to how many Americans were serving on British ships, they replied that "to answer this it will be necessary to examine the Books of every Ship in His Majesty's Service; which will require a considerable time and be attended with other inconveniences."

The commissioners then proposed a draft of an article in which Britain would abandon the practice of impressments on the high seas for a limited period. This would be accompanied by stricter regulations concerning the hiring of seamen of other nationalities and penalties for the shipmasters who did so. They also tentatively affirmed the British right of visit on the high seas. The American commissioners answered that they would accept the stricter regulations concerning hiring, but were opposed to any right of search on the high seas.

This sounded very favorable to the American position. But in the weeks following this draft, the British officials changed their attitude. The British decided that they could not give up their legal right to reclaim British citizens on the high seas. The opinion now held by the commissioners was that the high seas were extraterritorial and merchant ships sailing on the high seas could not protect British subjects from being reclaimed for service on British ships. The document further stated that there had been "no recent cases of complaint" and promised the greatest moderation and discretion in the exercise of the right in the future.[11]

The British consuls stationed in the United States sent their opin-

Introduction

ions. Thomas Barclay, the British consul in New York, wrote the following: "The wast [*sic*] of Seamen in the British Navy is well known, nor is this a matter of more notoriety, than that the British Navy is the sole remaining obstacle between the Emperor of France and universal domination.... Under these Circumstances, the American Government ought rather to wink at casual improper impressments, than to complain without cause and only to require the discharge of the Individual when his case was made evident."[12]

Then in 1807 another incident occurred. The USS *Chesapeake* under the command of Commodore Barron sailed out from Norfolk Roads. This was her first voyage since she had been repaired and refitted in harbor. As she passed Lynnhaven Bay, a British ship, the *Leopard*, left the British squadron and followed the *Chesapeake* out to sea. When both ships were about ten miles out, the *Leopard* signaled "Dispatches." The commander of the *Chesapeake* thought the British captain wished the *Chesapeake* to

Captain P.B.V Brooke commanding His Majesty's ship Shannon, *boarding the American frigate* Chesapeake (Library of Congress, Washington, D.C.).

Introduction

carry mail to Europe. This was a common courtesy of the time. So the American ship waited for the British to send someone aboard with the mail. Instead, the dispatches proved to be an order from the British admiral to search for and remove deserters. Commodore Barron refused and said the only deserters aboard were three Americans formerly impressed and he would not permit a search. He did not know that also onboard his ship was a British deserter, Jenkins Ratford, who was sailing under the assumed name of John Wilson.[13]

The British officer returned to his ship and eight minutes later the British began firing on the *Chesapeake*. Because they had just left home port after refitting, Commodore Barron's ship was not prepared for battle; many of the ship's supplies had not been stored away and the decks were littered with them. In addition, few of her guns were ready. After suffering twenty-one casualties, the *Chesapeake* lowered its flag. British officers then came on board and mustered the crew. The three Americans and Ratford were found and taken off the *Chesapeake*. The disabled *Chesapeake* then slowly returned to Norfolk. When news of this insult to the American flag spread in the United States, there was a great expression of anger. In Norfolk, Virginia, several thousand mourners attended the funeral of Robert McDonald, a sailor who had died as a result of wounds received onboard the *Chesapeake* in its one-sided battle with the *Leopard*. Three Americans had died that day and eighteen others had been wounded. Norfolk and nearby Portsmouth residents requested that all citizens wear crepe for ten days to honor the Americans who had died on the *Chesapeake*.

The incident aroused strong feelings across America. Americans regarded it as a national insult perpetrated by a Great Britain still unwilling to accord the country the rights of an independent nation. Norfolk residents destroyed casks of water intended for the British ship HMS *Melampus*. At a meeting in Williamsburg citizens pledged "our lives, our fortunes and our sacred honour to support our government." Another meeting of citizens in Washington, D.C., declared that "no sacrifice is too great to maintain our independence, national honor and character." A mass meeting was held in Boston to rally citizens behind the government. Another meeting was held in Philadelphia. Some of the residents in Philadelphia sawed the rudder off a British merchant ship and displayed it in front of the home of the British consul. Militia units began preparing themselves for war and President Jefferson ordered British naval ships to

Introduction

leave American waters.¹⁴ Jefferson wrote, "Never since the Battle of Lexington have I seen this country in such a state of exasperation as at present and even that did not produce such unanimity."¹⁵

Opinion concerning the American commodore James Barron was very critical. It embarrassed Americans that the *Chesapeake* had been so poorly prepared to oppose the British show of force. Barron was called before a naval court and suspended from service for five years. Following his sentencing he struggled to find employment. Officers and men from aboard the *Chesapeake* felt compelled to defend their honor in several duels following the incident.

Public opinion did not seem to focus on the four men taken off the *Chesapeake* by the British. Martin, from Westport, Massachusetts, was an African American; Ware, from Maryland, was an "Indian looking man"; while Strachan was a white man, also from Maryland. Ratliff was not an American. The four men were court-martialed in Halifax, Nova Scotia, and the three Americans were sentenced to 500 lashes, but their sentences were remitted. Ratford — the Englishman who had prevented a fellow deserter from rejoining the navy, proclaiming "they were in the land of liberty," and made a "contemptuous gesture" before a British officer — was sentenced to death and executed aboard the *Halifax*.¹⁶

President Jefferson wanted the practice of impressments stopped. He wanted the return of the three American sailors impressed from the *Chesapeake*. He also requested reparations to the families of the dead and injured crewmen and the removal of the British admiral who had commanded the ships that engaged in the attack and impressments.¹⁷ The British foreign minister, George Canning, was willing to return the impressed sailors and pay reparations, but he refused to stop impressments.

Following the president's order requiring British warships to leave U.S. territorial waters, the British ordered a more vigorous impressment of British subjects from neutral vessels. Frustrated, Jefferson sought to use economic pressure to force Great Britain and France to respect the neutral rights of the U.S. He sent a message to Congress encouraging the passage of an embargo. The bill was passed in December of 1807. The bill prohibited all U.S. vessels from leaving for foreign ports. There was much opposition to the Embargo Act, especially from the areas where shipping was very important (New England, New York, etc.). John Adams thought the embargo was a catastrophe, although his son John Quincy Adams, then in Congress, supported it. John Quincy Adams called it a "worthy experiment."[18] The president agreed to a revision, the Non-Importation Act, which reopened trade with neutral nations and promised to open trade with either Great Britain or France if they would cease violating neutral rights.

Napoleon seized upon this to have his foreign minister indicate to the United States that they had indeed ceased their violation of neutral rights. Members of Congress reacted to growing public anger over British violations of U.S. neutrality. A congressional committee on foreign relations remarked that the plight of impressed sailors was not always the main interest: "the cries of their wives and children in the privation of protectors and parents, have of late been drowned in the louder clamors at the loss of property."

The Portland newspaper, *Eastern Argus*, denounced "Man Stealing," saying that the British were "not content with robbing us at sea, they infest our coast, they molest our vessels at the entrance of our harbors, and drag from them our citizens who are merely passing from one port to another."[19]

John Diggio was a young apprentice shipwright who was traveling with his master aboard the merchant ship *Spitfire* between Portland and New York. The *Spitfire* was stopped off the coast of New York by HMS *Guerriere*. The British seized Diggio despite the pleas of Diggio's master and refused to relinquish him. When the matter was reported in the *New York Evening Post,* the editor commented, "What has it come to this, that the Americans must have written protections to enable them to sail along their own shores."[20] Diggio was released and returned home to tell of other Americans who were impressed on the *Guerriere*.

David Otis, the master of the brig *Charles Miller*, was appalled when his ship was stopped and Benjamin Rogers, a sailor, and Henry Brooks, a steward, were impressed. Otis wrote a letter to the newspaper warning that "man stealers" were operating off the American coast.[21]

Jonah Spock reported the capture and impressment of his fifteen-year-old son, James, in the spring of 1811. The writer of the *Essex Register*, of Salem commented: "When we record the stealing of one American from on board one of our vessels, two from another, four from another, and so on without number, whose names to us are not familiar and with whose characters we are not particularly acquainted, then our sensibilities are not excited in so great a degree as when the case is brought home to us — when

Introduction

it becomes our irksome task to stain our annals with the atrocious conduct of the British robbers stealing from our citizens and neighbors their children yet in the state of infancy and forcing them to board their floating dungeons to assist in robbing their brethren."[22]

The issue of impressment was very much on the minds of Americans. What was life like for the men who experienced it? Of course, many of those who were impressed could not read or write, so their stories have not been preserved. But some men did escape from British warships or prisons and wrote about it. The following chapters contain some of the accounts of impressed men. In many of these cases, those men led very difficult lives and made daring escapes.

The remembrance of the attack on the *Chesapeake* still rankled. And when the USS *President* fired on an unidentified ship which turned out to be a smaller British sloop, the *Little Belt*, Americans loved it. The captain of the *President* said that the *Little Belt* fired first. But this was not the account given by the captain of the *Little Belt* as they limped into Nova Scotia with thirteen dead and nineteen wounded. He said the Americans had fired first.

In American newspapers the incident was played up as a heroic feat. The commodore of the *President* was serenaded in New York. The local newspaper described it as "a token of respect for his spirited protection of the honor of his country flag on the late recontre with the USS *Little Belt*."[23]

Another paper, the *Centinel of Freedom,* praised the captain's use of his ship's guns: "He used them — and the result is no Barron expedition — no half way business — but such as reflects the highest honor on our flag, and it is a very tolerable offset to the *Chesapeake* affair."[24] Reluctantly, President Madison sent a war message to Congress, asking them to declare war on Great Britain. He gave Congress a list of four grievances: Illegal impressments, illegal blockades, refusal to recognize rights of neutrality and support of Indian attacks on American settlements in the West. Congress voted for war.

James Durand, who was being held against his will on a British ship during this time, relates his experiences: "All of us that were Americans impressed into the British Service were notoriously insulted and abused by the British officers and men. Often we were brought to the lash, so that they could vent their damnable fury upon us. 'You damned Yankee,' the

INTRODUCTION

Captain would say to me, 'We'll soon have all your ships in our ports and all your damned countrymen as our prisoners.'"25

But the first news that was received was that the USS *Constitution* had defeated the British ship *Guerriere*, and his angry captors "increased their ill usage of us."

After a time, the Americans aboard ship heard that American seamen impressed into the British navy were to give themselves up as prisoners of war and be sent to Dartmoor Prison. Since there were a great number (approximately 80) of impressed Americans aboard Durand's ship, they decided to select a spokesman and ask the captain to turn them over as prisoners of war. They went to the captain and he shouted at the spokesman: "Do you call yourself a Yankee, you damned Scotch rascal?" The captain knocked him down the ladder to the other deck, a distance of about eight feet. When the man recovered himself he offered to show his protection to the captain to prove that he was indeed an American citizen. But the captain refused to see it.26

The First Shot of the War of 1812, Clyde O. Deland, 1909 (Library of Congress, Washington, D.C.).

Introduction

After this, many of the impressed sailors were retained, including Durand, while others were sent away to Dartmoor Prison. As for other impressed men whose accounts will be told, Joshua Penny, who had escaped from impressment and returned home, was actively involved in the American navy during the War of 1812. Thomas Jervey also escaped and returned home to Charleston; after his homecoming he became a shipmaster and sailed from that city to various ports. He married and his first wife died of consumption only a few months after the wedding. He married a second time to the daughter of the Dutch governor of Aruba, Curacoa and Bonaire. During the War of 1812 Jervey was chosen to command a privateer schooner, the *Saucy Jack*. The ship had been built, and was owned, by the city of Charleston. Jervey and his crew were able to capture several British ships and bring them in to Charleston. He then left the *Saucy Jack* to become captain of a gunboat.[27]

American land forces did not do well in the War of 1812. Peace commissioners met in Ghent in 1814 and agreed on terms to end the war; the agreement said nothing about impressment. But with the defeat of Napoleon, the British did not need so many men in their navy and impressments became less of an issue.

Part I
Impressed

Chapter 1

John Newton

As this is a book about impressments, one would expect that Newton's recollections would include a more vivid description of the manner of his impressment. However, he only mentions it and then goes on to describe some of his experiences. Others will describe their first encounter with the press gang more graphically.

John Newton's father was a ship captain and John as a young man made several voyages on merchant ships. He also traveled in England and met and fell in love with a young woman, although his father did not approve. After one of his voyages, on returning home to England, he was caught by the press gang and impressed. In later years he wrote a series of letters to a fellow cleric telling about his life, including his impressment experience. His account follows.

"I was impressed, (owing entirely to my own thoughtless conduct, which was all of a piece), and put on board a tender; it was at a critical juncture, when the French fleets were hovering upon our coast, so that my father was incapable to procure my release. In a few days I was sent on board the Harwich man of war at the Nore; I entered here upon quite a new scene of life and endured much hardship for about a month. My father was then willing that I should remain in the navy, as a war was daily expected, and procured me a recommendation to the Captain, who took me upon the quarter-deck as a midshipman. I now had an easy life as to externals, and might have gained respect, but my mind was unsettled, and my behaviour was indifferent. I here met with companions, who completed the ruin of my principles, and though I affected to talk of virtue, and was not so outwardly abandoned as afterwards, yet my delight and habitual practice was wickedness. My chief intimate was a person of

PART I : IMPRESSED

exceeding good natural talents, and much observation: he was the greatest master of what is called the *free-thinking scheme* I remember to have met with, and knew how to insinuate his sentiments in the most plausible way—And his zeal was equal to his address; he could hardly had laboured more to the cause, if he had expected to gain heaven by it. Allow me to add, while I think of it, that this man, whom I honored as my master, and whose practice I adopted so eagerly, perished in the same way as I expected to have done. I have been told that he was overtaken in a voyage from Lisbon with a violent storm; the vessel and people escaped, but a great sea broke on board, and swept him into eternity—Thus the Lord spares or punishes according to his sovereign pleasure; But to return—I was fond of his company, and having myself a smattering of books, was eager enough to shew my reading. He soon perceived my case, that I had not wholly broke through the restraints of conscience, and therefore did not shock me at first with too broad intimations of his design; he rather as I thought spoke favorably of my religion; but when he had gained my confidence, he began to speak plainer; and perceiving my ignorant attachment to the *Characteristics*, he joined issue with me upon that book, and convinced me, that I had never understood it. In a word he so plied me with objections and arguments, that my depraved heart was soon gained, and I entered into his plan with all my spirit. Thus, like an unwary sailor who quits his port just before a rising storm, I renounced the hopes and comforts of the gospel at the very time when every other comfort was about to fail me.

"In December 1744 the Harwich was in the Downs, bound to the East Indies. The Captain gave me liberty to go on shore for a day; but without consulting prudence or regarding consequences, I took horse, and following the dictates of my restless passion, I went to take a last leave of her I loved. I had little satisfaction in the interview, as I was sensible that I was taking pains to multiply my own troubles. The short time I could stay passed like a dream, and on New-year's day 1745 I took my leave to return to the ship. The Captain was prevailed on to excuse my absence, but this rash step (especially as it was not the first liberty of the kind I had taken) highly displeased him, and lost me his favour, which I never recovered.

"At length we sailed from Spithead with a very large fleet. We put into Torbay with a change of wind, but it returning fair again, we sailed

1. John Newton

the next day. Several of our fleet were lost in attempting to leave that place; but the following night the whole fleet was greatly endangered upon the coast of Cornwall, by a storm from the southward. The darkness of the night, and number of the vessels, occasioned much confusion and damage. Our ship, though several times in imminent danger of being run down by other vessels, escaped unhurt; but many suffered much, particularly the Admiral. This occasioned our putting back to Plymouth.

"While we lay at Plymouth I heard that my father, who had interest in some of the ships lately lost, was come down to Torbay. He had a connection at that time with the African company. I thought if I could get to him, he might easily introduce me into that service, which would be better than pursuing a long uncertain voyage to the East Indies. It was a maxim with me in those unhappy days never to deliberate; the thought hardly occurred to me, but I was resolved to leave the ship at all events, I did so, and in the wrongest manner possible. I was sent one day in the boat, to take care that none of the People defected, but I betrayed my trust and went off myself. I knew not what road to take and durst not ask, for fear of being suspecting; yet having some general idea of the country, I guessed right, and when I had traveled some miles, I found upon inquiry, that I was on the road to Dartmouth. All went smoothly that day, and part of the next; I walked apace, and expected to have been with my father in about two hours, when I was met by a small party of soldiers: I could not avoid or deceive them. They brought me back to Plymouth: I walked through the streets guarded like a felon — My heart was full of indignation, shame, and fear. — I was confined two days in the guardhouse, then sent on board my ship, kept in irons, then publicly stripped and whipped, after which I was degraded from my office, and all my former companions forbidden to shew me the least favour, or even to speak to me — As midshipman I had been entitled to some command, which (being sufficiently haughty and vain) I had not been backward to exert. — I was now in my turn brought down to a level with the lowest, and exposed to the insults of all.

"And as my present situation was uncomfortable, my future prospects were still worse; the evils I suffered were likely to grow heavier every day. While my catastrophe was recent, the officers, and my quondam brethren, were something disposed to screen me from ill usage; but during the little time I remained with them afterwards I found them cool very fast in

PART I : IMPRESSED

their endeavours to protect me. Indeed they could not avoid it, without running a great risk, of sharing with me; for the Captain, tho in general a humane man, who behaved very well to the ship's company, was almost implacable in his resentment when he had been greatly offended, and took several occasions to shew himself so to me, and the voyage was expected to be (as it proved) for five years. Yet I think nothing I either felt or feared distressed me so much as to see myself thus forcibly torn away from the object of my affections, under a great improbability of seeing her again, and a much greater of returning in such a manner as would give me hopes of seeing her mine. Thus I was miserable on all hands as could well be imagined. My breath was filled with the most excruciating passions, eager desire, bitter rage, and black despair.—Every hour exposed me to some new insult and hardship, with no hope of relief or mitigation; no friend to take my part or to listen to my complaint. Whether I looked inward or outward, I could perceive nothing but darkness and misery. I think no case, except that of a conscience hounded by the wrath of God, could be more dreadful than mine: I cannot express with what wishfulness and regret I cast my last looks upon the English shore; I kept my eyes fixed upon it, till the ship's distance increasing, it insensibly disappeared; and when I could see it no longer, I was tempted to throw myself into the sea which (according to the wicked system I had adopted) would put a period to all my sorrows at once. But the secret hand of God restrained me....[1]

"I now return to my voyage. During our passage to Madeiera I was a prey to the most gloomy thoughts. Though I had well deserved all I met with, and the Captain might have been justified if he had carried his resentment still farther; yet my pride at that time suggested that I had been grossly injured; and this so far wrought upon my wicked heart, that I actually formed designs against his life; and this was one reason that made me willing to prolong my own. I was sometimes divided between the two, not thinking it practicable to effect both. The Lord had now to appearance given me up to judicial hardness, I was capable of anything. I had not the least fear of God before my eyes, nor (so far as I remember) the least sensibility of conscience. I was possessed of so strong a spirit of delusion that I believed my own lie, and was firmly persuaded, that after death I should cease to be,—Yet the Lord preserved me!—Some intervals of sober reflection would at times take place; when I had chosen death rather than life, a ray of hope would come in, (though there was little probability for

1. John Newton

such a hope), that I would yet see better days; that I might return to England, and have my wishes crowned, if I did not willfully throw myself away. In a word my love to [his sweetheart] was now the only restraint I had left. Though I neither feared God nor regarded men, I could not bear that she should think meanly of me when I was dead. As in the outward concerns of life, the weakest means are often employed by divine Providence to produce great effects, beyond their common influence, (as when a disease, for instance, has been removed by a fright), so I found it then; this single thought, which had not restrained me from a thousand smaller evils, proved my only and effectual barrier against the greatest and most fatal temptations. How long I could have supported this conflict, or what, humanly speaking would have been the consequence of my continuing in that situation, I cannot say; but the Lord, whom I little thought of, knew my danger, and was providing for my deliverance.

"Two things I had determined when at Plymouth, that I would not go to India, and that I would go to Guinea; and such indeed was the Lord's will concerning me, but they were to be accomplished in His way, not my own. We had now been at Madeira some time; the business of the fleet was completed, and were to sail the following day. On that memorable morning I was late in bed, and had slept longer, but that one of the midshipmen (an old companion) came down, and between jest and earnest bid me rise; and as I did not immediately comply, he cut down the hammock or bed in which I lay, which forced me to dress myself. I was angry, but durst not resent it. I was little aware how much his caprice affected me, and that this person, who had no design in what he did, was the messenger of God's providence. I said little, but went upon deck, where I that moment saw a man putting his cloaths into a boat, who told me, he was going to leave us. Upon inquiring, I was informed that two men from a Guinea ship, which lay near us, had entered on board the Harwich, and that the Commodore (the present Sir George Pocock), He ordered the Captain to send two others in their room. My heart instantly burned like fire.—I begged the boat might be detained a few minutes, I ran to the Lieutenants, and intreated them to intercede with the Captain that I might be dismissed upon this occasion. Though I had been formerly upon ill terms with these officers, and had disobliged them all in their turns, yet they pitied my case, and were ready to serve me now. The Captain, who when we were at Plymouth had refused to exchange me, though at the

Part I : Impressed

request of Admiral Medley, was now easily prevailed on. I believe, in little more than half an hour from my being asleep in my bed, I saw myself discharged, and safe on board another ship. This was one of the many critical turns of my life, in which the Lord was pleased to display his providence and care, by causing many unexpected circumstances to concur in almost an instant of time. These sudden opportunities were several times repeated; each of them brought me into an entire new scene of action, and they were usually delayed almost the last moment in which they could have taken place.

"The ship I went on board was bound to Sierra Leon, and the adjacent parts of what is called the *windward coast of Africa*. The commander, I found, was acquainted with my father; he received me very kindly, and made fair professions of assistance; and I believe would have been my friend: but without taking the least advantage of former mistakes I pursued the same course; nay, if possible, I acted much worse. On board the Harwich, though my principles were totally corrupted, yet, as upon my first going there I was in some degree staid and serious, the remembrance of this made me ashamed of breaking out in that notorious manner I could otherwise have indulged. But now entering amongst strangers, I could appear without disguise, and I well remember, that while I was passing from one ship to the other, this was one reason why I rejoiced in the exchange, and one reflection I made upon the occasion, viz. That I now might be as abandoned 'as I pleased, without any controul'; and from this time I was exceedingly vile indeed, little if anything short of that animated description of an almost irrecoverable state, which we have in *2 Peter* ii, 14. I not only sinned with a high hand myself, but made it my study to tempt and seduce others upon every occasion; nay I eagerly sought occasion, sometimes to my own hazard and hurt. One natural consequence of this carriage was, a loss of the favour of my new Captain; not that he was at all religious; or disliked my wickedness any further than it affected his interest, but I became careless and disobedient; I did not please him, because I did not intend it; and as he was a man of an odd temper likewise, we the more easily disagreed. Besides, I had a little of that unlucky wit, which do little more than multiply troubles and enemies to its possessor; and, upon some imagined affront, I made a song, in which I ridiculed his ship, his designs, and his person and soon taught it to the whole ship's company. Such was the ungrateful return I made for his offers

1. John Newton

of friendship and protection. I had mentioned no names, but the allusion was plain, and he was no stranger either to the intention of the author.— I shall say no more of this part of my story; let it be buried in eternal silence — But let me not be silent from the praise of that grace which could pardon, that blood which could expiate, such sins as mine: Yea the Ethiopian may change his skin, and the 'leopard his spots,' since I, who was the willing slave of every evil, possessed with a legion of unclean spirits, have been spared, and saved, and changed to stand as a monument of his almighty power for ever.

"Thus I went on for about six months, by which time the ship was preparing to leave the coast. A few days before she sailed the Captain died. I was not upon much better terms with his mate, who now succeeded to the command, and had, upon some occasion, treated me ill. I made no doubt but if I went with him to the West Indies, he would put me on board a man of war; and this, from what I had known already, was more dreadful to me than death. To avoid it, I determined to remain in Africa, and amused myself with many golden dreams, that here I should find an opportunity of improving my fortune.

"There are still upon that part of the coast a few white men settled, (and there were many more at the time I was first there, whose business it was to purchase slaves, etc. in the rivers and country adjacent, and sell them to the ships at an advanced price). One of these, who at first landed in my indigent circumstances, had acquired considerable wealth; he had recently been in England, and was returning in the vessel I was in, of which he owned a quarter part. His example impressed me with hope of the same success; and upon conditions of entering into his service, I obtained my discharge. I had not the precaution to make any terms, but trusted to his generosity. I received no compensation for my time on board the ship but a bill upon the owners in England, which was never paid, for they failed before my return. The day the vessel sailed, I landed upon the island of Benanoes, with little more than the cloaths upon my back, as if I had escaped shipwreck....[2]

"There seems an important instruction, and of frequent use, in these words of our dear Lord, 'Mine hour is not yet come.' The two following years, of which I am now to give some account, will seem as an absolute blank in a very short life; but as the Lord's hour of grace was not yet come, I was to have a still deeper experience of the dreadful state of the heart of man when left to itself; I have seen frequent cause since to admire the mercy of the lord, in banishing me to those distant parts, and almost excluding me from human society, at a time when I was big with mischief, and like one infected with a pestilence, was capable of spreading a taint where ever I went. Had my affairs taken a different turn, had I succeeded in my designs, and remained in England, my sad story would probably have been worse. Worse in myself, indeed, I could have hardly been; but my wickedness would have had greater scope; I might have been very hurtful to others, and multiplied irreparable evils. But the Lord wisely placed me where I could do little harm. The few I had to converse with were too much like myself, and I was soon brought into such abject circumstances, that I was too low to have any influence, I was rather shunned and despised than imitated; there being few, even of the negroes themselves (during the first year of my residence among them) but thought themselves too good to speak to me. I was yet an 'outcast lying in my blood,' (Ezek. xvi.) and, to all appearances, expected to perish — But the Lord beheld me with mercy — he did not strike me to hell, as I justly deserved; 'he passed by me' when I was in my blood, and bid me 'live.' But the appointed time for the manifestation of his love, to cover all my iniquities with the robe of his righteousness, and to admit me to the privileges of his children, was not till long afterwards; yet even now he bid me live, and I can only ascribe it to his secret upholding power that what I suffered in at part of this interval, did not bereave me either of my life or senses; yet, as by these sufferings, the force of my evil examples and inclinations was lessened, I have reason to count them amongst my mercies.

"It may not, perhaps, be amiss to digress for a few lines, and give you a very brief sketch of the geography of the circuit I was now confined to, especially as I may have frequent occasion to refer to places I shall now mention; for my trade afterwards, when the Lord gave me to see better days, was chiefly to the same places and with the same persons, where and by whom I had been considered as upon a level with their meanest slaves. From Cape de Verd, the most western point of Africa, to Cape Mount, the whole coast is full of rivers; the principal are Gambia, Rio Grande, Sierra Leon, and Sherbro. Of the former, as it is well known, and I was never there, I need say nothing. The Rio Grande (like the Nile) divides into many branches near the sea. On the most northerly, called *Cacheo*, the Portuguese, have a settlement. The most southern branch, known by

1. John Newton

the name of *Rio Nuna*, is, or then was, the usual boundary of the white man's trade northward. Sierra Leon is a mountainous peninsula, uninhabited, and I believe inaccessible, on account of the thick woods, excepting those parts which ly near the water. The river is large and navigable. From hence, about twelve leagues to the south-east are three contiguous islands, called the *Benanoes*, about twenty miles in circuit: this was about the centre of the white men's residence. Seven leagues farther, the same way, ly the Plantanes, three small islands, two miles distant from the continent at the point, which form one side of the Sherbro. This river is more properly a *sound*, running with a long island, and receiving the confluence of several large rivers, '*rivers unknown to song*' but far more deeply engraven in my remembrance than the Po or Tyber. The southernmost of these has a very peculiar course, almost parallel to the coast; so that in tracing it a great many leagues upwards, it will seldom lead one above three miles, and sometimes not more than half a mile from the sea-shore. Indeed I know not but that all these rivers may have communications with each other, and with the sea in many places, which I have not remarked. If you cast your eyes upon a large map of Africa, while you are reading this, you will have a general idea of the country I was in; for though the maps are very incorrect, most of the places I have mentioned are inserted, and in the same order as I have named them.

"My new master had formerly resided near Cape Mount, but now he settled at the Plantanes, upon the largest of the three islands. It is a low sand island, about two miles in circumference, and almost covered with palm-trees. We immediately began to build a house, and to enter upon trade. I had now some desire to retrieve my lost time, and to exert diligence in what was before me; and he was a man with whom I might have lived tolerably well, if he had not been soon influenced against me; but he was much under the direction of a black woman, who lived with him as a wife. She was a person of some consequence in her own country, and he owed his first rise to her interest. This woman (I know not for what reason) was strangely prejudiced against me from the first; and what made it still worse for me, was a severe fit of illness, which attacked me very soon, before I had opportunity to shew what I could or would do in his service. I was sick when he sailed in a shallop to Rio Nuna, and he left me in her hands. At first I was taken some care of, but as I did not recover very soon, she grew weary, and entirely neglected me. I had sometimes not

Part I : Impressed

a little difficulty to procure a draught of cold water when burning with a fever. My bed was a mat spread upon a board or chest, and a log of wood my pillow. When my fever left me, and my appetite returned, I would gladly have eaten, but there was no one gave unto me. She lived in plenty herself, but hardly allowed me sufficient to sustain life, except now and then, when in the highest good humour, she would send me victuals in her own plate after she had dined; and this (so greatly was my pride humbled) I received with thanks and eagerness, as the most needy beggar does an alms. Once, I well remember, I was called to receive this bounty from her own hand, but being exceedingly weak and feeble, I dropped the plate. Those who live in plenty can hardly conceive how this loss touched me; but she had the cruelty to laugh at my disappointment; and tho the table was covered with dishes, (for she lived much in the European manner), she refused to give me any more. My distress has been at times so great, as to compel me to go by night, and pull up roots in the plantation (though at the risk of being punished as a thief), which I have eaten raw upon the spot, for fear of discovery/ the roots I speak of are very wholesome food, when boiled or roasted, but as unfit to be eaten raw in any quantity as a potatoe. The consequence of this diet, which, after the first experiment, I always expected and seldom missed, was the same as if I had taken *tartar emetio*; so that I have often returned as empty, as I went, yet necessity urged me to repeat the trial several times. I have sometimes been relieved by strangers, nay even by the slaves in the chain, who have secretly brought me victuals, (for they durst not be seen to do it), from their own slender pittance. Next to pressing want, nothing sits harder upon the mind than *scorn* and *contempt*; and of this likewise I had an abundant measure. When I was very slowly recovering, this woman would sometimes pay me a visit, not to pity or relieve, but to insult me. She would call me worthless and indolent and compel me to walk, which, when I could hardly do, she would set her attendants to mimic my motion, to clap their hands, laugh, throw limes at me; or, if they chose to throw stones (as I think was the case once or twice), they were not rebuked: but in general, though all who depended on her favour must join in her treatment, yet, when she was out of sight, I was rather pitied than scorned by the meanest of her slaves. At length my master returned from his voyage; I complained of ill usage, but he could not believe me; and as I did it in her hearing; I fared no better for it. But in his second voyage he took me with him. We did pretty well

1. John Newton

for a while, till a brother-trader he met in the river persuaded him that I was unfaithful, and stole his goods in the night, or when he was on shore. This was almost the only vice I could not be justly charged with: the only remains of a good education I could boast of was, what is commonly called *honesty*; and as far as he had intrusted me, I had always been true, and though my great distress might, in some measure, have excused it, I never once thought of defrauding him in the smallest matter. However, the charge was believed, and I condemned without evidence. From that time he likewise used me very hardly; whenever he left the vessel, I was locked upon deck, with a pint of rice for my day's allowance, and if he staid longer, I had no relief till his return. Indeed I believe I should have been nearly starved, but for the opportunity of catching fish sometimes. When fowls were killed for his own use, I seldom was allowed any part but the intrails to bait my hooks with; and at what we call *slack water*, that is, about the changing of the tides, when the current was still, I used generally to fish (for at other times, it was not practicable) and I very often succeeded. If I saw a fish upon my hook, my joy was little less than any other person may have found in the accomplishment of the scheme he had most at heart. Such a fish, hastily broiled, or rather half burnt, without sauce, salt, or bread, had afforded me a delicious meal. If I caught none, I might (if I could) sleep away my hunger till the next return of slack water, and then try again. Nor did I suffer less from the inclemency of the weather and the want of cloaths. The rainy season was now advancing: my whole suit was a shirt, a pair of trowsers a cotton handkerchief instead of a cap, and a cotton cloth, about two yards long to supply the want of upper garments; and thus accoutered I have been exposed for twenty, thirty, perhaps near forty hours together, in incessant rains, accompanied with strong gales of wind, without the least shelter, when my master was on shore. I feel to this day some faint returns of the violent pains I then contracted. The excessive cold and wet I endured in that voyage and so soon after I had recovered from a long sickness, quite broke my constitution and my spirits; the latter were soon restored, but the effects of the former still remain with me, as a needful memento of the service and wages of sin.

"In about two months we returned, and then the rest of the time I remained with him was chiefly spent at the Plantanes, under the same regimen as I have already mentioned. My haughty heart was now brought down, not to a wholesome repentance, not to the language of the prodigal; this was far from me; but my spirits were sunk; I lost all resolution, and almost all reflection. I had lost the fierceness which fired me on board the Harwich, and which made me capable of the most desperate attempts; but I was no further changed than a tyger tamed by hunger — remove the occasion, and he will be as wild as ever.

"One thing, though strange, is most true. Though destitute of food and cloathing, depressed to a degree beyond common wretchedness, I could sometimes collect my mind to mathematical studies. I had bought *Barrow's Euclid* at Plymouth; it was the only volume I brought on shore; it was always with me, and I used to take it to remote corners of the island by the sea-side, and draw my *diagrams* with a long stick upon the sand. Thus I often beguiled my sorrows, and almost forgot my feeling — and thus, without any other assistance, I made myself master in a good measure of the first six books of *Euclid*....[3]

"There is much piety and spirit in the grateful acknowledgment of Jacob, 'With my staff I passed this Jordan, and now I am become two bands.' They are words which ought to affect me with a peculiar emotion. I remember that some of those mournful days, to which my last letter refers, I was busied in planting some *lime* or *lemon trees*. The plants I put in the ground were no longer than a young gooseberry bush: my master and his mistress passing by the place, stopped a while to look at me; at last, 'Who knows,' says he, 'who knows but by the time these trees grow up and bear, you may go home to England, obtain the command of a ship, and return to reap the fruit of your labours, we see strange things sometimes happen.' This as he intended it, was a cutting sarcasm. I believe he thought it full as probable that I should live to be king of Poland; yet it proved a prediction, and they (one of them at least) lived to see me return from England, in the capacity he had mentioned, and pluck some of the first limes from those very trees. How can I proceed in my relation till I raise a monument to the divine goodness, by comparing the circumstances in which the Lord has since placed me, with what I was at that time! Had you seen me, Sir, then go so pensive and solitary, in the dead of night, to wash my one shirt upon the rocks, and afterwards put it on wet, that it might dry upon my back while I slept; had you seen so poor a figure, that when a ship's boat came to the island, shame often constrained me to hide my self in the woods from the sight of strangers; espe-

1. John Newton

cially had you known that my conduct, principles and heart, were still darker than my outward condition — how little would you have imagined that one, who so fully answered to the [Greek word meaning hateful and hating one another] of the apostle, was reserved to be so peculiar an instance of the providential care, and Exuberant goodness of God. There was at that time but one earnest desire in my heart, which was not contrary and shocking, both to religion and reason; that one desire, though my vile licentious life rendered me peculiarly unworthy of success, and though a thousand difficulties seemed to render it impossible, the Lord was pleased to gratify. But this favour, tho' great, and greatly prized, was a small thing compared to the blessings of his grace: he spared me to give me 'the knowledge of himself in the person of Jesus Christ'; in love to my soul, he delivered me from the pit of corruption, and cast all my aggravated sins behind his back. He brought my feet into the paths of peace. — this is indeed the chief article, but it is not the whole. When he made me acceptable to himself in the Beloved, he gave me favour in the sight of others. He raised me new friends, protected and guided me through a long series of dangers, and crowned every day with repeated mercies. To him, I owe it that I am still alive, and that I am not still living in hunger, and in thirst, and in nakedness, and the want of all things; into that state I brought myself, but it was He delivered me. He has given me an easy situation in life, some expericiental knowledge of his gospel, a large acquaintance amongst his people, a friendship and correspondence with several of his most honored servants — But it is as difficult to enumerate my present advantages, as it is fully to describe the evils and miseries of the preceding contrast.

"I know not exactly how long things continued with me thus, but I believe near a twelvemonth. In this interval I wrote two or three times to my father; I gave him an account of my condition, and desired his assistance; intimating, at that same time, that I had resolved not to return to England, unless he was pleased to send for me. I have likewise letters wrote by me to Mrs. N**** in that dismal period; so that at the lowest ebb It seems I still retained a hope of seeing her again. My father applied to his friend in Liverpoole, of whom I have spoken before, who gave orders accordingly to a Captain of his, who was then fitting out for Gambia and Sierra Leon.

"Some time within the year, as I have said, I obtained my master's

Part I : Impressed

consent to live with another trader, who dwelt upon the same island. Without his consent I could not be taken, and he was unwilling to do it sooner, but it was then brought about. This was an alteration much to my advantage; I was soon decently clothed, lived in plenty, was considered as a companion, and trusted with the care of all his domestic effects, which were to the amount of some thousand pounds. This man had several factories, and white servants in different places, particularly one in Kittam, the river I spoke of, which runs so near along the sea-coast. I was soon appointed to go there, where I had a share in the management of business jointly with another of his servants. We lived as we pleased, business flourished, and our employer was satisfied. Here I began to be wretch enough to think myself *happy*. There is a significant phrase frequently used in those parts, That such a white man is grown *black*. It does not intend an alteration of complexion, but disposition. I have known several who, settling in Africa after the age of thirty or forty, have, at that time of life, been gradually assimilated to the tempers, customs, and ceremonies of the natives, so far as to prefer that country to England; they have even become dupes to all the pretended charms, necromancies, amulets, and divinations of the blinded negroes, and put more trust in such things than the wiser sort among the natives. A part of this spirit of infatuation was growing upon me (in time perhaps I might have yielded to the whole); I entered into closer engagements with the inhabitants, and should have lived and died a wretch amongst them, if the Lord had not watched over me for good. Not that I had lost those ideas which chiefly engaged my heart to England, but despair of seeing them accomplished made me willing to remain where I was. I thought I could more easily bear the disappointment in this situation than nearer home. But so soon as I had fixed my connections and plans with these views, the Lord providentially interposed to break them into pieces, and save me from ruin in spite of myself.

"In the mean time, the ship that had orders to bring me home arrived at Sierra Leon: the Captain made inquiry for me there, and at the Benanoes; but understanding that I was at a great distance in the country, he thought no more about me. Without doubt the hand of God directed my being placed at Kittam just at this time; for as the ship came no nearer than the Benanoes, and staid but a few days, if I had been at the Plantanes I could not perhaps have heard of her till she had sailed. The same must have certainly been the event, had I been sent to any other factory,

1. John Newton

of which my new master had several upon different rivers. But though the place I was at was a long way up a river, much more than a hundred miles distance from the Plantantes, yet by the peculiar situation which I have already noticed, I was still within a mile of the seacoast. To make the interposition more remarkable, I was at that very juncture going in quest of trade, to a place at some distance from the sea, and should have set out a day or two before, but that we waited for a few articles from the next ship that offered, to complete the assortment of goods I was to take with me. We used sometimes to walk on the beach, in expectation of seeing a vessel pass by, but this was very precarious, as at that time the place was not at all resorted to by ships for trade. Many passed in the night, others kept at a considerable distance from the shore. In a word, I do not know that any one had stopped while I was there though some had before, upon observing a signal made from the shore. In February 1747, (I know not the exact day), my fellow servant walking down to the beach in the forenoon, saw a vessel sailing past, and made a smoke in token of trade. She was already a little beyond the place, and as the wind was fair, the Captain was in some demur whether to stop or not; however, had my companion been half an hour later, she would have gone beyond recall; but he soon saw her come to an anchor, and went on board in a canoe; and this proved the very ship I have spoken of. One of the first questions he was asked was concerning me, and when the Captain understood I was so near, he came on shore to deliver his message. Had an invitation from home reached me when I was sick and starving at the Plantanes, I should have received it as life from the dead; but now, for the reasons already given, I heard it at first with indifference. The Captain, unwilling to lose me, told me a story altogether of his own framing; he gave me a very plausible account how he had missed a large packet of letters and papers which he should have brought with him, but this, he said, he was sure of, having had it from my father's own mouth, as well as from his employer, that a person lately dead had left me 400£ *per annum*; adding further, that if I was in any way embarrassed in my circumstances, he had express orders to redeem me, though it should cost one half of his cargo. Every particular of this was false; nor could I myself believe what he said about the estate; but as I had some excitations from an aged relation, I thought a part of it might be true. But I was not long in suspense; for though my father's care and desire to free me had too little weight with me, and would

PART I : IMPRESSED

have been insufficient to make me quit my retreat, yet the remembrance of Mrs. N****, the hopes of seeing her, and the possibility that accepting this offer might once more put me in a way of gaining her hand, prevailed over all other considerations. The captain further promised, (and in this he kept his word), that I should lodge in his cabin, dine at his table, and be his constant companion, without expecting any service from me. And thus, I was suddenly freed from a captivity of about fifteen months. I had neither a thought nor a desire of this change one hour before it took place. I embarked with him, and in a few hours lost sight of Kittam.

"How much is their blindness to be pitied who can see nothing but chance in events of this sort! So blind and stupid was I at that time: I made no reflection, I sought no direction in what had happened; like a wave of the sea driven with the wind, and tossed, I was governed by appearances, and looked no farther. But He, who is eyes to the blind, was leading me in a way that I knew not.

"Now I am in some measure enlightened, I can easily perceive, that it is in the adjustment and concurrence of these seemingly fortuitous circumstances that the ruling power and wisdom of God is most evidently displayed in human affairs. How many such casual events may we remark in the history of Joseph, which had each a necessary influence on his ensuing promotion! If he had not dreamed, or if he had not told his dream;— if the Midianites had passed by a day sooner, or a day later, if they had sold him to any person but Potiphar; if his mistress had been a better woman; if Pharaoh's officers had not displeased their lord; of if any, or all these things had fell out in any other manner or time than they did, all that followed had been prevented; the promises and purposes of God concerning Israel, their bondage, deliverance, polity, and settlement, must have failed: and as all these things tended to and centered in CHRIST, the promised Saviour, the desire of all nations would not have appeared.[4]

"The ship I was now on board, as a passenger, was on a trading voyage for gold, ivory, dyers-wood, and bees wax. It requires much longer time to collect a cargo of this sort, than of slaves. The Captain began his trade at Gambia, had been already four or five months in Africa; and continued there a year, or thereabouts, after I was with him; in which time we ranged the whole coast as far as Cape Lopez, which lyes about a degree south of the Equinoctial, and more than a thousand miles farther from England than the place where I embarked. I have little to offer worthy of your

1. John Newton

notice in the course of this tedious voyage. I had no business to employ my thoughts, but sometimes amused myself with mathematics; excepting this, my whole life, when awake, was a course of most horrid impiety and profaneness. I know not that I have ever since met so daring a blasphemer; not content with common oaths and imprecations, I daily invented new ones; so that I was often seriously reproved by the Captain, who was himself a very passionate man, and not at all circumspect in his expressions. From the relation I at times made of my past adventures, and what he saw of my conduct, and especially towards the close of the voyage, when we met with many disasters, he would often tell me, that, to his great grief, he had a Jonah on board, that a curse attended me where-ever I went; and that all the troubles he met with in the voyage, were owing to his having taken me into the vessel. I shall omit any further particulars, and after mentioning an instance or two of the Lord's mercy to me, while I was thus defying his power and patience, I shall proceed to something more worthy of your perusal.

"Although I lived long in the excess of almost every other extravagance; I never was fond of drinking; and my father had often been heard to say, that while I avoided drunkenness, he should still entertain hopes of my recovery. But sometimes I would promote a drinking-bout, for a frolic sake, as I termed it; for though I did not love the liquor, I was bold to do iniquity, and delighted in mischief. The last abominable frolic of this sort I engaged in was in the river Gabon; the proposal and expence were my own. Four or five of us one evening sat down upon deck, to see who could hold out longest in drinking geneva and rum alternately; a large seashell supplied the place of a glass. I was very unfit for a challenge of this sort; for my head was always incapable of bearing much strong drink. However I began, and proposed the first toast, which I well remember was some imprecation against the person who should *start first*— This proved to be myself— my brain was soon fired — I arose, and danced about the deck like a madman; and while I was thus diverting my companions, my hat went overboard. By the light of the moon I saw the ship's boat, and eagerly threw myself over the side to get into her, that I might recover my hat. My sight in that circumstance deceived me; for the boat was not within my reach, as I thought, but perhaps twenty feet from the ship's side. I was, however, half over board, and should in one moment more have plunged myself into the water when somebody caught hold of my

PART I : IMPRESSED

cloaths behind, and pulled me back. This was an amazing escape; for I could not swim if I had been sober; the tide ran very strong; my companions were too much intoxicated to save me; and the rest of the ship's company were asleep. So near was I to appearance of perishing in that dreadful condition, and sinking into eternity under the weight of my own curse.

"Another time, at Cape Lopez, some of us had been in the woods, and shot a buffalo, or wild cow; we brought a part of it on board, and carefully marked the place (as I thought) where we left the remainder. In the evening we returned to fetch it, but we set out too late. I undertook to be the guide, but night coming on before we could reach the place, we lost our way.—Sometimes we were in swamps, up to the middle in water, and when we recovered dry land, we could not tell whether we were walking towards the ship, or wandering farther from her.—Every step increased our uncertainty.—The night grew darker, and we were entangled in inextricable woods, where perhaps the foot of man had never trod before him. That part of the country is entirely abandoned to wild beasts, with which it prodigiously abounds. We were indeed in a terrible case; having neither light, food, or arms, and expecting a tyger to rush from behind every tree. The stars were clouded, and we had no compass, to form a judgment which way we were going. Had things continued thus, we had probably perished; but it pleased God, no beast came near us; and after some hours perplexity the moon arose, and pointed out the eastern quarter. It appeared then, as we had expected, that instead of drawing nearer to the sea-side, we had been penetrating into the country; but by the guidance of the moon we at length came to the water-side, a considerable distance from the ship. We got safe on board, without any other inconvenience than what we suffered from fear and fatigue.

"Those, and many other deliverances, were all at that time entirely lost upon me. The admonitions of conscience, which, from successive repulses, had grown weaker and weaker, at length entirely ceased; and for a space of many months, if not for some years, I cannot recollect that I had a single check of that sort. At times I have been visited with sickness, and have believed myself near to death; but I had not the least concern about the consequences. In a word, I seemed to have every mark of final impenitence and rejection; neither judgments nor mercies made the least impression on me.

"At length, our business finished, we left Cape Lopez, and, after a few days stay at the island of Annabona, to lay in provisions, we sailed homewards, about the beginning of January 1748. From Annabona to England, without touching any intermediate port, is a very long navigation, perhaps more than seven thousand miles, if we include the circuit necessary to be made on account of the trade winds. We sailed first westward, till near the coast of Brazil, then northwards, to the banks of Newfoundland, with the usual variations of wind and weather, and without meeting anything extraordinary. On these banks, we stopped half a day to fish for cod; this was then chiefly for diversion; we had provisions enough and little expected those fish (as it afterwards proved) would be all we could have to subsist on. We left the banks March 1, with a hard gale of wind westerly, which pushed us fast homewards. I should here observe, that with the length of this voyage in a hot climate, the vessel was greatly out of repair, and very unfit to support stormy weather; the sails and cordage were likewise very much worn out, and many such circumstances concurred, to render what followed more dangerous: I think it was on the 9th of March, the day before our catastrophe, that I felt a thought pass through my mind, which I had long been a stranger to. Among the few books we had on board, one was Stanhope's *Thomas a Kempis*: I carelessly took it up, as I had often done before, to pass away the time; but I had still read it with the same indifference, as if it was entirely a romance. However, while I was reading this time, an involuntary suggestion arose in my mind, What if these things should be true? I could not bear the force of the inference, as it related to myself, and therefore shut the book presently. My conscience witnessed against me once more, and I concluded, that true or false, I must abide the consequences of my own choice. I put an abrupt end to these reflections, by joining in with some vain conversation or other that came in the way.

"But now *the Lord's time was come*, and the conviction I was so unwilling to receive was deeply impressed upon me, by an awful dispensation. I went to bed that night in my usual security and indifference, but was awakened from a sound sleep by the force of a violent sea, which broke on board us. So much of it came down below as filled the cabin I lay in with water. This alarm was followed by a cry from the deck, that the ship was going down, (or sinking.) As soon as I could recover myself, I essayed to go upon deck, but was met upon the ladder by the Captain, who desired me to bring a knife with me. While I returned for the knife, another per-

Part I : Impressed

son went up in my room, who was instantly washed overboard. We had no leisure to lament him; nor did we expect to survive him long; for we soon found that the ship was filling with water very fast. The sea had torn away the upper timbers on one side, and made the ship a mere wreck in a few minutes. I shall not affect to describe this disaster in the marine dialect, which would be understood by few; and therefore I can give you but a very inadequate idea of it. Taken in all circumstances, it was astonishing, and almost miraculous, that any of us survived to relate the story. We had immediate recourse to the pumps, but the water increased against all our efforts; some of us were set to bailing in another part of the vessel, that is, to lade it out with buckets and pails. We had but eleven or twelve people to sustain this service; and notwithstanding all we could do, she was full, or very near it; and then with a common cargo she must have sunk of course; but we had a great quantity of bees-wax and wood on board, which were specifically lighter than the water; and as it pleased God that we received this shock in the very crisis of the gale, towards morning we were enabled to employ some means for our safety, which succeeded beyond hope. In about an hour's time the day began to break, and the wind abated. We expended most of our cloaths and bedding to stop the leaks (although the weather was exceedingly cold, especially to us who had so lately left a hot climate); over these we nailed pieces of boards; and at last perceived the water abate. At the beginning of this hurry, I was little affected; I pumped hard, and endeavoured to animate myself and my companions: I told one of them, that in a few days this distress would serve us to talk of over a glass of wine: but he being a less hardened sinner than myself, replied with tears, 'No, it is too late now.' About nine o'clock, being almost spent with cold and labour, I went to speak with the Captain, who was busied elsewhere, and just as I was returning from him, I said, almost without any meaning, 'If this will not do, the Lord have mercy on us.' This (though spoken with little reflection) was the first desire I had breathed for mercy in the space of many years. I was instantly struck with my own words, and as Jehu said once, *What hast thou to do with peace?* So it directly occurred, *What mercy can there be for me?* I was obliged to return to the pump and there continued till noon, almost every passing wave breaking over my head; but we made ourselves fast with ropes, that we might not be washed away. Indeed I expected, that every time the vessel descended in the sea, she would rise no more, and though I dreaded death

1. John Newton

now, and my heart foreboded the worst, if the scriptures, which I had long since opposed, were indeed true; yet still I was but half convinced, and remained for a space of time in a sullen frame, a mixture of despair and impatience.[5]

"The 10th (that is in the present style the 21st) of March, was a day much to be remembered by me, and I have never suffered it to pass wholly unnoticed since the year 1748. On that day the Lord sent from on high, and delivered me out of deep waters.— I continued at the pump from *three* in the *morning* till near *noon*, and then I could do no more. I went and lay down upon my bed, uncertain, and almost indifferent, whether I should rise again. In an hour's time I was called, and not being able to pump, I went to the helm, and steered the ship till midnight, excepting a small interval for refreshment. I had here leisure and convenient opportunity for reflection. I began to think of my former religious professions, the extraordinary turns in my life; the calls, warning, and deliverances I had met with, the licentious course of my conversation, particularly my unparalleled effrontery in making the gospel history (which I could not now be sure was false, though I was not as yet assured it was true) the constant subject of profane ridicule. I thought, allowing the scripture premises, there never was nor could be such a sinner as myself; and then comparing the advantages I had broken through, I concluded at first that my sins were too great to be forgiven.... Thus, as I have said, I waited with fear and impatience to receive my inevitable doom. Yet though I had thoughts of this kind, they were exceeding faint and disproportionate; it was not till long after (perhaps several years) till I had gained some clear views of the infinite righteousness and grace of Christ Jesus my Lord, that I had a deep and strong apprehension of my state by nature and practice; and perhaps till then I could not have borne the sight. So wonderfully does the Lord proportion the discoveries of sin and grace, for he knows our frame, and that if he was to put forth the greatness of his power a poor sinner would be instantly overwhelmed, and crushed as a moth. But to return; when I saw, beyond all probability, there was still hope of respite, and heard about six in the evening, that the ship was freed from water — there arose a gleam of hope. I thought I saw the hand of God displayed in our favour: I began to pray — I could not utter the prayer of faith: I could not draw near to a reconciled God, and call him father. My prayer was like the cry of the ravens, which yet the Lord does not disdain to hear. I now

Part I : Impressed

began to think of that Jesus whom I had so often derided; I recollected the particulars of his life, and of his death; a death for sins not his own but, as I remembered, for the sake of those who in their distress should put their trust in him. And now I chiefly wanted evidence.— the comfortless principles of infidelity were deeply riveted, and I rather wished than believed these things were real facts. You will please to observe, Sir, that I collected the strain of the reasonings and exercises of my mind in one view, but I do not say that all this passed at one time. The great question now was, how to obtain faith? I speak not of a appropriating faith (of which I then knew neither the nature nor necessity), but how I should gain an assurance that the scriptures were of divine inspiration, and a sufficient warrant for the exercise of trust and hope in God.... The wind was now moderate, but continued fair, and we were still drawing nearer to our port. We began to recover from our consternation, though we were greatly alarmed by our circumstances. We found that the water having floated all our moveables in the hold, all the casks of provisions had been beaten to pieces by the violent motion of the ship: on the other hand our livestock, such as pigs, sheep, and poultry, had been washed overboard in the storm. In effect, all the provisions we saved, except the fish I mentioned, and some food of the pulse kind, which used to be given to the hogs (and there was but little of this left) all our other provisions would have subsisted us but a week at scanty allowance. The sails too were mostly blown away, so that we advanced but slowly even while the wind was fair. We imagined ourselves about a hundred leagues from the land, but were in reality much farther. Thus we proceeded with an alternate prevalence of hopes and fears.— My leisure time was chiefly employed in reading and meditating on the scripture, and praying to the Lord for mercy and instruction.

"Things continued thus for four or five days, or perhaps longer, till we were awakened one morning by the joyful shouts of the watch upon deck proclaiming the sight of land. We were all soon raised at the sound. The dawning was uncommonly beautiful, and the light (just strong enough to discover distant objects) presented us with a gladdening prospect: it seemed a mountainous coast, about twenty miles from us, terminating in a cape or point, and a little further two or three small islands, or hummocks, as just rising out of the water; the appearance and position seemed exactly answerable to our hopes, resembling the north-west extremity of

1. John Newton

Ireland, which we were steering for. We sincerely congratulated each other, making no doubt but that, if the wind continued, we should be in safety and plenty the next day. The small remainder of our brandy (which was reduced to little more than a pint) was, by the Captain's orders, distributed amongst us; he added at the same time, 'We shall soon have brandy enough.'—We likewise ate up the residue of our bread for joy of this welcome sight, and were in the condition of men suddenly reprieved from death. While we were thus alert, the mate, with a graver tone than the rest, sunk our spirits, by saying, that 'he wished it might prove land at last.' If one of the common sailors had first said so, I know not but the rest would have beat him for raising such an unreasonable doubt. It brought on however warm debates and disputes whether it was land or no; but the case was soon unanswerably decided for the day was advancing fast; and in a little time one of our fancied islands began to grow red from the approach of the sun, which soon arose just under it. In a word, we had been prodigal of our bread and brandy too hastily, our land was literally *in nubibus*, nothing but clouds, and in half an hour more the whole appearance was dissipated.—Seamen have often known deceptions of this sort, but in our extremity we were very loath to be undeceived. However, we comforted ourselves, that tho' we could not see the land yet, we should soon, the wind hitherto continuing fair; but alas! We were deprived of this hope likewise.—That very day our fair wind subsided into a calm, and the next morning the gales sprung up from the south east, directly against us, and continued so for more than a fortnight afterwards. The ship was so wrecked, that we were obliged to keep the wind always on the broken side, unless the weather was quite moderated: thus we were driven, by the wind fixing in that quarter, still further from our port, to the northward of all Ireland, as far as the Lewis or western islands of Scotland, but a long way to the westward. In a word, our station was such as deprived us of any hope of being relieved by other vessels; it may indeed be questioned, whether our ship was not the very first that had been in that part of the ocean at the same season of the year.

"Provisions now began to grow very short; the half of a salted cod was a day's subsistence for twelve people, we had plenty of fresh water, but not a drop of stronger liquor; no bread, hardly any cloaths, and very cold weather. We had incessant labour with the pumps to keep the ship above water. Much labour and little food wasted us fast, and one man died under the hardship. Yet our sufferings were light in comparison of our just fears; we could not afford this allowance much longer, but had a terrible prospect of being either starved to death, or reduced to feed upon one another. Our expectations grew darker every day, and I had a further trouble peculiar to myself. The Captain, whose temper was quite soured by distress, was hourly reproaching me (as I formerly observed) as the whole cause of the calamity, and was confident, that if I was thrown overboard, (and not otherwise), they should be preserved from death. He did not intend to make the experiment, but the continued repetition of this in my ears gave me much uneasiness, especially as my conscience seconded his words; I thought it very probable that all that had befallen us was on my account. I was at last found out by the powerful hand of god, and condemned in my own breast. However, proceeding in the method I have described, I began to conceive hopes greater than all my fears; especially when at the time we were ready to give up all for lost, and despair was taking place in every countenance. I saw the wind come about to the very point we wished it, so as best to suit that broken part of the ship which must be kept out of the water, and to blow so gentle as our few remaining sails could bear; and thus it continued without any observable alteration or increase, though at an unsettled time of the year, till we once more were called up to see the land, and were convinced that it was land indeed. We saw the island Tory, and the next day anchored in Lough Swilly in Ireland. This was the 8th of April, just four weeks after the damage we sustained from the sea. When we came into this port, our very last victuals was boiling in the pot; and before we had been there two hours, the wind which seemed to have been providentially restrained till we were in a place of safety, began to blow with great violence, so that if we had continued at sea that night in our shattered enfeebled condition, we must in all human appearance have gone to the bottom. About this time I began to know that there is a God that hears and answers prayer. How many times has he appeared for me since this great deliverance.— Yet, alas! How distrustful and ungrateful is my heart unto this hour.[6]

"I have told you, that in the time of our distress we had fresh water in abundance. This was a considerable relief to us, especially as our spare diet was mostly salt fish without bread; we drank plentifully, and were not afraid of wanting water, yet our stock of this likewise was much nearer to an end than we expected; we supported that we had six large butts of water on board, and it was well that we were safe arrived in Ireland before we discovered that five of them were empty, having been removed out of their place, and stove by the violent agitation when the ship was full of water. If we had found this out while we were at sea, it would have greatly heightened our distress, as we must have drunk more sparingly.

"While the ship was refitting at Lough-Swilly, I repaired to Londonderry. I lodged at an exceeding good house, where I was treated with much kindness, and soon recruited my health and strength. I was however a serious professor, went twice a day to the prayers at church, and determined to receive the sacrament at the next opportunity. A few days before, I signified my intention to the minister, as the rubric directs, but I found this practice was grown obsolete. At length the day came: I arose very early — was very particular and earnest in my private devotion, and with the greatest solemnity engaged myself to be the Lord's for ever and only his. This was not a formal, but a sincere surrender, under a warm sense of mercies recently received; and yet, for want of a better knowledge of myself, and the subtilty of Satan's temptations, I was seduced to forget the vows of God that were upon me. Upon the whole, though my views of the gospel salvation were very indistinct, I experienced a peace and satisfaction in the ordinance that day, to which I had been hitherto a perfect stranger.

"The next day I was abroad with the mayor of the city, and some other gentlemen, shooting; I climbed up a steep bank, and pulling my fowling-piece after me, as I held it in a perpendicular direction, it went off so near my face as to burn away the corner of my hat. — thus when we think ourselves in the greatest safety, we are no less exposed to danger than when all the elements seem conspiring to destroy us. The divine Providence, which is sufficient to deliver us in our utmost extremity, is equally necessary to our preservation in the most peaceful situation. During our stay in Ireland I wrote home. The vessel I was in had not been heard of for eighteen months, and was given up for lost long before. My father had no more expectation of hearing that I was alive, but he received my letter a few days before he left London. — He was just going Governor of York Fort in Hudson's Bay, from whence he never returned. He sailed before I landed in England, or he had purposed to take me with him; but God designed otherwise, one hindrance or another delayed us in Ireland until it was too late. I received two or three affectionate letters from him, but I never had the pleasure of seeing him more. I had hopes, that in three years more I should have had an opportunity of asking his forgiveness for the uneasiness my disobedience had given him; but that ship that was to have brought him home came without him. According to the best accounts we received, he was seized with the cramp when bathing, and drowned a little before her arrival in the bay.—Excuse this digression.

"My father, willing to contribute all in his power to my satisfaction, paid a visit before his departure to my friends in Kent, and gave his consent to the union which had been so long talked of. Thus when I returned to____, I found I had only the consent of one person to obtain, with her I as yet stood at as great an uncertainty as on the first day I saw her.

"I arrived at____ the later end of May 1748, about the same day that my father sailed from the Nore, but found the Lord had provided me another father in the gentleman whose ship had brought me home. He received me with great tenderness, and the strongest expressions of friendship and assistance, yet not more than he has since made good, for to him, as the instrument of God's goodness, I owe my all. Yet it would not have been in the power of this friend to have served me effectually, if the Lord had not met with me on my way home, as I have related. Till then, I was like the man possessed with the legion.—No arguments, no persuasion, no views of interest, no remembrance of the past, or regard to the future could have constrained me within the bounds of common prudence. But now I was in some measure restored to my senses. My friend immediately offered me the command of a ship; but upon mature consideration, I declined it for the present. I had been hitherto always unsettled and careless, and therefore thought I had better make another voyage first, and learn to obey, and acquire a further insight and experience in business, before I ventured to undertake such a charge. The mate of the vessel I came home in was preferred to the command of a new ship, and I engaged to go in the station of a mate with him. I made a short visit to London, etc. which did not fully answer my views. I had but one opportunity of seeing Mrs. N****, of which I availed myself very little, for I was always exceeding awkward in pleading my own cause viva voce.—But after my return to L____, I put the question in such a manner, by letter, that she could not avoid (unless I had greatly mistaken her) coming to some sort of an explanation. Her answer (though penned with abundance of caution), satisfied me, as I collected from it, that she was free from any other engagement, and not unwilling to wait the event of the voyage I had undertaken. I should be ashamed to trouble you with these little details, if you had not yourself desired me."[7]

Following this, Newton obtained a position as first mate aboard the Brownlow. This was a slave ship. It was several years later before he renounced the slave trade.

Chapter 2

Joshua Davis

Joshua Davis wrote an account of his experiences in a book entitled *A Narrative of Joshua Davis, an American Citizen, Who Was Pressed and Served on Board the Ships of the British Navy*. The subtitle states that he was in *Seven Engagements, Once Wounded, Five Times Confined in Irons, and Obtained His Liberty by Desertion*. He begins his narrative: "I Joshua Davis, was born in *Boston*, in the Commonwealth of Massachusetts on the 30th of June 1760. On the 14th of June 1779, I entered on board of the Privateer Jason, of 20 guns commanded by commodore John Maney, bound on a cruise." After a battle, his ship was captured and he was forced to go on board a guard ship and there became ill. He continues as follows:

> One day as I was drinking beer in the galley, I was taken ill on a sudden, and fell backward — when I was taken up and carried to my hammock. I was insensible for about 8 hours, when my senses returned; and the doctor asked me how I felt — I told him I had a violent pain in my head and back. He said, "you are young and likely to get over the fever if you will mind my directions." the fever broke in about 48 hours, when I was ordered on shore to the hospital with a few men that had recovered of the fever. We were all put in a sick ward, I recovered very fast; But unhappily had a relapse, by going out and sitting on the grass; which made me so crazy, that when the doctor came to give me some physick, I bit him in the hand. However in the course of three weeks I recovered so as to be able to walk under the piazza. One day, walking alone, and reflecting on my unhappy situation, I cast my eyes round and saw two men coming towards me, who proved to be the doctor's mate and the midshipman who put me on board of the guard ship. as they passed by me, the midshipman said to the doctor, "is not that that Davis which I put on board of the guard ship?" "No replied the doctor, he died long since" The midshipman stepped up to me and clap-

2. Joshua Davis

ping me on the shoulder, said "Davis, is this you or your ghost?" I replied "it was what was left of me." They left me at that time but next morning a boat came after me, with the doctor and lieutenant of the Surprize who sent a porter for me to go to them at Mr. Shuffler's office under the middle sentry I obeyed the order and went with him to see the gentleman.[1]

While I was before them, the doctor asked me how I did—to which I replied, that I did not feel very well; but he insisted that I was well enough to go on board with them. I made answer, "gentlemen I m [sic] not well enough to go at present." He then told me I must go on board on the morrow, when they sent the boat for me. The next morning the porter came for me, when I told him I would go with him, if he would let me get my clothes, which he gave me liberty to do But instead of returning I secreted myself behind the chimney until he was gone.

The next morning, while I was at breakfast, he came and took me with him to Mr. Shuffler. "You d__d rascal," said he, "why did you not come when I sent for you? I will make you pay dearly for this"—and ordered the porter to call the sergeant of the guard, who soon came, and was ordered to take and confine me in the guard house. I was taken there, and confined for the space of fourteen days, without provisions or bedding being allowed me—yet the guard helped me to provisions, or I should have suffered much.[2]

Another example of the sort of discipline aboard ship is related by Davis:

One morning the hands were piped on deck and ordered to wash the decks, as usual. The men being ordered aft to haul the Holy Stone. Charles Mansfield, our third lieutenant, came on deck, and called the list over. Two men, belonging to the main-top were missing; he told the boatswain's mate to send them aft. On going to the quarter deck, he lieutenant says, "you d__d rascals, why were you not on deck before," and not waiting for an answer, sings out "main deck, there! Come aft, boatswains mates, take these fellows, and give them a d__d hiding." they collared each of them, and beat them with a supple-jack until they were so tired that they could do it no longer. The lieutenant then bid the men go to their duty—but as they grumbled a little when they went to the gangway, they were called back again, and the boatswain and his other mate were ordered on the quarterdeck, when the lieutenant said, "take these fellows and give them another hiding, for grumbling." They took hold of them and beat them so unmercifully, that the men begged for mercy, and requested to be tried by a court martial. "I'll court martial you," said he, "call the master at arms and tell

Part I : Impressed

him to put these rascals in irons," who took the men down below decks, and put them both in feet cuffs, in which situation they were kept three days. On the fourth morning they were taken up on deck; Mr. Westcott, the first lieutenant, said, "men you may go to your duty again," they took off their hats and thanked him and went below.

Davis continued to have problems with his health, which he exaggerated to try to get out of work on occasion: "My bed was sent on board the next day, without being smoked; through which neglect I caught the fever again. The doctor ordered me to be put down in the ship's hold, over the water casks, fearing the whole crew should take the disease. In the mean time the ship was got under way to convoy a number of merchantmen to Halifax, N.S. The doctor attended me day to day—and at times I was very much deranged—in which situation I continued for 21 days, when the fever broke, and I recovered as to go upon deck—and in a few days more we arrived at Halifax. Capt. Reves asked me how I felt—to which I replied that I did not feel very strong yet."

Apparently, the captain tried to win his confidence and made him some promises, but Joshua had little confidence in what the captain said because he had made similar promises before. Joshua writes:

And from that day I was determined to feign myself sick, and accordingly took my hammock. The doctor came and asked me how I felt—when I told him that I had a languid and weak feeling in my stomach. He told the captain that he was afraid I was in consumption. "If that is the case, says he, he shall go on shore before the ship leaves the harbour."

On the 27th June, the ship sailed for Newfoundland. I was called on deck, and the Captain asked me how I was. "Very weak in the stomach, sir," said I. He said, "not so weak but that you can do duty again; come, give us a tune on your fife." I played a tune very faintly—when he said, "you are either d__d weak or lazy," and told me to get my hammock and go on shore with the pilot, to whom the Captain said, "take this Yankee dog to prison"—and turning round to me, said, "get into the boat, and if ever I catch you privateering again, I will hang you on the yard arm." I went into the boat, and rowed on shore with the pilot, who carried me to the house of the commissary of prisoners. This was about 2 o'clock in the morning. We knocked at the door—the commissary looked out of the window, and the pilot told him he had a prisoner, and wished to know what to do with him. He was ordered to put me on board of the Pembroke, a 71 gun ship then lying in the stream.

2. Joshua Davis

Later, Davis served onboard a ship which was laid up for repairs:

I went on board the ship the next day, where I found every thing in confusion. The ship was built by contract, and had lain in the river only four years. When the carpenters knocked away the knees of the upper deck, they were all found to be rotten, which took some time to replace them. I was determined to quit the ship as quick as I could and formed a plan accordingly. I went to my messmate, (Mr. John Reeves, of Philadelphia, and captain of the hold) and told him my plan was to feign myself sick, then go to the hospital and get discharged. He said he would all he could. I told him I would go to my hammock, drink a pint of vinegar a day, rub allum on my tongue to make it white, and rap my elbow against the ceiling to make the pulse beat. Reeves said it was a good plan, if it did but take. I accordingly took to my hammock, and sent for the doctor's first mate. He came to me, and took hold of my wrist, saying my pulse beat quick; then told me to put out my tongue, and said, "I appeared to have symptoms of fever; have you any pains?" I told him I had pains in my back and head. He left me a few minutes and returned with a liquid, which he gave me to take. I filled my mouth with it and turned round, to go to sleep. Says he, "you will feel better after this," and went away — when I spit out his medicine. Next morning he brought the doctor with him; when I saw him coming I knocked my elbow again, put allum on my tongue, and quivered my limbs. He took hold of my wrist, and turning round to his mate, says, "this man has got a fever and ague on him, and must be sent to the hospital tomorrow. The next morning I was ordered to get into the boat — and my appearance, I think, was rather singular; I had a large great coat on, full of holes, and dragging behind me full 6 inches; an old black handkerchief on my head, and led to the boat between two men. On getting into the boat, the officers said, "Davis, you will hardly weather this." To which I replied, "I do no know whether I shall or not." When I got to the hospital, I went to the keeper of the place, and asked him in private whether he knew, if I bribed the doctor's mate, I could get my discharge "Yes," says he "I will insure your discharge if you will give me half a guinea." The doctor's mate came to me and asked me how I did. I told him I should feel better after I had little of his assistance — to which he said, he would help me all he could — when I told him my plan. He said I should have my discharge for one guinea, which I agreed to give him — when he told me there would be a discharge in a few days.[3]

Apparently, he was caught, because later the master at arms was called:

PART I : IMPRESSED

[W]e were accordingly put into irons by the feet. The next day our commodore came on board with a number of ladies and gentlemen to see the ship; on passing us, the Commodore's Lady asked him what we had done, that we were confined in irons? He told her that we had deceived the doctors. On her inquiring what was to be done with he replied, "They must be punished for it." She said, "I pity them." An Irishman that was in irons with us, says "God bless you Madam; I hope you will live to bless th Commodore all the days of your life." In about ten minutes Mr. King, the second lieut. Came down with the master at arms and said to him "Take these men out of irons, and let them go to their stations again." Our irons were then knocked off, and we were ordered by the boatswain to go to work. The ship being nearly ready for sea, I was determined not to go in her, at the risk of my life; and was contriving another plan how I should get out of her.

The day before we sailed, a number of pressed men were brought on board, and put into different divisions. The second division had to row the guard that night. When they were called upon to answer to their names, I took particular notice of one of the men, was called out to row in the second watch. After the officer had discharged the division. I went up to the man, and told him he had to row the boat that night and asked him if he knew how — to which he said no; when I offered to do it for him, if he would lay in his hammock when the second guard-boat's men were called, and I would answer to his name. He wished to know why I wanted to do it for him — I said "because I have a good reason for it; we were to sail early in the morning and my clothes were all on shore. [I]f he let me do his duty in the board I would [bring] some gin on board and treat him to this he immediately consented.[4]

When the call came for the second guard-boat's men, Davis took the other man's place and when the boat landed he was able to make his escape. But not for long. He and some others appropriated a small boat to carry them on their way:

[B]ut when we were passing by a number of merchantmen, about abreast of Cole stairs, I saw a boat with 12 oars muffled rowing down the river. As soon as they perceived our boat, they made for us. I saw a sculler about 20 yards a head of us, and called him alongside — when I sprung into his boat, and told him to pull as hard as he could (I pushing with him at the same time.) He was very anxious to know my hurry; but I begged of him not to stop to ask questions, but put me on shore, and I would give him whatever he asked. In the meantime the other boat had got alongside of the boat I had left. Directly we saw the boat making after us — when I advised my

2. Joshua Davis

friend (for he was one) to run his boat between the two tier of shipping. He did so — I jumped out of the boat and he followed me — I lost both my shoes in the mud and had not time to step again, before the boat in search of us was close in shore We then agreed to lay down close to the mud. The boat struck to the shore and one of the people said, "Cockswain, where is that other boat gone to?" Luckily for us, it was the dark of the morning and they could not perceive us. When they found that we were not to be seen, they said, "d__n them, let them go; pull away, my lads" and went down the river leaving us to help each other out of the mud — for the tide had got up to me. He, having long boots on, did mind it so much, and helped me out. As soon as we reached the wharf, we went to a tavern to wash ourselves, the landlord of which said to my companion, "Tom, where have you been, that you are so full of mud?" He said, "this man has led me a fine jaunt this morning from the Gravesend boat," and then told him the particulars, pretty much as I have related it. I then asked the boatman what I had to pay; but he refused to take anything until I told him where I came from, and why I had hurried him so, which I promised to do on condition that he should keep it secret. Says he, "you have run away from a man-of-war, and if you have you are welcome to the pay; I was yesterday a man-of-war's man but a landsman to-day; I have been on board his majesty's ships, and know how to pity those that are there."— Our conversation ended there, and I went out to the pump, to wash myself. I treated the boatman, and went down to the widow Bell's, where I found Captain Cushing who said to me, "you have come in good time to help us get our goods in, for I lost all my men last night, by the press gang, except my first mate, and one man who jumped into the ship's hold, and broke his leg." I then went on board his ship (the Nonpareil of Boston) and went to work. Our captain had to hire men from the shore to help in with the cargo, until he could get a crew, which was finally made up of men who had been hiding themselves from the press-gang. After getting our cargo and passengers on board, we set sail, on the 2nd Oct. 1787, for Boston.[5]

Chapter 3
Joshua Penny

This account of Joshua Penny is taken from a book entitled *The Life and Adventures of Joshua Penny, a Native of Southold, Long Island, Suffolk County, New York, Who Was Impressed into the British Service*:

"The publication of this narrative has unavoidably been delayed. Poverty has hitherto prevented the narrator from discharging his duty to the public and yielding to the repeated solicitations of his friends....

"His country has waged war, principally for the security of commerce and the protection of her seamen; it therefore has become a duty to publish to the world the imperious and barbarous conduct of the common enemy, on the great highway of nations.... The British 'maritime code' is diametrically opposed to the rights and immunities of every other nation on the terraqueous globe. Those who regard the rights of an American sailor as those of an American citizen, and who can sympathise in the sufferings of their fellow men, will listen to my story and overlook the necessary imperfections.

"My father, Edward Penny, lived and is yet living at Southold in the county of Suffolk on Long-Island where I was born on the 12th of September, 1773.—My parents had nine children, and like most others with numerous progeny, they were very poor. My mother at an early period summoned her boys to attend her, for the purpose of determining their future pursuits for a livelihood. She examined us in rotation, and on asking me, 'Well, Joshua, what will you do for a living in the world?' I answered that I intended to go as far as sea and land would carry me.

"At fourteen years of age, I was bound by indenture to Dr. John Gardiner, who lived in that place with the reputation of being an excellent physician, and was, certainly a good man. At the expiration of one year,

3. Joshua Penny

I urged my father to cause my indenture to be cancelled, because I was anxious to try my fortune at sea. This was done, and I entered on board of a sloop under command of Capt. Webb, and sailed to Guadaloupe. On our return to New-York, I visited my friends, who were rejoiced at my safe arrival, expecting to find me disgusted with a seafaring life. In vain they pressed me to remain quietly at home until I should be better educated. They were disappointed; my fondness for the sea was undiminished.

"I solicited for and obtained leave to visit my brother, in Philadelphia, but on my arrival at New York, went from one vessel to another inquiring if a cabin boy was wanted, without ever asking to what port they were bound; when at last I went on board the brig *Perseverance* George Lippencott, master. Being very small for one of my age; he asked me whose child I was, and if I had my parent's liberty to go to sea? I told him that I had been once with their permission, and wished to do the same again. Upon this he shipped me at two and a half dollars per month, which I thought great wages, and must confess that for once I did feel proud. The brig sailed for Port Royal, Virginia, up the Rappahannock river.[1]

"On this passage I was maltreated by the mate, who happened to be a rough Irishman. I had complained to the captain of his ill usage, but the mate, after receiving a reprimand, grew worse, and threatened to throw

Sailor, Thomas Rowlandson (National Maritime Museum, Greenwich, London).

Part I : Impressed

me overboard, if I should enter any more complaints against him. In the evening when the brig was ready to pursue her voyage to Portugal, the captain and mate both went on shore, and gave me an opportunity to desert.

"My chest, with a codfish and half a dozen biscuits in it, was put into a boat which took me on shore. I buried my chest in the sand, and traveled all that night in the woods. The next morning I was in the road and discovered two men on horseback: They hailed and asked me whither I was traveling? I answered that 'I knew not where I was going, and hardly knew from what place I had come.' One of these men (laughing) said, 'well then, my lad get on my horse and I will soon show you where you came from.' He then inquired how far I had traveled since nine o'clock the preceding night, and on my telling him, he demanded the reason for leaving captain Lipincott. He asked me if the captain was not a clever man? 'very clever and fatherly (said I) but the mate is an Irish bull-dog, he has beaten me almost to death.' [T]hese men took me to the captain, who sent us all on board, and there demanded the cause for thus absconding. I told him the mate had treated me so ill that I was afraid to go with him. He next inquired for my chest; and I pointed out the place where it was buried.

"The mate in my absence, had accused me of stealing some articles that were missing, and now jumped into the boat to go on shore, but the captain choosing to go without him, proceeded to the chest, which he found to contain no other plunder than the codfish and biscuits, as I had represented. He commended me for providing as I had done previous to the escape; and turning to the mate, charged him to prefer no more such accusations against me, on peril of being kicked overboard.

"The brig was laden with corn, and sailed for Oporto, but on her passage she encountered many severe gales of wind; in one of which she lost a deck load of oars and sweeps. This happened in the Gulf, but was not the only damage she sustained. Laden with corn, in bulk it became necessary to scuttle her deck and throw over the swelling corn. We reached Figura in distress, and there discharging the residue of her cargo, loaded with salt. We reached the port of Norfolk after a long tedious passage, on an allowance of water. Here we remained only twenty-four hours, and sailed for New York, where the captain paying me something more than the amount of my wages, discharged me.

"From this time I went occasionally to the West Indies, and coasted

3. Joshua Penny

from New York to Charlestown. In the last of these trips two Irish gentlemen, passengers, prevailed on my captain to release me, as they had agreed conditionally with me, that if I would accompany them to their intended trading establishment, they would instruct me as far as they were able to read, write, &c. [T]heir names were Parsons Pan, and Anthony Carrol. With these gentlemen I went to a spot forty miles west of Augusta, in Georgia, where they pitched their tents and trafficked with both whites and Indians. A residence there of twelve months was long enough for one of my roving disposition.

"The time had as yet passed agreeably enough with men like these, but my fortune was unmade. Nothing was neglected which wore the charm of novelty. I was often out on hunting parties, and one day while in pursuit of game, we had caught a large Opossum. Mr. Carrol being unused to the pranks of this animal insisted on carrying it upon his shoulder. The Opossum who had feigned death without any advantage to himself, fastened his teeth upon the Hibernian's neck. He was largely terrified at this unexpected assault — threw himself on the ground and rolling over in anguish and affright, exclaimed, 'I'm dead! I'm dead!' He was not relieved by his companions, until experience had taught him a severe lesson on hypocrisy. On leaving these men, I led to Augusta, a young wolf, which they had purchased of an Indian, and gave me on My intended trip to Ireland. With this they assured me my fortune would be made in their native country. At Augusta I embarked for Savannah, with my wolf, a few clothes and a trifling sum in cash.

"The brig Minerva, of Portsmouth, N.H. captain E. Schofield, was lying at Savannah, bound to Cork. In her I took passage and was within three days sail of our destined port, when the brig was boarded from a French privateer. The precious wolf, chained on deck, attracted the first notice of our Frenchman, the officer particularly amused himself by pricking it with his sword. They retired soon after to the cabin, where they examined Minerva's papers, drank freely of porter, and returned carelessly on deck. The officer inadvertently approached too near the offended wolf who revenged the affront received, by thrusting his teeth through the boot of his antagonist. The wound was inflicted near the officer's heel, from which blood started over his boot. This enraged him — he drew a pocket-pistol with which the wolf was instantly dispatched. Thus were my prospects of amassing wealth blasted in a moment!

Part I : Impressed

"This was the first year of their revolutionary war (1793) with England. They had already manned so many prizes, as they informed us, that we were suffered to proceed without further molestation. In three days more we were in Cork, when the captain told me that 'since my wolf was lost I could not do better than to tarry with him.' But I wished to travel, and had a certificate given me by Messrs, Pan and Carrol, which was directed to their friends at Nenagh, in the county of Tipperary. The wolf skin was sold for three of their seven shillings. No sooner was I in readiness to commence the journey, than a press gang took me to a 74: the captain of this ship looked at my certificate, and humanely ordered me to be set again on shore. On the road I was often taken up on suspicion of being a deserter. Dressed in a rifle frock (hunting shirt) my appearance there was novel, and in passing the houses of the rich, was invited to enter. Here I was uniformly well treated — furnished with meat, bread, and butter — a guinea or half guinea to defray expenses on the road. For about three weeks, however, I was among the poorer class, where the only food is milk and potatoes. They received me hospitably, and never insulted me with the opprobrious epithet of yankee.

"I soon formed a very favorable opinion of the Irish character, which opinion to this day remains unchanged. The elder brothers of Messers. Pan and Carrol were living in affluence at Nenagh. They received me kindly — told me I should be welcome to stay with them, and amuse myself as long as I thought proper. Six months residence was sufficient for one whose fortune was yet to make; things around me were robbed of all their novelty, and a recruiting serjeant appeared at the nick of time. This man stimulated me too freely. I enlisted, and went to Dundagh where the regiment lay. There I immediately caught the itch, and was sick of a pleurisy. The doctor, when I had remained three weeks in the hospital, reported me well. I drew shirts, shoes and stockings — the taylor also had taken the measure for a red coat. With him I left the measure — and that night shipped on board a brig which sailed directly for Liverpool. The captain on our arrival, paid me to my satisfaction, and urged me to return with him; but I had fallen out with Ireland — and declined.

"This affair should have remained unpublished, were it consistent with my design. It is however, some apology for a young man unskilled in the arts employed to entrap mankind, that the recruiting officer had first intoxicated its prey, and took advantage of his weakness. In my senses

3. Joshua Penny

I should not have enlisted — but I must not conceal or misrepresent, however the naked truth will affect my character. Experience is a stern instructor, and I have profited from this quarter.

"Among other things, I had discovered that an American in the dominions of his Britannic majesty, should be provided with a protection — even then his safety is not ensured. Proof being made of my citizenship, before James Murray, Esq. American Consul at that place I ventured to continue in Liverpool for two weeks. Although lodged in the press-room as often as every other night, I never produced my protection until the regulating captain came to examine us in the morning, because I had frequently seen the papers of neutrals torn in pieces by the press gang, and thrown into the fire — declaring their protections good for nothing; that 'they could buy them any where for a quarter of a dollar.' How wretched is that government, which compels men to become murderers of their countrymen, and exerts her power to entrap and enslave those whom she professes to preserve free! A government of force, like that of England, is worse than the government of the American Indians.[2]

"Liberty is mocked by that nation which enslaves her subjects on pretence of rendering their condition more prosperous. Compel a man, whom you stile free, to abandon his wife, his children, and every thing else he values in this world, to become your slave on shipboard! How dare you call that a land of freedom where this practice prevails, countenanced by its laws? 'Where liberty dwells, there is my country.'

"Those in America who chime with this foe to the human race, are fit subjects for an English ship of war; they deserve to be under discipline in a floating purgatory, until they have learned to unite in support of the only government where liberty delights to dwell — There they shall, with my petition be sent, until they have learned to commiserate the fate of an impressed sailor. My indignation must be suppressed.

"Tired of being haunted by a press-gang, I engaged with captain Matthews of the ship Budd, bound to the African Slave coast. Our voyage to *Annamaboo* had been tedious, but we were not long detained there. We sailed with a cargo of 382 slaves for Jamaica. Nothing remarkable happened on the passage, except that we descried a sail at such a distance, that it was impossible to ascertain her colors. Our ship had 14 guns, which were fired at the strange sail as long as she could be seen: this courageous attack lasted about an hour: but our imaginary enemy did not appear to take the

Part I : Impressed

least notice of us. The captain, at Port royal, reported this affair; and according to his account, we had beaten off a French privateer of 18 guns. His report acquired him great credit there.

"Soon after our entry in that port, the captain called the doctor, and said in the presence of the ship's company, 'See here are no less than eleven of these wenches pregnant by me, for which I shall get the more by fifty guineas per head. I have never had a less number of any voyage I ever made; yet I have one of the handsomest of women, for a wife in Liverpool who has never had a child.'

"Not many days had passed after our arrival, ere we were again haunted by press-gangs, and our whole crew impressed. We were put into the Alligator frigate of 28 guns, under the command of captain Africk. Four of us were Americans; the others chiefly Danes and Swedes. A fever raged in this ship and out of forty men, there were eleven corpses to be interred on the first morning.

"No sooner was the captain on deck in the morning, than we were ready with our American protections. He said, 'Men I will not look at your protections — my ship is in distress, and I will have men to carry me to England.' He refused to hear a word on the subject of liberating any one of our number. The ship got under way, and the next morning went into Montego Bay, and anchored in the harbour at 8 o'clock in the evening; her boats were manned to board the merchant's ships lying there; and impressed from them without discrimination. This business of kidnapping continued until daybreak, when they got under way in season to prevent applications for relief. There were forty men impressed that night, some of whom were American mates and supercargoes — some had been taken out of their beds on shore, without liberty to dress themselves. We ran down to the fleet in the offing, of 114 sail of merchantmen waiting for this ship to join the convoy of two ships of the line and the brig Jack Tar. The next day, however, our ship was dispatched by order of the admiral, on a commission to Havanna; we lay twenty-four hours at the Moro-Castle, then went to sea and rejoined the fleet.

"The next day I was taken sick of a fever — was soon deprived of my senses, and when I first recollected myself, was out of my hammock and attempting to walk on deck; suddenly blindness prostrated my feeble frame, when I heard a general shout, 'there goes another dead yankee.' I was returned to my hammock; the doctor shortly after came along, and

3. Joshua Penny

on finding a corpse next to me, he called his lob-lolly boy and chid him for not seeing that dead man's hammock cut down; adding, 'that other man (meaning me) will be dead before 12 o'clock; and you ought to have the dead removed immediately, to make room for me.' My fever was broken, so that the doctor's prophetic sentence was entirely harmless.

"On our passage to England we fell in with an American schooner, laden with poultry, apples and cider. She was brought to, and her whole cargo purchased by the fleet. This yankee vessel was saved the trouble of going to the West-Indies — returning with casks of sea-water for ballast. One of our convoy, a king's transport of 14 guns, took fire suddenly in drawing spirits. Many persons, even ladies, jumped overboard, no lives were lost.

"The sick had recovered after reaching the English Channel, and all the impressed seamen taken from Jamaica, were ordered on the quarter deck. The captain then addressing himself to us, said, 'I want to know who of you impressed in Jamaica, are willing to take his majesty's bounty; it is customary to allow impressed men twenty-four hours to consider whether they will accept this privilege; if not, they are on arriving at Spithead, to be put on board some vessel bound to foreign parts, where they shall not have opportunities to write to the d__d consul.' He called me singly and said, 'You have been the sickest, and I have been a father to you; do you refuse the king's bounty?' I answered (pointing to an arm chest), if he would give me that chest full of guineas and a lieutenant's commission, he could not tempt me. He replied, 'you had every day for two months, a dish from my own table, which no other man in this ship has had, and now you refuse to take the king's bounty! You are a d__d yankee rebellious rascal!' At Spithead we were called on deck with our baggage: What was next to be done with us we were left to conjecture. A part of our company expected to be set on shore — others had previously written letters to be sent to the consuls of their respective nations; but all were disappointed. A launch conveyed us along side of the *Stately* 64, captain Douglas. In two hours our squadron was ordered to sea. This squadron consisted of the America 64, commodore Blanket, Ruby 64, Rattlesnake sloop of war, and two frigates, beside the *Stately*, whose names I have forgotten. We had put our letters on board of a passage boat. And were sailing to some unknown part of the world. The officers alike ignorant with the men, bet on our destination. Bets were laid on Batavia, Botany Bay, &c. but

Part I : Impressed

after being at sea ten weeks, we made the *Table Mountain*; and every preparation was made for action. The next morning at day-break, we were joined by Admiral Elphintstone, with three 74's, three frigates, two sloops of war, and a gun brig. At 8 o'clock, the signal to Clear away for action was hoisted on board the admiral's ship, and repeated by the commodore. We entered False Bay, where the Dutch had one fort of 8 guns, and another of four. Fifty men, who composed the whole force there, spiked their cannon and retreated to Cape Town, leaving our fleet to take possession of everything. A frigate and man of war brig lay in the harbour. We pillaged the East-India stores on shore — stove the casks of wine and spirits, which ran like rivlets to the sea. The liquor was said to be poisoned by the Dutch. English sailors would have drank the spirits, with permission, if they had really believed it, to be poisoned; provided they could have got fairly drunk before they died. Our land forces were on shore the next day.

"One evening, shortly after our arrival here, while hoisting in our boats, we were alarmed by the cry of fire! The surgeon's mate in a fit of intoxication, let a candle fall into the surgeon's chest, which was open. The candlestick in its fall had broke some bottles, the contents of which instantly took fire. The flame rushed out, streaming from under the after hatchways to the quarter-deck. Orders were immediately given to hoist out all the boats. The order was executed with dispatch; but the boats no sooner struck the water, than they sunk with the crowd of men jumping into them. Few had the presence of mind to assist in extinguishing the fire.

"I had jumped overboard and hoped to effect my escape, but when within gun-shot of the shore was picked up by another ship's boat. All were taken and saved by the boats, except the captain's steward — he was a Guinea negro, who is as often steward of a ship as a fool is employed in the palace of a British king. The fire was extinguished without any other loss.

"Having often witnessed the *great* alarm at a *little* fire in a British ship, I am not at a loss to account for the horrors inspired by an American Torpedo.

"Col. McKenzie's regiment marched from Simon's Town to attack a garrison at Muisenburgh, on the road to Cape Town. There our regiment was repulsed with the loss of sixty Highlanders. While we continued at Simon's Town 3,200 sailors were landed to reinforce the regular troops they

3. Joshua Penny

drilled us every day for five weeks, and general Craig with admiral Elphinstone and commodore Blanket, reviewed us once in every week.

"One day a serjeant undertook to drill our sailor corps, when we threw down our arms, refusing any longer to be under land officers. General Craig thereupon wrote to the admiral that the sailors were mutinous, and refused obedience to his officers. The admiral sent him word that the sailors were in the right, and they should be commanded by their own lieutenants, or if that would not do the captains should take charge of their own men. The lieutenants took command, but they had to go through the process of drilling before they were capable of instructing us.

"Provisions became scarce, we were on an allowance of half a pound of salt meat and three-fourths of a pound of bread. The general's cow approaching too near a sailor sentinel, and not giving the countersign, was of course killed upon the spot. Pigs suffered death in the same way; thus we procured a seasonable supply of fresh meat. We were led by the guard to our ships, all in irons and fastened to a rope. The admiral instantly released us, and sent us ashore with a letter addressed to the general, informing him that 'the sailors had as much right to eat fresh meat as himself.' From that period there was a misunderstanding and coolness between those officers.

"In the rear of this town there was a large green with a high spot where stood an hospital; this was our parade ground; and we were marching at a review around this hospital, the day previous to our contemplated march for Cape Town, when one of our ship's lieutenants, crowded at one corner of the building, in his haste to give the word of command, 'left wheel!' cried 'luff you buggars and weather the hospital!' The general laughed; and falling, rolled over in the dirt in his convulsions. We were pronounced fit for action, but must be exercised in shooting at a target. Accordingly a rock was fired at which was in the water. The admiral had given out that whenever an American should fire, the rock would smoke. About one of ten who fired, drew smoke from the rock; and on being asked by the general, 'What countryman are you?' His answer uniformly was, 'I'm an American.'

"The army, (as I must call it) marched to make a new attack on the Dutch garrison at Muisenburgh, a distance of eight miles. Our main body proceeded by the shore, under cover of a sixty-four and a sloop of war, while a picket guard pushed their way over part of the mountain, to the

Part I : Impressed

camp which was at its foot. To make head against our main force, were ten of the Dutch artillery with two 24 pounders, 1 howitzer, and 2 smaller pieces. Their guns were on a platform, but exposed as they were they threw ten shot into the Stately's hull, which killed ten of her men. One of their shot split an 18 pounder of the Stately. None of the Dutch were killed, but it was imprudent to oppose our overwhelming force: and they retreated to Constantia plantation.

"The militia (for there were no regulars here) were either Dutch or civilized Hottentots, with whom we contended at Muisenburgh. We captured it without difficulty, and lay there or near it for three months, waiting for a reinforcement. We had frequent skirmishes on our foraging parties, in which I frequently volunteered; because vegetables were to be found in the deserted gardens; besides I was intent on the discovery of some convenient place for concealment, when ever I could make my escape from these man-stealers.

"A party of eight under a sergeant, traveled to the top of a neighboring mountain in the rain. One of our party mounted to a rock and cried out 'Dutchmen coming!' The sergeant flying, ordered us to follow him; but two of this party were Dutch, and we had discovered ourselves to the English enemy as we had preconcerted. The Dutch soldiers supposed us to be deserters and were marching towards us. When they were at gun shot distance from us, we laid down arms and met them. They took us to their camp — treated us with Constantia wine and mutton tails of the best quality. In short they had nothing too good for us. They knew we had deserted, for this was not the first party; and asked us the cause of our desertion? We answered them truly, that we had been impressed and wished to return home. They sent us to Cape Town in a wagon without a guard, the inhabitants on the road where we halted, treated us very handsomely.

"When we had arrived in town we were taken before the governor who ordered us clothed and victualled at a boarding house. He told us we had our choice to go into the garrisons or amuse ourselves in town. We had as much wine as we could drink, and ran about the streets as we pleased, until the Cape should be surrendered. Here we had remained two months, when the governor called all who were deserters (about 40) and told us that a British reinforcement of 14,000 men had arrived, on their way to India; and had summoned the garrison to surrender; that it would be given up the next morning at 8 o'clock; and that we might retire into the country where we would be well received by the inhabitants. Our knapsacks were loaded out of the Company's stores, with as much as we could carry away. We retired to the bushes on a hill about two miles from town, and drank Dutch wine that night. The next morning at 9 o'clock the British made their entry within the walls of that town, which was strongly fortified and said to have 500 cannon mounted for its defence. The Dutch governor betrayed the town; yet the English might have captured it with their 20,000 men.

"Our party traveled two days in company, to a Dutchman's house. This man could not speak English, but through our interpreters, he advised us to separate in squads of three each. After that time, whenever we came to a cross road a section filed off, until I was one of the last three. We had frequently called at the dwelling houses of the inhabitants, who always came to the door with wine and brandy, but dared not entertain us. They were kind enough to direct us on our way, and give us the distance to the next house.

"Water was so rarely found, that we took that in calibashes. There was plenty of tropical and other fruits. Our trio, ie. Jacob Cogwell, of Boston, one Vanderweit a Dutchman, and myself, continued its course for four days, when we arrived at the house of a farmer named Saerl Overalsten. This man informed us that this place was 100 miles from the Cape, that it was at the head of the Klanvis Riviere, which emptied into the sea at 50 miles distance. We continued here ten days, hunting with his sons and otherwise amusing ourselves. The sons of our host went on their annual visit to this river's mouth, in quest of fish; on this occasion we joined their company. We had been two weeks at the river's mouth, living on fish and ostrich eggs, when this course of life became an old affair. The ostriches were always in sight, and in such numbers that at a distance they appeared like a drove of cattle. While fishing one day we discovered two men walking on the beach, which at first alarmed us. They approached us, and being interrogated, stated that they 'had deserted from the whaling ship John of London, which was then lying 40 miles from us — that captain Gardiner, formerly of Nantucket, commanded her — that he had killed one man and split the head of another with a broad-axe — that they had left the ship at anchor and were very hungry.' They lodged with us that night; for if they were English, they had also suffered under the tyranny exercised on board an English ship. They had been advised by a Hottentot of the capture of

PART I : IMPRESSED

the Cape, and we confirmed the account which been given; their tongues were in their element that night.

"Cogswell and myself took it into our heads to visit this ship at anchor, whose crew were waging war with whales. We set off the next morning with fish and a calibash of water, reached the ship in twenty-four hours. A whale-boat at the mouth of the Groot Vis-Riviere, which belonged to the John, was watering. The crew confirmed the story which the two deserters related. They said it was a murdering ship, and they had calculated to leave her, but had heard of the surrender of the Cape to the English. With them we went on board and satisfied the inquiries of the captain. He said he was much in want of men; for two of his d__d rascals had deserted from him. He said they had ten days more of whaling to be done before they sailed for St. Helena. We shipped; and a few days after she was discovered to be so leaky that it was doubtful she would reach St. Helena. The character of the captain was correctly given. One evening after killing two or three whales, I asked Cogswell whether he preferred to remain here or go among the Hottentots? He chose to stay. I went on shore to get some fresh water, since the scurvy had rendered the crew nearly incapable of duty. The best of my way was made for the fishing party, and on finding the wagons had left there, pursued the track until I reached them. I went with them to their home. Mr. Ovalstein inquired what had become of *Yacoub*? I told him how it was, and that I would sooner continue with the Africans than go to sea with an Englishman. True, I had heard that captain Gardiner was a yankee, but who does not know that a renegade is a refined aristocrat. Jonas, said the good Dutchman, you have done right — you shall want nothing as long as you stay with me. He called me Jonas because my name here was Jonas Ingelbergh; he had from the first learned that I was from Long Island, and perhaps of Dutch extraction.

"We lived with this honest Dutchman two or three months, and during this time were frequently visited by a neighbour whose name was Frederick Leemburgh. This man wished me to live with him. He owned 50 or 60 slaves, and told me I should have nothing to do at his plantation but oversee a little his negroes. He would give me victuals and clothes but nothing more.

"With him I had been six months, when his wagons returning from the Cape, brought newspapers containing a public notice that the English had possession of the district, and that if any inhabitant while under

English laws, should entertain a deserter, he should be transported to Botany Bay for life. He then told Vanderwiet and me, that he was in such dread of the British tyrannical laws, he dared not entertain us any longer, but advised us to travel into the interior, as long as inhabitants were to be found.

"The *Bosjesmen* were at that time making inroads on the frontiers, and our company was very acceptable to the Dutch party who were forming to act on the defensive, at Cold Bockveld. People at this place very willingly entertained us, and we joined them on their march to attack the enemy's camp. These Bosjesmen or Boschmen are savages. In that vicinity they had lately pierced a stake through the body of a woman — murdered all her children and drove off her flock. We marched in the tracks of wild beasts about three weeks; the Hottentots on bullocks, subsisting on flour conveyed in sacks, wild honey, and roots resembling American ground nuts. Our force was 40 men exclusive of 50 or 60 Hottentots; the latter were our scouts, and brought us intelligence in the night, that they had discovered our enemy dancing about their fires, and drinking a liquor made of honey. They piloted us within gun-shot of the encampment, where we laid in ambush until sunrise. The Bosjesmen had poisoned arrows, and our Hottentots were armed with arrows of reed, pointed with steel fastened into bone. Our foes slept in huts or tents, and the first one who showed himself was a boy stirring the coals. He was shot down. This brought them out of their tents like a swarm of bees. They threw showers of arrows at us while we lay among the rocks; but our fire dispersed them. Of our party one Dutchman was killed and two wounded. One Hottentot refusing to have the poison cut from his wound also died. We found in the hostile camp twenty or thirty dead bodies, and a woman with nine children. The woman was shot, because no prisoner can be admitted into any settlement over the age of eleven years. This was the same party that had impaled the woman above mentioned and murdered her family.

"These Bosjesmen are from four feet four inches to five feet high. They have no chief or political head, but rove in hordes much like the other inhabitants of the forest. We returned to Cold Bekeveld with the nine captive children in baskets, slung on the oxen by a girth which passed around the bodies five or six times, and drawn *taut* by two Hottentots. These oxen will carry four hundred weight, and in traveling five or six weeks will tire a horse carrying one hundred.

PART I : IMPRESSED

"The poison used by the wild Hottentots is of two sorts; the one is the sap drawn from an incision made on the north side of a certain tree, into which the arrow's point is dipped. The other is taken from a snake. During my continuance here, a party returned from a tour to the country where they kill sea-cows.

"The Caffrees sometimes come here to trade with the Christians, who described to me their persons and character. These Caffrees were much larger than the white inhabitants with whom they trafficked. They are black as jet, dressing themselves with burnt roots, charcoal and stinking grease, like the Hottentots. In hunting the whole Kiraal, armed with spears, (not with bows and arrows likes the Bosjestmen) inclose the wild beasts and drive them to the center. They keep themselves at the distance of a rood between person, and no one animal of all the various kinds must be suffered to pass on penalty of death. The person who flies is instantly massacred as a coward. Their spears are made of bamboo poles with a feather to keep its course, and a harpoon or lance at the other end. They obtain their iron from the wrecks of ships. In the punishment they inflict they seem to imitate the lion. A Hottentot shepherd informed me, that 'sitting on a mountain near a precipice, he had seen a lioness bring her prey toward her young, and when near their bed spring suddenly upon them, those young who sneaked off in fear, she killed for cowardice, but kindly fed the remaining.' My informant was seventy years old, and worthy, I believe, of implicit confidence.

"I had been one year or longer absent from the Cape, and grew weary of the interior country; I had advanced a few days on my way back, when I met an inhabitant who said, he had a man on his plantation who deserted from Cape Town at the time of its surrender to the English. I found this man, who told me his name was John Johnston of Bristol in R.I. He joined me in hopes of reaching our beloved country.

"After two or three days travel from the town we halted at the house of John Van Reinesburgh. Here we refreshed ourselves at the desire of our host, for three or four days, and then traveled toward the town till within three or four miles of it. On this road in with another fellow-deserter; he could pass for a Dutch African, and we sent him on to reconnoitre. He came back next day and reported that the fleet we had left in the bay were all gone except the Stately (the ship from which I had taken leave) and the Rattlesnake, sloop of war; but a number of other ships had arrived there in our absence. He further stated, that seven men had been recently shot for desertion, and there had been a great naval mutiny in England. On the arrival of this news at the Cape, the sailors hoisted a sailor's jacket — gave three cheers on board each ship, and adopted the same regulations which had been adopted in England.

"We went into the town at mid-day, dressed like the inhabitants of the country. The landlord at whose house we were, said there were some merchant ships in want of men, but it was impossible to avoid the English patrols, who were searching every house for deserters. I asked the landlord if the captain of the Robert Morris was living? He answered me, that the captain was dead. That ship was cast away on the evening of my escape; and I thought to tell them, in case of being apprehended, that I belonged to that ship and had been in the country to procure a livelihood. That night the patrol came and demanded what countrymen we were. We all answered that we were American. Johnson and myself were lodged in jail that night. The next morning we were told by the Fiscal, that every such character in town, who could not give a *correct account* of himself, must be kept in jail until the trials of the sailors for mutiny were terminated. There were about twenty in confinement on suspicion of having deserted. Our bed was the naked stone floor; and our rations of provisions were nothing but bread and water and one spoon full of salt.

"Admiral Clark ordered the prisoners to be examined by each guard-ship, until the whole had gone through, so as to ascertain whether there were any who had ever belonged to any ship with their knowledge. Every day three or four lieutenants made us stand up for examination. They asked our names and what countrymen we were? How we came there? &c. All of us had come there in ships: but none happened to be English. I told them of the Robert Morris, whose wreck was then in sight. The officers told each of us that they knew us; and we had belonged to the same ships, or certainly the same squadron with themselves. They promised we should not be hurt *if they could help it*. We knew the consequences of detection as well as they could tell us; and if we prevaricated or concealed the truth, we acted as most others do who endeavour to *preserve their lives*.

"It is the duty of every American to avoid impressments in a British ship of war. It ought to be the first article of the impressed seaman's creed, that a British vessel of war is a Pandora's box — a nefarious floating dungeon, freighting calamities to every part of this lower world.

PART I : IMPRESSED

"One day, looking through the grates I espied an officer whom I knew to be a lieutenant of the Stately! Judge of my feelings when I knew that if I was detected, I should be lashed to the cannon's mouth and blown in pieces, for having deserted in an enemy's port! I lost my courage at the sight of the officer; but before he entered the prison door fear forsook me, and I was perfectly at ease. The officer, tapping me on the shoulder, asked if I was an American? Yes, I answered. 'Is not your name Joshua Penny?' My name is Jonas Inglesburg; I never deny my name nor country. He continued, 'can you deny that I know you?' No sir, I replied angrily, every officer who has been here these three weeks has known me, and of course you must know me.

"None except two Englishmen had confessed desertion; and the Fiscal was ordered by the admiral to ship the rest on board the first merchant ship which should arrive. We were then put onboard of an Indiaman at this time lying in port, where we remained a few days making preparation to sail. The admiral told our captain that two men had deserted from his ship the preceding night; and he was correctly informed they were in our ship — he must have them delivered to him, else he would take the whole crew. This was a finesse of the admiral. Villainy often assumes the regular form of law and right, with these tyrants of the sea. Our captain could do no otherwise than tell the admiral 'to search and welcome.'

"All of us who had been liberated from the jail, were now taken on board of the admiral's ship, TORMENTOR 74. I was transferred to the Sceptre 64, and after lying in Table Bay four or five months, was drafted to cruise in the Rattlesnake, off the Isle of France (Mauritius) under commodore Luzaco, of Guernsey, who commanded the Jupiter 54. The Rattlesnake, a few days after she sailed, parted from the fleet in a gale of wind, and did not rejoin it until eight days after the squadron had commenced the blockade of Port Louis, the only harbour and town of that island. Soon after this, we captured a Danish cutter laden with silks and satins, and I was immediately put into the prize, which sailed for the Cape. This pleased me, for I hoped to have another opportunity to get from the fangs of these harpies. This was a tedious passage, and when we were four days sail from port we had only one junk bottle of water to a man. It was calm when the fleet hove in sight, but we hoisted signals of distress and boats came off which towed us in.

"The prize was stripped, and we were returned on board the ships to

3. Joshua Penny

which we had respectively belonged; and thus my hopes of escape were again blasted. I was drafted to the Sphinx, a ship of 20 guns, bound to cruise off St. Helena. An American whaling ship lay near us at St. Helena, and four of us who messed together, all Americans, agreed to escape to the whaler; and after bribing the sentinel, plunged into the water. The others succeeded; but not being a good swimmer, I rested on our buoy and got with difficulty into the ship's head by climbing on the cable.

"One of the three who effected their escape was James Hall. He attempted to escape on board the Sceptre, before our draft from that ship, by swimming to an English Indiaman. He stowed himself on board the Indiaman but when the watch list was called the next morning, The captain of the Sceptre, on receiving the report of Hall's absconding, ordered all boats out to search the ships in port. He was found in the first ship they searched, and was of course to be punished. All hands were called to see the culprit flogged; and stood as usual with their hats off. Hall was young, with thin skin; and on receiving three strokes of the cat, cried out, 'Oh captain! For God's sake forgive me!' The captain then suspending the punishment, asked the unfortunate young man, if he would now promise to attempt no more to runaway? To which Hall answered *'No, by G-D captain, I will never give it up for one bad job.'* As often as this solemnity occurs, the surgeon stands by the captain, to give notice of the man's fainting. After three strokes more were given, the surgeon communicated the danger of the patient; upon which the cat was again arrested. Hall, scarcely able to articulate; addressing himself to the captain said, *'Captain, we Americans can't bear flogging like Englishmen, we are not used to it.'* The captain turned, and walking off, with difficulty refrained from laughing aloud; but the whole ship's company smiled, though they dared not laugh. Hall was released because this captain did not happen to be a barbarian. I have always noticed that when an American was whipped he fainted.

"A few days after my unsuccessful attempt to reach the American ship in St. Helena all hands were called to get our ship underway, and on calling the fore-top-men, the three Yankees were missing. The captain then called the purser's steward to ascertain the missing Yankee's mess. I was then called upon to relate what I knew of their running off. I told the captain as a number of men had been on shore watering the ship I thought they had been on duty. That was a falsehood, but *was not malicious*.

PART I : IMPRESSED

Lieutenant, Thomas Rowlandson (National Maritime Museum, Greenwich, London).

He asked me if I could swim? No, I answered. He then took a book out of his pocket and said, 'You are a yankee, sir, and have been seven years in the navy without ever being flogged, and *now I'll flog you if you are God Almighty's first lieutenant.*'

"All hands were now called on deck to witness my punishment; and I was immediately seized up. My senses left me when I had received three strokes of the cat. I fell (so I was afterwards informed), hanging by the wrists with my head on one shoulder. The surgeon informed the captain of my condition, when the captain said, 'he shall take his dozen, dead or alive!' I was cut down, and at the first recollection of myself, they were washing my face with a tub of water.

"We sailed for the Cape, but on the way fell in with a French privateer. The privateer brought us to action; we exchanged a few shots and ran. The Frenchman had a less number of guns and was of inferior force — none of us were hurt. On our arrival at the Cape, Captain Alexander was taken out of his ship and sent to England to be tried for cowardice. Cowards are always cruel. I shall forbear to dwell on this wretch's character, in order to shun the censure of being revengeful.

3. Joshua Penny

"I was drafted a second time from the Sceptre, and with fifty others put on board the Jupiter, after she returned from the Isle of France, with some other commander, whose name I do not remember. Information came to hand that a French frigate was cruising off the Cape, and as we were leaving the land in pursuit of her, she hove in sight, standing for us. Our drum beat to quarters and we prepared for action. A few broadsides were exchanged — seven of our men were killed and fourteen wounded; the first lieutenant's arm was shot off, and he died the day following. This was the same man who came out with me in the Stately, and who examined me in the prison at Cape-Town. The captain on his return was tried by court-martial. He pleaded that the weather was so rough he could not work his lower deck guns; but his men proved his plea unfounded. The French frigate followed our ship to the port, and the admiral hoisting his flag on another ship ordered his ship to the Isle of France since he knew the Frenchman belonged there. The admiral's ship had Port Louis blockaded three days before the French frigate appeared at the harbor's mouth. She was captured by the 74; and on arriving at the Cape, the admiral asked the French captain why he did not fight his 74? 'Because,' said the Frenchman, 'I have manned so many of your Indiamen, that I had not men enough; Beside, my ship is old, not good for much.' Our two decker ship had 54 guns; yet, we ran from this French frigate of only 44 guns.

"Commodore Luzac's squadron brought in 40 sail of prizes, in about five months from his departure for the Isle of France. The admiral ordered the smallest prize to be sold, and the money to be distributed among the sailors in that squadron. The prize money amounted to eight dollars per man. The first installment we received and were to receive the other four dollars at some time after; but when the second payment became due I was not to be found and four dollars is all I have ever received for my services rendered his majesty.

"A packet arrived from England with the important intelligence, that a British sloop of war, of 18 guns, had captured a Spanish 74! On the receipt of this news the yards of every ship were manned and three cheers given. Our captain said, 'Huzza! My boys! If this is the way our seamen fight, the wars will soon be over. And we shall be paid off!' A person who was present at that splendid affair, informed us a little after, that this was the fact: A British 74, a frigate, and a sloop of war were in company, and the Spanish ship under the guns of them all; when the sloop of war

PART I : IMPRESSED

was ordered to go along-side the Spaniard, and order him to strike his colors!

"Not long after this the 4th of June came, when the seamen were allowed to get drunk, because this is their king's birth day; and when the 4th of July came, I applied to Lt. Pingally for liberty to get drunk. He said 'go along forward, you yankee rascal.' The captain then spoke to him, when he, as I suppose, informed him of my request. He called me to him, and asked — What do you mean, sir, by asking permission to do what you know is contrary to the regulations of this ship? I recollect sir, said I, that about a month ago you gave the English liberty to get drunk because it was their king's birthday; and now I want the liberty to rejoice on my nation's birth day. The captain laughing heartily, ordered that two gallons of wine and one of brandy be procured from the shore for me and my *yankee mess* to rejoice. We all liked this captain. The glass passed merrily round in our *yankee mess*, of thirty in number, and they began to sing *Hail Columbia, happy land*! A north countryman, who called himself the bully of the ship, came along for the purpose of fomenting a quarrel, and told us — 'get out of the way, you d__d yankee buggers.' This was consequently, taken as an insult. I gave him an unceremonious box on the ear, and asked if that was what he meant. Yes, he answered, it is exactly what I want. A few blows were passed between us, when the officer between the decks coming us, ordered *fair* play — he had observed that several others were aiding my antagonist by pelting me. A few more passes were made at each other; at last I struck him with the left hand, and in drawing back found two of the bully's teeth sticking in the joint of one of my fingers. My antagonist, on losing his front teeth, yielded immediately.

"I was then put on the surgeon's list as unfit for duty. The finger is stiff to the present time. This appeared to me a good opportunity to improve for my deliverance, so that I resolved to counterfeit inability, if necessary to attain this end. I continued six months under the doctor's care, and he reported me incurable; but the captain said 'the yankee feigns his sickness, so as to get at liberty — to run away from the hospital.' This the surgeon told me; but soon after put me once more on the list of incurables. The captain then told the surgeon that I was not so sick as I represented. — The surgeon replied, he understood his own business, and I was immediately ordered into the boat with a sick company going to the hospital, under the care of the surgeon's mate, who was to attend us on shore.

3. Joshua Penny

The hospital was situated at the foot of Table mountain, half a mile from the shore. I was put into a blanket, slung on an oar and carried by two men.

"The doctor's mate, ordered the men to follow him through town in single rank, and I was in the rear of this procession. We had not proceeded far before we came to a wine-house, where I begged the sailors to set me down, as I was very *thirsty*. They very readily complied, knowing they would get some wine.—I called on the landlord, as we entered his house, for a bottle of Constantia wine and three tumblers. I took my glass, and paid the landlord while the sailors were drinking theirs. I proposed going immediately, judging however that they would never budge while any wine remained. As soon as they became engaged, I pretended an occasion of necessity to retire out of the back door, and helped myself by the chairs until fairly out, and it was safe to become as well as ever I was in my life. I went hastily through the back yard into another street, which enabled me to get through the town and reach the thicket of bushes at the skirts of Table mountain, which I had often looked to as a place of refuge. I had this in contemplation long before, because I had been acquainted with the mode of living in similar places, and had taken the precaution to provide myself with a belt to fasten around me, containing a knife, a small brass tinder-box, and eleven dollars.

"Here, feeling myself secure from pursuit, I meditated leisurely, and at length determined to spend the residue of my days on this mountain, if the British ships should not leave the Cape. I resolved to become a breakfast for a lion, sooner than be taken to another floating dungeon.

"I returned into the town in the dark, and laid in my supply of goods — this was two loaves of bread, a calabash of brandy and a flint. This was as much as I could take, although my money was not all spent, which had been saved out of my rations of grog for this purpose. My dress was composed of one shirt, one Guernsey frock, and one pair of duck trowsers, with a hospital cap.

"Thus equipped I marched on my tour up the mountain, without waiting to hear what return the doctor's mate would make to our captain of the sick *Jonas Ingleberg*, for that was my name on board the ship. My destiny seemed providential; for the first news I had of the Sceptre, was that she sunk soon after I left her, in a gale of wind without weighing her anchors, and every soul on board perished in her.

Part I : Impressed

"There are no trees on Table mountain, and I climbed the cragged rocks through the bushes, and ascended, or attempted to ascend, all night; yet frequently returned to the place last left. I was much fatigued, and sometimes found a spring of water, where my calabash was very useful. It was unsafe to make a fire that night on the mountain fronting the ships, yet I was in danger from the wild beasts, who were often near me and seemed reluctant to get out of my way. I knew the wild beasts were numerous here, and of almost every species. The next morning, I perceived that the ships lay far below, and could not discover me.

"This mountain is green in every season, and it seems, from the water, that a cat might be discovered upon it: but I found nothing else than gullies, cragged rocks piled on each other, and scrubby bushes in their crevices. Here I began to think of preparing for subsistence, and, on searching, soon found a hive of bees among the rocks. This wild honey is so plenty, that a man from Cape Town will return home, loaded, the same day he leaves it. The Hottentots had taught me the process of obtaining this honey, and having a wooden pipe, I proceeded to the cavity of the rock, covered with wax, and introducing the stem of my pipe through the entrance of the bees, blew in the smoke, which caused the bees to retreat into the interior. The second night I could make a fire under the cover of a rock, and regale myself with brandy and honey.

"When I had ascended four days from the mountain's foot, I lost sight of the fleet and the bay. My course now was over level rocky spots, of 30 or 40 feet in width, on which I saw innumerable herds of goats, hosts of antelopes, wolves, tigers, and leopards. The three latter are the only animals considered dangerous here, except the venomous snakes. The baboons are here numerous and large. At first they would apparently take no notice of me; but soon after would be seen on a precipice, 100 feet above, throwing stones at me.

"At last I reached the summit, and selected a spot, in view of the Western Ocean, for my residence. I occupied a cavern which secured me from storms, near a spring of good water. My whole stock of provisions being nearly exhausted, I thought it time to recruit. Necessity invents the means in these cases. I sallied out with a stone in my hand, and had not advanced a great distance when I espied an antelope on the brow of a precipice. I threw the stone at the back of his head and tumbled him to the bottom; where, by a circuitous route, I found my game, whose skin I drew over his head, and cutting the meat into strings, hung it on sticks put into the crevices of my habitation. This meat when dried, I broiled and eat with toad-sorrel for my sauce. Besides this I had honey and good water. It seemed rather hard at first, to live without bread, salt, and articles deemed necessary in former days; but at the end of two or three weeks I lived very contentedly. While among the Hottentots I had learned their method of making a very pleasant beverage resembling metheglin. I was fortunate enough to find an old hollow tree, which I cut off with my knife, and seized a green tree, which I cut off with my knife on one end for a bottom. Into this tub honey and water was put to stand twenty-four hours; then was added some pounded root to make it foment. This root, in use among the frontier Hottentots, does not resemble any of my acquaintance in America, but makes an excellent drink in this preparation. I had ground-nuts and a root with a stem one inch above the ground, with three leaves as small as those of the garden pink. This root, of the size of a junk bottle, is eatable; yet it is not as good as the water-melon, which the Dutch call it. It is probable the kameroo from the description given me of its size and shape.

"My clothes, by creeping through the rocks and bushes, were so tattered that I had become almost naked. In this extremity I made a needle from the bone of a beast; the eye of which being made with my sharp pointed knife, enabled me to sew with the sinews of my antelopes. With the skins I equipped myself completely from head to foot. The skins were dressed by rubbing sand on the flesh side with a stone; and furnished me with moccasins, shin-fenders, or leggings to the knee; a short petticoat fastened round my waist, and a hunting frock. The hair was worn inside when cold, and turned outside when warm. It is almost unnecessary to add that I wore a superb cap.

"Thus accoutered, it is natural to suppose me somewhat elevated, although without a looking-glass. Pride must have a fall — I was soon afflicted with lice. By procuring an entire new suit, and changing my residence, these tenants of the skin abandoned me. It was not troublesome to change my quarters; and by often shifting my abode for a new tenement, I acquired by occupation dwellings enough to make my territory called a city. Thus I lived, unannoyed by wild beasts or press-gangs; until one day I crept out of some cragged rocks, and came inadvertently into a large concourse of wolves, in their season of making love. They soon sur-

Part I : Impressed

rounded me, some within 20 feet. I stood ready with my knife to defend myself; when at last, one turned off, another followed, till they all had sneaked off apparently ashamed of themselves and left me alone. I used to kill darsies or mountain rats, which eat grass, and are choice food.

"At each full moon I cut a notch in the root which hung to a silken cord around my neck; and this was the only account I kept of time.

"Once I undertook to descend the western side of the mountain to the sea shore, where I could often see vessels in clear weather, but the mountain being very steep on that side, with so many rocks that I frequently let myself down by taking hold of bushes, until I seemed sliding to the sea without power to stop. In two days I returned and gave up experiments in that direction. My practice was to eat twice in the day; and when cooking in the evening always heard the howling of wild beasts, and often saw the light of their eyes when attracted about me by the smell of meat.

"My residence was not on the summit, but in a convenient place for hunting; near some height, on which I could cramp my game. I often went over to the eastern front to view the ships; and continued to do so until twelve notches were made upon the calendar fastened to my neck. I had become perfectly reconciled to my condition — had abundance of meat, sorrel, honey and water; and every night could sing my song with as much pleasure as at any period of my life. In fine, I never enjoyed life better than while I lived among the ferocious animals of Table Mountain; because I had secured myself against the more savage English. I now discovered some vessels at sea, on the western side of the mountain, but was unable to distinguish them as ships or other vessels, the clouds being so far below me. However, I suspected the fleet had sailed from the Cape — mustered my provisions and stowed them in a knapsack, made of a skin drawn over the head, after splitting on the hind-legs. The skin of each hind-leg was tied to that of the fore-leg on the same side, and my arms passed through the loop, the neck hung at the bottom down my back.

"I now left my numerous habitations for the last time. During my residence I had never been able to discover the vestige of a human being, except myself having ever ventured here. I traveled one day and part of a night, without being able to discover any shipping, on account of intervening clouds. I often was compelled to travel five miles on the mountain, without gaining in descent one hundred rods. The second day in my descent, the air being clear, I saw the bay, and one vessel only. I concluded

3. Joshua Penny

to pursue my course until I could ascertain her character. Continuing on the next day, I perceived that vessel to be a brig; and having no top-gallant-masts, took her for a merchantman.

"Determined to push for her immediately, I descended to the foot of the mountain, and rested there til after day break. It was only half a mile to the shore. A British regiment I supposed to be stationed in the town; yet I thought no person would know me after so long an absence, especially in my mountain dress. But to avoid their notice of my uncouth habit, I turned the hair side inwards. I marched through the town unobserved by any one except two or three servants, who continued to gaze obliquely at me as long as I could see them. The boat was coming to the shore as I approached it with two men and the captain, as I supposed.

"I tried my power of speech to prepare myself. The captain landing advanced guardedly towards me, I stepped up to meet him and asked if he wanted to ship a man? He was surprised to hear me speak, and asked 'What in the name of God are you! Man or beast?' He at last stepped up to me and giving me his hand, said 'this is no place to talk — jump into the boat and go on board.' The boat was ordered to return for him in half an hour; into it I sprung, and was soon snug on board.

"When the captain returned he sent for me in the cabin and ordered me two suits of clothes. I put them on, and took my beard off for the first time in fourteen months. He then heard a short story of myself, and said he supposed me to be a deserter; but that I had nothing to fear if I would go with him.

"This brig was under Danish colors, but the captain and property were English, as he told me — and was bound to St. Helena, and thence to London. On learning that I had deserted the Sceptre, he informed me that she had been sunk fourteen months; he pointed to a monument on shore over the bodies of her crew which had been driven on shore and there interred. We were a few days making ready to sail for St. Helena, which place we reached without accident. The governor detained us here until the India fleet arrived to take us under convoy. Lying here four months, I found this captain to be a truly good, humane man. He let me have money to spend there, and although no agreements was made for any wages he had compassion on me. While we lay there the India ship called the Indian Chief, of Philadelphia, lay near us. I wished to return home in her; yet I could not without deserting — and who would be so ungrateful

Part I : Impressed

as to desert from such a captain. At sight of the American flag tears streamed from my eyes. I rushed on board, and every American I saw seemed nearer of kin than any brother I left at home. The conversation which ensued may be conjectured. Among other things I told them of the loss of my protection, and asked if they had lost a hand? A young man answered, 'yes, we have lost my brother John Porter, of your height and complexion.' Taking his protection, I went to our brig and told the captain to put me down on the log book, John Porter. He laughed and said it was well thought of. The India fleet arrived and I was taken into the Admiral Hughes, an India built ship of 2200 tons, which took our captain's brig in tow to England. It was a very boisterous passage, and the brig often hoisted signals of distress. Her hands were nearly worn out at the pumps; but received only 20 dollars per month; while those of us who had been transferred at St. Helena, were paid 22 dollars and fared well. When I was taken out of the brig and along side of the Admiral Hughes — who should I behold but Lieutenant Pingally, 1st of the Sceptre, which had foundered when he was on shore. He was the first person who spoke to me. He stood on the gang-way; called me aside and said, 'Inglesberg, don't you know me?' 'Yes, your honour, perfectly.' The first opportunity that offered so as not to expose me, he asked where I had been, &c. I hope said he it was nothing that I had done which made you desert. He then told me what had happened after I left the Sceptre. He said that the surgeon's mate was unable to give a satisfactory account of the dead Inglesbergh. You and I said he, 'seem to be born for some fortunate end. I went on board of that ship and had returned on shore not two hours, before it blew so hard that it was impossible for a boat to reach her. At 4 o'clock that (Sunday) afternoon she hoisted signals of distress; and fired distress guns until 8 o'clock in the evening, when we heard no more from her, and suppose she sunk immediately.' That harbour, for six months in the year, is as unsafe to lie in as the Gulf of Mexico.

"We arrived at the Downs, the boisterous weather notwithstanding. A French fishing row-galley had taken one of our India ships with the chops of the English Channel. This I had from the captain of the brig, after our arrival in London, who said letters from their friends in France stated their capture and arrival there.

"The regulating captain at the Downs made us all pass in review before him and answer his interrogatories. He catechized me and received

3. Joshua Penny

my answers, thus — 'What countryman are you?' An American sir. 'Where is your protection?' here it is, said I, (showing him the one obtained at St. Helena.) 'How did you come here?' I told him I entered at St. Helena. Lieutenant Pingally stood all this while looking at me, over the interrogating captain's shoulder, and laughed. He, however, after seeing me clear of these fellows clutches, called me aside and told me that 'he was appointed to the command of a 20 gun ship, and if I would go along with him, I should have as good an office as I could merit. I refused, and he said, 'Well, I wish you safe home; If I can never man my ship without impressments I never wish her manned. I knew you to be an American, or perhaps I should not have suffered you to get off as you have.' This was a good Englishman, and any one who was acquainted with him would gladly leave any other, and run to him. The captain of our brig, at Deptford, was glad to see us once more. He paid us all off, with two dollars extra to those who had fared so well in the 'Admiral Hughes,' and then discharged us.[3]

"We went to London with too much money not to loose a little. I had lived so long without the privilege of spending anything that I, too, was a gentleman while my money lasted. Two ladies sitting by a window, said, 'There goes two sailors, gentlemen for a week.' 'Yes,' said one, 'and there sits two strumpets for life.' No man spends his money more to his own notion than a sailor.

"At length I sought a birth in an American vessel; but there were so many Americans waiting to go home that I could get no chance to work my passage. Fortunately I found the ship Dauphin of Boston, bound to Charleston, South Carolina. In her I had a pleasant passage to Charleston.

"When I beheld my native country I was in an ecstasy of joy. Here I found Mr. Enoch Rider of Sag-Harbor, on Long Island, and who is living now. With his assistance I procured me a better protection than the borrowed one at St. Helena. I had engaged to return to England in the Dauphin, because I was with my countrymen, was poor, and was ambitious to try my fortune once more. The captain had paid me fourteen dollars per month, and engaged to give me 48 dollars per month if I would return with him. Captain Wallace, considering my situation favored me with a month's advance pay while the ship took in her cargo of cotton.

"We experienced heavy gales of wind on this voyage. Our boats and anchors were lost in the English Channel, and we put into Dartmouth to repair our damages whence we proceeded to London. Here the cargo was disposed of and the vessel sold. Thus I was again set adrift; but soon after learned that it was a common practice with some merchants to make a sham sale of their vessels, and get a new crew to work their passage home. By this *yankee trick* they gained, in the whole voyage, notwithstanding the high wages in a southern port.

"I expended all my money while waiting for an opportunity to return. At last I went to Wappingstairs, where I found an American schooner, which had come from France expressly to procure American seamen. Captain Charles Smith of North-Carolina, who had commanded a French privateer, been taken three times by the English, and as often escaped from prison, now commanded this schooner. On this passage, an English frigate brought us to, and ordered us on board. The captain of this frigate had been once taken by captain Smith, and now observed to him that he had left off privateering and become merchantman. 'Yes,' replied captain Smith, 'but this does not afford me pocket-money, and I'll soon try it again.' On this the Englishman threatened to flog him, but looking at his clearance, set him at liberty, telling him, 'You are an insolent rascal.'

"In two hours more we were at Morlaix: from this we were conveyed thirty miles to Brest. The ship in which we were to enter was called LaDiable a Quatre [the devil on all fours]. She had been captured by the English and by them called the Danae: converted into a sloop of war, under the command of lord Proby; and sent to cruise off the coast of France. He was called the greatest tyrant in the British navy. Two men whom he punished with the cat jumped overboard the same in consequence of his tyrannical conduct — the seamen in their rage rose upon him, and run the ship in Brest. There she was exposed to sale — purchased by the American consul, and made an American ship. The sailors called her former commander Dog Toby. But we entered her under captain Edward_____ from Virginia.

"The French suspecting us on intending to be captured by the English, would not suffer us to go to sea for a twelvemonth. She was known to be a remarkable fast sailing ship. While we lay thus, at this port, news reached us of the treaty of peace at Amiens, Brest and the fleet was brilliantly illuminated; and great rejoicing took place over this nest-egg of future wars.

"An armament was fitted out for St. Domingo under general Le Clerk, the brother-in-law of Bonaparte. Our ship was freighted thither, and we had on board a Mr. Cooper with his family. One of his daughters died

3. Joshua Penny

and was thrown overboard near Teneriffe, and another of them ran off with a French officer at St. Domingo. We sailed in the month of December 1801; and he entered the bay of Samiana on the 28 of the same month, but we put into Cape Francois. The general had 20,000 troops. As our squadron was entering, we received a few guns from the fort, but on returning a broadside the blacks blew up the fort: as we continued our course the negroes blew up another magazine, said to contain 1500 barrels of powder, and set the town on fire. The sailors were permitted to plunder on shore; and entering houses in flames, we forced open desks and bureaus with the chimney crane. Buckets of melted dollars were taken on board; but the officers seized the whole as we threw them on deck. Three of us had found a bag of plate; and when the officers took this from us to divide among themselves, we mutinied and were for some days kept in irons. After my discharge, at this port I lived on shore to speculate. Such scenes of murder and rapine as were witnessed, are too shocking to relate. *Pandemonium* seemed let loose. A city laid in ashes was to be rebuilt, and after this commenced boards were 100 dollars per 1000. The high prices on everything, at first rendered it difficult to obtain sustenance on the land: but I lived there to see the markets glutted. It was so unhealthy, that for some time there were hardly well enough to bury the *dead*."

Joshua continues with his account of his adventures in sailing on a number of ships. Storms and cheating masters beset him. He does return home to see his family, but then returns to the sea.

Chapter 4
Pirates!

In an age when pirates were more prevalent it should come as no surprise that they also engaged in impressments. When a pirate ship captured a merchant vessel, it seems to have been rather common practice to force some of its crew to leave their old ship and join up with the pirates. Those most likely to be impressed were young men. Newspaper advertisements of the times often mention the ages of those transferred from merchant ships to pirate ships, and these men often were 17, 18, 20, 23, 27 years old.

The wide number of advertisements in American newspapers attest to this, as in the *Boston News Letter*:

> Public Notice is hereby given, that one Daniel Starr of Boston, by Trade a Joyner, but lately a Mariner, on board the Brigt. Essex, whereof Robert Pest was a Commander, in his Voyage from Ireland to Salem, on the 17th of July last, was taken by one Thomas Roberts Commander of a Pirate Ship and Sloop of 150 men and forced the said Starr to go along with them, against his Will, as the said Pest and William Barnes his Mate have testified upon Oath, before Lawful Authority at Boston, the 7th of October 1720.[1]

A few months later a similar advertisement appeared:

> The Deposition of Capt, Thomas Richards, Master of the Ship Two Sisters of Topsham, and the Subscribers his Crew, given in to the Hon. Major Lawrence Armstrong, Commander of Fort Philip. Dated the 12th of May 1721. On the 21st of April 1721. A Pirate Briganteen of 20 guns and 35 Men, about two in the Afternoon, in 30 Deg. N. Lat. 500 Leagues W. of the Maderas, the last Port we parted from, came up with us. Fired a Shot, hoisted a black Flagg with Death's Head, took and plundered our Ship and forcibly carried away Five M, viz William Palfrey Mate, aged 17 Years, born at Limston in Devon, John Phillips Carpenter, aged 27 years, born at Painton

4. Pirates!

near Tangmouth in Devon, Daniel Glitton, Boatswain 35 years, born at Appledore in Northam Parish, Devon. John Hopping, aged 23 Years, born near Limsten, Devon, and Carey Cafworth, born in the County of Cornwall.[2]

This was followed by a list of crew members who attested to the above statement. In August of 1721 another similar advertisement appeared:

Be it known unto all People whom it may concern. That Captain Benjamin Norton, Mariner, Archibald Hammull, Mariner, Christopher Penny, Mariner, all of New Port in the Colony of Rhode Island and Province Plantation in New England, being on the Fifteenth day of January 1st at Anchor at St. Lucia one of the Caribee Islands in the West Indies, in a Briganteen whereof the said Benjamin Norton was Master, and on board whereof was John Daw of Newport aforesaid, Mariner and Mate of the said Briganteen was taken by Roberts and Company of said Island, on said Fifteenth day of January, and that on the Third day after they were taken by the said Pirates at St. Lucia, they took the aforesaid John Daw and asked him, Whither he would sign to their Articles or no. And he refused. Whereupon they cut the said John Daw over the Head in several places with a Cutlas, and tyed him to the Maintop sail Sheet, and there they whipped him almost to Death, so that he could hardly stand alone, and the same time while they were whipping him, they held a Pistol loaded to his head, and said They would kill him unless he would sign their Articles; which he refused to do; and after their repeating so much cruelty on him, they Compelled the said John Daw to sign their Articles, and kept him on board when they dismissed these Deponants. The said John Daw was born in the west of England, and is a Man of short Stature, pretty thick and well set and of a Light Complexion and fresh Colour.[3]

A pirate named Phillips impressed several sailors in September of 1723. The advertisements in the newspaper recorded the following:

Francis Palmer & Philip Stokes Mariners, late belonging to the Schooner Nymph of the Harbour of St. Peters in Newfoundland, Jethro Furber late Master: severally declare and say: That on the Sixth Day of September last, the said Scooner lying at an Anchor in the Harbour Briton in Newfoundland aforesaid, a Scooner came into the said Harbour, Commanded by John Phillips a Pirate, Manned with nine Men; and surprised and took the said Scooner Nymph & Company; and by Force & Violence compelled John Burrell of Boston in New England, Mariner (then belonging to the said Scooner Nymph) to go with said Pirate Phillips contrary to the said Bur-

PART I : IMPRESSED

rell's Will, who was under great concern of Mind & Distress, when forced away by the said Pirate. And the said John Phillips ordered the said Furber to declare upon his return home, that the said Burrell was a Forced Man; and that if the said Furber should neglect to do it, when he met with him again the said John Phillips would Cut off his Ears.[4]

In the same issue of the *Boston Newsletter*, Robert Ford, Mariner, declared "that on the Eighteenth Day of September last, he was taken in the Briganteen Mary by one John Phillips a Pirate who then commanded a Scooner, that he said on board the said Scooner John Burrell, who was called a Forced man, who was very kind to this Declarant and gave him his Hat again, which had been taken from by a French boy."[5] At least one of the pirate captains first came on board as a forced man. Bartholomew Roberts was captured by the pirate Captain Davis on June 5, 1719. Roberts was forced on board the pirate ship and at first would have little to do with the pirate crew members. He was accounted a religious man who read the Bible, observed the Sabbath, and did not drink, swear or dance. This was very different from the way of the pirate crew. But he was an experienced and skillful mariner and as time went by these characteristics were recognized and appreciated by the crew. When the captain of the pirate ship was killed, the pirates elected Roberts captain. It may be that he accepted the offer because he realized that because of his lower class background this was his only chance to captain a ship and also that if the ship were captured it would be assumed that he was a pirate. He would later remark, "It is better to be a commander than a common man, since I have dipped my hands in muddy water and must be a pirate."[6]

A century later, Aaron Smith, sailing from England to the West Indies, was on the *Zephyr* when it was captured by pirates. The captain of the pirate ship needed a navigator and the *Zephyr*'s captain, in order to prevent the pirates from keeping him, had told the pirate captain that Smith was an "excellent one" and also had some medical knowledge. So Smith was forced to serve on the pirate's ship. In *The Atrocities of the Pirates* (1824), a book he later wrote, Smith described his emotions at the time: "The horrors of my situation now rushed upon my mind. I looked upon myself as a wretch, upon whom the world was closed forever; exposed to the brutality of a ferocious and remorseless horde of miscreants, doomed to destruction and death, and perhaps worse to disgrace and ignominy; to become the partaker of their enormities; and be compelled I knew not how

4. Pirates!

soon to imbue my hands in the blood of a fellow-creature and perhaps a fellow countryman."[7]

Smith goes on to describe his activities aboard the pirate ship. He was called upon by the captain to make drinks for Spanish visitors who came aboard the ship to bid for the pirate's plunder. The captain ordered that the drinks were to be especially intoxicating so that the visitors would bid high prices for even trivial items. The drinks had the desired effect upon the bidders and also intoxicated members of the crew. Two of the drunken crew members began to quarrel and fought each other. No one stopped them. The fight was observed by all the others on board. When one of the combatants fell with a severe stab wound in his chest, Smith was called upon to bandage him. Smith protested that he "knew nothing of the healing art." But the captain told Smith that the master of the ship from which Smith had been taken had informed him that he had cured and saved the life of a member of that ship. So Smith "dressed his wounds" as well as he possibly could. At various other times Smith was called upon to minister to the wounded. He also served as a sailmaker. He observed several times when officials from the local area traded with the pirates. He wrote about it: "For I am convinced from personal observation, that from the governor to the mere clerk or officer, all derive some degree of benefit from the acts of those lawless ruffians, and therefore it is against their interest to injure them."[8]

When the captain fell ill, he asked his prisoner to cure him. He also promised him his liberty if he cured him. Smith did not believe this promise and so "resolved to take advantage of his illness" to make his escape. He told the captain to stay in his cabin. Two fishermen came on board the next day and the pirates and the fishermen became very drunk. Smith then drugged the medicine he was giving the captain and while the pirates and fishermen were asleep, he made his escape: "At midnight all were asleep. The inclemency of the night had driven the usual sleepers on deck below and therefore no one could see me. Not a sound was heard save the sullen roar of the waters around me or the wind and the rain beating against the shrouds. Not a star was to be seen and the scud was flying thick and heavy. With a palpitating heart, I seized my bag that held my instruments, and in which I had secured some biscuit, and crept softly letting myself down, the companion ladder and from thence to the stern of the corsair, where the fishermen's canoe was moored. Into this I gently dropped my bag, and then letting myself down, cut the painter and let her drift away with the current in order not to rouse them by any noise."⁹

Another account of capture by pirates is given by Captain George Roberts, who described his capture in his book, *The Four Voyages of Capt. George Roberts ... Written by Himself.* Captain Roberts described his captors as attempting to persuade him to join them, especially since they were in need of someone who knew the coast of Brazil, toward which they were heading. But Roberts refused their offer. Following this there ensued a discussion among the pirates. Some of the pirate sailors had sailed with Roberts on an earlier voyage. They told him that, according to their rules, it was wrong to force a married man to join them. These men suggested that Roberts tell the pirate captains, Low and Russell, he had a wife and five or six children. Roberts was not mistreated by the pirates but one of the captains, who called himself John Russell, argued mightily that Roberts should be compelled to go with them.¹⁰ Failing to persuade Low and the rest of the pirates to this point of view, Russell did succeed in setting Roberts adrift in his sloop with no supplies, few sail, and only his two boys and himself to man it.¹¹

According to David Cordingly in his book, *Under the Black Flag: The Romance and the Reality of Life among the Pirates,* many pirate captains preferred to recruit men who were unmarried. One study of Anglo-American pirates, which examined 521 who were active from 1716 to 1726, found that 23 of the pirates were known to be married.¹² When one pirate ship was wrecked on the coast of Cape Cod, the governor of Massachusetts ordered that the men should be questioned. Their confessions indicate that married men were not encouraged to join the pirate crew. One sailor said that when he and nine other men were on a ship that was captured, the other men "were sent away being married men." Another testified that "no married men were forced," which meant that they were not compelled to sign the pirate's articles and join the crew.¹³

When Philip Ashton was captured by pirates, the captain, Edward Low, questioned him as to whether he or any of the five men who were with him were married. None of them replied. This so angered Captain Low that he came up to Ashton and pointed a pistol to his head and shouted, "You Dog! Why don't you answer me?" When he found that none of the men were married, Captain Low's anger subsided. Ashton later learned that Low's wife had died a short time before Low became a pirate.

4. Pirates!

It was Ashton's belief that this was the reason why Low would only take unmarried men, "that he might have none under him under the influence of such powerful attractive as a wife and children, lest they should grow uneasy in his service and have an inclination to desert him, and return home for the sake of their families."[14]

Edward Lucie-Smith writes in his book, *Outcasts of the Sea, Pirates and Piracy,* that pirate ships often followed a seasonal pattern. They would winter in the Caribbean and when good weather came, they would sail north looking for new men to impress. Often they would find willing recruits among the fishing stations of Newfoundland. There the men were paid so poorly that they were deeply in debt and this looked like a way out. Other men were "forced" from captured ships. Men who possessed special skills, such as coopers and carpenters, or as we have seen, navigators and doctors, were especially to be desired and once taken were unlikely to be easily released.[15]

When men were enticed or forced to join up with the pirates they generally signed an agreement. These agreements differed from crew to crew but here is one example:

    I. Every man has a vote in affairs of moment; as equal title to the fresh provisions or strong liquors at any time seized....

    II. Every man to be called fairly in turn by list on board of prizes....

    III. No person to game at cards or dice for money.

    IV. The lights and candles to be put out at eight o'clock at night....

    V. To keep their piece, pistols and cutlass clean and fit for service.

    VI. No boy or women to be allowed among men....

    VII. To desert their ship or their quarters in battle was punished with Death or Marooning.

    VIII. No striking one another on board, but every man's quarrels to be ended on shore, at sword or pistol.

    IX. No man to talk of breaking up their way of living till each had a share of L, 1000....

    X. The Master and the Quartermaster to receive two shares of a prize....

    XI. The musicians to have rest of the Sabbath day.[16]

These articles of the pirates were considered important in their trials if any pirate ship or pirate crew member were captured and brought to justice.

PART I : IMPRESSED

When brought to trial some of the prisoners claimed that they were only unwilling prisoners and as proof of this they said they had never signed the articles.

In a trial of pirates at Newport in 1723 a number of their former captives were questioned. Captain Welland, formerly of the ship the Amsterdam Merchant said he recognized six of the men. John Mudd said that he remembered one pirate because the pirate had taken "the buttons out of his sleeve."[17] Another sailor, Benjamin Weekham testified that he had smallpox when his ship was captured and that one of the prisoners had carried him on board the pirate ship and when he had asked for a shirt the pirate had sworn at him.[18]

When the prisoners were asked if they had anything to say in their defense, William Blades said he was forced on board the pirate ship and that he had never signed the articles nor had he partaken of a share of the pirate spoils. Thomas Huggett said he had never shared with the pirates, as did Peter Cues. William Jones said he signed the articles only about three weeks after he was taken by the pirates and that he had been forced by the pirate captain to be with them. John Brown said that he had been beaten black and blue in an effort to make him sign the articles. Thomas Jones said he was only seventeen years old and had been taken off a ship at Newfoundland. Thomas Mumford, an Indian, said he had been a servant onboard a fishing boat and was taken off the ship by the pirates. The pirates hanged two Indians but kept him but did not share their prizes with him. He had about six bits when taken.

Next, John Kencate, a doctor onboard the pirate ship, was then brought to trial. The prosecutor charged that the pirates confided their cure and life in the doctor's hands, "and in this trust and dependence it is that they enterprise these horrid depredations." Therefore he should also be judged guilty. But Captain Welland testified that while he was on the pirate ship, the doctor seemed to be solitary, and others said the doctor was there against his will and had never signed the articles. Others testified that the doctor had been very courteous to the prisoners taken by the pirates. When called on to testify in his own behalf, the doctor said that he had been a doctor onboard a ship that was captured by the pirates off the Cape Verde Islands. He said the pirates had kept him ever since but that he had never shared with them nor signed their articles. The court then declared that Thomas Jones, Thomas Mumford, Indian, and Dr.

4. Pirates!

Kencate were innocent. The rest were judged guilty and sentenced to be hanged.[19]

The next day Dr. Kencate was called on to testify concerning three other members of the pirate crew, Thomas Powell, Joseph Sweetser and John Libbey. Kencate said that he had seen Thomas Powell acting as a gunner onboard the pirate ship and that he went on board several ships taken by the pirates and participated in the plunder of them, and that Joseph Libbey was also an active member of the crew and participated in taking goods off captured ships. But he said he had never seen Joseph Sweetser use his arms. Furthermore he refused to go on board any ship taken by the pirates. When Thomas Mumford was questioned, an interpreter was used since Mumford did not speak good English. Speaking through the interpreter, Mumford said that he saw Powell use his gun but once when he shot a Negro but never a white man. And he saw Libbey go on board a captured ship and bring back a pair of stockings. As to Sweetser, Mumford said he cooked on board the ship sometimes and also helped with the sails and once he saw him clean a gun but he never saw him fire it, and Sweetser once told him that he wanted to leave the ship and had also asked the captain if he could go ashore before they fought with the ship that eventually captured them, but had been refused. Sweetser produced an advertisement to show that he had been forced to join the pirates. Sweetser was found not guilty. Several of the men produced advertisements to prove they had been forced. But unless there was corroborating evidence they were judged guilty.

The gallows were set up on a point of land projecting into the harbor and a crowd gathered to witness the execution. Most of the prisoners had something to say before the execution. Mostly they cautioned young people not to follow in their footsteps and to beware of the sins that had led to their downfall. Twenty-six men were hanged on July 19, 1723, for piracy.[20]

Pirates were active all up and down the coast of North America. In Charles Town, South Carolina, one inhabitant noted that "the greatest Plague to us now is by Piracy on our Coast."[21] In June 1718, the famous pirate Blackbeard appeared in the Charles Town harbor with four ships and proceeded to plunder ships in the harbor and seize some of their passengers. Blackbeard demanded a chest of medicine as a ransom for the passengers. If the governor of the province did not give in to his demands,

PART I : IMPRESSED

Blackbeard promised to cut off the heads of his captives, including Sanuel Wragg, a member of the council, and Wragg's young son. While the governor and council were deliberating, Blackbeard and his pirates paraded through the streets of the town. The governor gave in and sent Blackbeard nearly 400 pounds of medical supplies. Before the pirates left, they took jewelry, rich clothes, and the like from their captives before releasing them.[22]

Although the governor asked the Proprietors for ships and soldiers to protect the city and its harbor from pirates, none arrived. Finally, after several more ships were seized by pirates, the town's merchants commissioned William Rhett a captain and outfitted two ships with 130 men to go after the pirates. Rhett and his men found Steve Bonnet, a notorious pirate, and his crew repairing their ship. After a bloody battle, Bonnet and his crew surrendered. Rhett returned to Charles Town with thirty-five prisoners.

In the trial that ensued on October 29, 30, 31 of 1718, the pirate crew offered their defenses. N. Paterson said that he had been on board a ship that had been captured by the pirate Blackbeard. The pirates took some of their best men and left the rest marooned on an island. When Major Bonnet came and told them he was planning to go to St. Thomas to apply for a commission to go privateering, Paterson said he was willing to go. It was only after he was on board that Bonnet "forced me to do what he pleased, for it was against my Will." When Paterson was asked if he was forced, he answered, "But Sir, it was in a strange Land, nor nothing left, and I had no money and I was willing to do something to live; but it was against my Will to go a pirating."[23]

Witnesses for one member of the pirate crew, Thomas Nichols, said that he was much discontented. But Major Bonnet said he "would force him to go."[24] According to other crew members he would not "join with the rest of the men, but instead separated himself from the company." Captain Read, who had been captured by the pirates and held hostage for a time, declared that Nichols behaved himself differently from the rest and did not join with them. Captain Manwaring, who also had been held captive, testified that Nichols had told him that he hoped it would soon be over, "for he hoped to get clear of them and looked very melancholy, and never joined with the rest in their Cabals when they were drinking, and when Major Bonnet sent for him he refused to go and said he would die

4. Pirates!

before he would fight."[25] Then Nichols was allowed to question some of the other members of the crew. He asked a pirate named Killing, "Did you never hear me say I would leave that Course of Life?" Killing answered, "When he came on board, he told me he would give the whole World if he had it to be free from them.... And he was not with them when they shared ... and he never was at their Cabals as the rest were."[26]

The judge then remarked, "He seems to be under a constraint indeed, and [it] therefore must be taken into Consideration." When other members of the crew attempted to plead they not be judged guilty since they had not been part of the party that boarded Captain Manwaring's ship, the judge said, "That is no Excuse, it is not such or such a one that goes on board only, but those that stand ready to assist them, have as great a hand in the Fact as the other; for Men would not be taken by two or three, if they had no more help, so that the whole Crew are equally concerned at such a time."[27] When the jury deliberated and reached their decision, Thomas Nichols was judged not guilty.

Following this the jury turned to considering several other members of the pirate ship. Captain Read said that Brierly acted as the rest of the company, but as for Boyd, "I thought him to be a Prisoner and discoursed freely with him, which if he had discovered it had done me an Injury, for I heard him wish we might meet with a Thirty Gun Ship, and I told him I should be glad of it as well." The foreman asked, "What did he wish to meet with a Thirty-Gun Ship for?" Captain Read answered, "To free us from the Pirates."[28] Brierly was judged guilty and Boyd was acquitted. The several groups of pirates were hanged on November 8 and November 19, 1718. They were buried below the high water mark off White Point, Charles Town.[29]

Then the trial of Major Bonnet took place. He had come from a good English family. It was said of him that he was a "gentleman that has had the Advantage of a liberal Education, and being generally esteemed a Man of Letters." He owned a sugar plantation on the island of Barbados. But he surprised his neighbors by purchasing a ship and naming it the *Revenge*. He paid wages out of his own pocket to the men he recruited to go with him. However, he proved a poor sailor and soon lost the confidence of his crew. For a time he joined up with the pirate Blackbeard, but eventually the two separated. When he and his crew were captured, they had beached their ship for repairs.[30] At his trial Bonnet pleaded not guilty but he had no real defense. Judge Trott sentenced him to be executed. The execution took place at White Point on December 10. After his body was taken down, it was buried near the bodies of the men of his crew.[31]

In April of 1724, Skipper Andrew Haradan, who commanded the ship *Squirrel*, was attacked by Captain John Phillips, a pirate. After Haradan surrendered, he was taken aboard the pirate ship and forced to remain. Haradan soon discovered that about half of Phillips' crew had been forced and were only waiting for a chance to escape. Edward Cheeseman, the ship's carpenter, was one of the first to discuss this with Haradan. The forced men had been contemplating some way to free themselves. The crew used their carpentry tools — axes, adzes, etc. — to overcome the pirate captain and his supporters. One of Haradan's supporters was John Filmore, a fisherman who had been captured by the pirate captain Phillips while Filmore was fishing off the coast of New Foundland. Filmore was married to Mary Spiller of Ipswich and their son Nathaniel was the grandfather of Millard Fillmore, who became president of the United States.[32]

Aaron Smith, whose capture by pirates in 1821 has previously been described, escaped successfully from pirates only to be arrested as a pirate and brought to London for trial. At his trial several men who had been captured by the pirates testified against him, saying that he acted as though he was a willing member of the pirate crew. When Smith was called to testify in his own defense, he said that he had been carried aboard the ship by the pirates and was tortured by them before he would do their bidding and navigate. He had been held in a solitary dungeon, flogged, powder placed at his feet and set fire to, among other inducements. He had not participated in the division of spoils of the pirates from their various captures, and in fact was nearly penniless when he eventually escaped from them. Aaron Smith then called twenty witnesses in his defense. One of them was his beautiful fiancée, who said that she had been waiting for him for three years. She said, "I expected on the prisoner arriving in England that I should become his wife." The she broke down and cried. The jury found Smith not guilty because they determined that he was a forced man. A number of observers felt that the testimony of Smith's fiancée had determined their decision.[33]

According to a leading authority on piracy, Hugh H. Rankin, piracy in North American waters waned following the capture and death of the most famous pirates — Roberts, Rackham, Van, Lowther and Low. From

4. Pirates!

1728 on there were fewer pirates operating off the North American coast.[34] Rankin believes that several causes contributed to the end of piracy. First, the piracy act was broadened to include as accessories any persons who traded with the pirates. Eliminating markets for pirates' plunder made their trade less profitable. Second, merchants in the colonies resented piratical activity upon their coast; it interfered with trade. Third, gradually the pirates had been excluded from their bases on islands in the Caribbean. Fourth, proprietary charters in the colonies had been revoked, and royal governors had been installed. These royal governors seemed to have been less inclined to leniency and cracked down on pirate adventurers who ventured into their territories. Fifth, the West Indies captains of guard ships were chosen more carefully. They often found and captured pirate ships. Rankin concludes: "Only when England and her colonies put behind them the idea that they could afford crime better than they could afford an adequate police force did affairs take a turn for the better. Merchants in the home country were effective in their influence on the government to remove the causes of economic isolation in the colonial trade. Put in its simplest terms, once a congenial atmosphere was eliminated, piracy collapsed of its own weight."[35]

Chapter 5

John Stradley

Abandoned as an infant, John Stradley was placed in a foundling hospital and then sent to live with a large family until he was eight years old, when he was apprenticed to a blacksmith. After serving his time and learning a trade, he decided to look for another position. He served for a time on board a merchant ship and then at the end of the voyage headed for London. Here is his account:

"So I took a place in the Coach to come up to London but was stopped by the Pres Master about fore miles from the Gasport who opened the Coach door and told me I must come out and give an account of myself— who I was and where I was going. I told him I had been Armorer of the Grafton and had returned my arms and had my certificate and a letter of Recommendation and was going to the tavern to apply for an oather Ship, he took my letter and looked at the Directions and examined the Seal and turned it Over and Over several times and I stood trembling all the while for fear he should open it. If he had I should have been told for there was not a word in it. But he gave me my letter and certificate and told me I might go about my business. So I came into London the Next Day and a fresh trouble came to know how I was to go through London to Woolrich, and as I had to pass over Tower Hill I thought the safest way to escape notis of the Press gang was to go right into the house where they was sitting for I was very Decently dressed and had very little of the appearance of a Seaman.[1]

"So I went boldly in and called for something to drink and asked one of them to drink with me which I did and I pay my reckoning and came right through them for they did not enquire who I was or what I was. So I came to Woolrich that Day and as I had no Relations and all I thought

5. John Stradley

I would go to see my Master and Mistress that I served my time to with an intention to take up my residence with them, but just as I entered the door I saw a number of men dressed in black. I asked for my former Master. They told me that he was ded and pointed me to the Coffin and said they was just agoing to carry him to the grave. This gave me a very suding shok which occasioned me to weep very much and to think my case was distressing on every quarter. But the Corps being buried and I began to recover the shok, I began to Inquire of my Old acquaintance but was Informed that some wore ded and to those gone away I found a Strong alteration....

"But I pressed On, I got a Comfortable situation in the Arsenal at Woolstock and continued there about eight months. We ust to go to work at five oclock in the morning and one Morning I went to the Arsenal gate with an intant to go to work but all at once the thought struck my mind that I would go to London to see one of my old shipmates that had escaped from the Ship he was turned over to when our ship was paid off.

"And I was going along the lone road that looks to Rotherhitte just opposite the St. Liemer hous I was stopt by a press Gang and took on bord the tender called the Night and laying at the tower to reserve presmen and here begun another Scene of troble I was stolen away like a Dog and lockt down in the hole with a sentinel over me with a drawn sword as if I had been a thief or a Murderer, from then I was Convoid to the Guard Ship laying at the Hoar which was a wretched sink of Iniquity. Their did I lay six week without anything to shift myself or any bed to lay on untill I was dirty and lousey and had spoilt all of my Clothes, after this the Armourer of the Ship was taken sick and was sented on shore and was Invalided and I applied for the situation and got a warrant for the Ship and Continued the station ten months then the ship was ordered up to Deptford to be Paid off for the war was over for a short time

"But while we lay at the Nor I was ordered on shore to Sheernefs to do som work for the Ship which I could no do on bord, and when I had finished it was quite dark and I had to go through the yard to look for the boat which was to fetch me on bord, but as I was coming through the yard I mist my way and fell into the dock and here is another Act of a merciful God I did not know him I was preserved in Christ Jesus for had it not bee the water was just comin to the Dock to break my fall I must surtinly have dast my life to Piaces against the bottom of the Dock but finding

Part I : Impressed

myself in the water I swam in the oather side of the Dock and got into a fishing boat which carried me to the stairs and landed me again in the yard where I had been walking all day,

"Anoathr time when I had been working on Shore on Sheernefs I was coming on bord with 14 oather men and it was very dark and the wind blew very hard and we had six miles to go before we could reach the ship the man at the bow of the boat laid in his oar too soon and took up the boat hook to stick at the ship but mist his mark and the boat went from the side of the Ship we was bloed about the sea all night in the open boat not knowing what to do or whar we ware and expecting the boat to sink for we shipt so much water that it was with great difficulty we could keep her above warter, but mercifully Preserved again and brought on bord the next morning.

"O the dangers of the sea and O Wonderful the mercy of God.

"We went up to Depthford and was Paid off the Depthford yard and here again I got clear of the miserable situation of a seafaring life, and was reentered in the Arsenal, I again rejoiced to my liberty and thought it a great hapiness to be from Perantile Constraint or the constrant of Tiranecle Officers, I therefore was determined to take my full swing of follar and vanity but my old tormenter so haunted me in all my Promised Pleasures that I could not find them as I had promised myself I should, for my conscience told me I was a guilty sinner and that God was angry with me, which alarmed me very much and made me think that if I did not Reform from my wicked ways I must go to hell, thus did I labour under the tormenting form of a guilty Conscience for many many months, so at last I began to think that I would go to sea again for their I should not have it in my power to Sin, I therefore indevered to git a Ship that was going to the West Indies but was Mercifully Disappointed for the Day of Gods Power was at hand, for the Lord afflicted my by taken all the use of my lims so that thay ware obliged to feed me as they did a child that had no help of himself,

"In this State of affliction I was often afrade to shut my eyes for fear of Pins and gasly figures that was painted in my emagenation,

"O the terrors of a guilty Conscience, Sinner be sure your sin will find you out was Stampt on my Verry Hart, but the Lord beheld my distress and brought me again from death to health and strength and one of my friends that layed in the haus with me lent me a book called Midetations, but being brought up ignerent that I could not read it so as to understand the meaning of it but I got a man to reade it to me and as he Red I struck with such astonishment and greatly wondered how it was Possible a man should attain to such Degree of Knoleg as to write such Owfull grand and pleasing things as I heard. Shurly thought I There is something in this world to be learnt which I had never heard of before and so I found at last for the book was the means in the hands of the Divine Spirit of Instructing in the true Knowledge of Salvation the way that God gives Sinners when all Oathers fail for very soon after I heard this book read my mind was forcable struk by that ever memorable Blessed Passage of Scripture, 'I will arise now and go to my father and will say father I have sind against haven and in thy sight and am not worthy to be called thy son,' and her I date that Happy Day Never to be forgotten in t[ime] or eternity."

Stradley II

Stradley continues to discuss religion and doctrinal matters. He writes: "I thought I would go to the place of worship in Plumeted rode whare I continued going for several months and Partook of the Ordinance of the Lord Supper with them." He relates arguing with a young friend about baptism until he sees that the bible teaches baptism: "At the time this change took place in Our minds we were both members of the Chappel in Plumsted road, but as soon as they under stood what was in our intention they were very much alarmed and said one to the oather, they have been among the Baptist and their minds are poisoned O let us pursued them of from it, But all in vain."

Stradley's own account ends there but attached to the handwritten biography is a note: "Thomas Stradley 1800–1888 Arrived at Asheville, N.C. in 1840." Also attached is this note: "The subject of this memoir used to smoke tobacco as a relief from asthmatic attacks, he called for a smoke of pipe which was speedily given by his long loved wife, after a few puffs he put the pipe aside, leaning on mother's bosom, he said: 'I have fought a good fight, I have kept the faith, henceforth' (here the Spirit passing the port-hole of life stopped at the finish of the shout of victory,) and Mother finished the strain of triumph, and lay his head on his pillow, 'There is laid up for me a Crown of Righteousness which the Lord the

PART I : IMPRESSED

righteous judge shall give me at that day, and not to me only but All them also that loves his appearing.'

"(signed) TS

"Note — Thomas Stradley, 1800–1888, Arrived at Asheville, NC in 1840 and was the first Baptist Minister there."

Eventually one of his descendents passed the manuscript describing his experiences on to the National Maritime Museum in London.[2]

Chapter 6

Jacob Nagle

Jacob Nagle, a young man from Reading, a small town in Pennsylvania, at fifteen joined George Washington's army during the American Revolution. Within a year, he entered service aboard several American ships. Captured aboard an American privateer, in December 1781, Jacob was taken to a prison on the island of St. Eustatius in the Caribbean. His fortunes changed rapidly in the days that followed. In his account of his adventures, he describes his life as a prisoner:

"Having no yard, we ware confined in the rooms upstairs. Our prisoner allowance was three quarters of a pound of bread pr day, salt codfish one day and salted horse meat on the next day. The jailor informed us that the sailors had no better. I could not relish the horsemeat, therefore I made practice of selling my allowance to the Negroes for sugar, I used with bread and water. In this disagreeable manner I lived. Our boatswain thought to rule us in prison as he thought fit and as he did in the schooner. He was one of the seven Englishmen, all seamen, that run from the *Royal Oak* before mentioned. One day he undertook to flog me. Though I was young, I engaged him til some of his old shipmates finding I was too smart for him, one of them came behind me and nocked me down. One of his old shipmates that had been on board of the man-a-war with the whole of them, being unwell, and laying on his bed, was looking at the treatment that I received from them. He jumped up and came to me and swore If I did not flog the boatswain he would flog me. He stood my second, and at it we went. In about ten or twelve minutes he gave it up, and the rest was afraid to say any more, as they found Jack was my friend.

"Jack was an able man and a good seaman. He shamed sick to get to

PART I : IMPRESSED

the hospital. In a few days he got liberty to work on board the merchant ships. One day a British man of war came into the roads and let go her anchor. She was called the *Blind Russel,* 74 gun ship. The captain going on shore in his barge spied Jack working on board, came along side, and ordered him into the boat. He went in and they pulled for shore. The captain landed and was giving the coxwain orders to carry the man on board. The captain was standing on the beach with his cane in his hand. Jack was in the bow of the boat and leaped on the gang board, and from thence on shore, and snatched the cane out of the captain's hand and knocked him down and then took to his heels and run for it, and the whole barges crew after him, crying out 'Stop him' running through the market place, but the blacks knowing they wanted to press him, cried out 'Run Massa, run Massa, no ketche, no have,' and Jack got into a sugar cane patch where they could not find him. So the captain went on board with a broken head and lost his man into the bargain. Jack then came into prison and remained there.[1]

"My companion and myself had the privilege of taking the boat and go on shore when we pleased. The schooner laying within hail. During the time we lay here, the anchors were sold, and we rec'd the prize money, but how much I do not recollect. One day, being on shore, we came down to the boat to go on board, when we were accosted by a sailor [who] prayed that we would give him some relief, as he had been three days on shore without any subsistence whatever excepting water. We took him into a wine house on the beach and call'd for as much as he thought fit to eat and drink. He hailed for Philadelphia, was taken by the British and kept him, and then taken by the French and was on board of the line a battle ships laying then in the harbour as as prisoner and had got on shore in hopes of getting on board sum America ship bound home. We agreed to take him on board with us and inform'd the mate that he was American and wanted to go to St. Pieres with us to go on board the *Holker.*

"Being on shore one day, and putting off to go on board again, the three of us, this Thos. Moody by name, a French boat was then landing full of men and officers.

"The bowman hailed him. 'A Jack, how you do?'

"'Very well.' said Jack.

"I said then, 'Jack, you are sold' not dreaming it would be any determent to us.

98

6. Jacob Nagle

"'O no' says Jack, 'that was my best friend on board.'

"I said, 'I would not trust him.'

"They landed and we went on board, but they took notice what vessel we went on board of, we thinking no more of it, but about 10'o clock at night, to our surprise, a serjents guard came on board us and demanded the three of us. The mate told him that he knew two of us was Americans.... The sarjent told him he had orders to take all three of us, and we must go to prison. We packed up our clothes, and a few dollars of our prize money, and they took us to prison that night.

"They unlocked a room that was so full that we could scarcely find a place vacant to lay down. In the morning the doors was unlocked and all hands had the privilege to go into the yard during the day.

"Our allowance was three quarters of a pound of bread and about 3 ounces of meat but no liquor. We sold our meat to the convicts which was in the same prison but confined below for about 2 dogs, which is about 2 pence, and a stampee is 3 halfpence. With this we could buy fruit or such other articles as we thought fit. The jailor was very strict in respect of liquor but you could by as much wine from as you please, but allowing no other person.

"Our chief amusement was the cudgels with baskets on the handels. In the morning, coming down into the yard, I admired these handsome straight sticks with baskets on the handels, and not knowing the meaning of their laying across each other. I took up one to view it, a hundred sailors sitting round on the benches. One young man jumped up from his seat, ketched up the other, and struck me over the head. I returned the blow. He guarded it off. I knew nothing about cudgeling, but I thrashed away without any guard, and when he struck at me, I struck him at the same time, which put us much upon a par, but he soon got tired of this sport and told me I did not play fair and I should guard myself. I told him it was not fair to hit me over the head, a stranger as I was, and knew nothing about cudgeling. Therefore we dropped the sport, with a hearty laugh among the seamen. However, I practiced and soon learnt to play a good stick with my old antagonist.

"In a few days after, the French commissary came into the prison and I informed him of my situation, and that I was an American and taken out of English prison. He told me that the man that we supported was taken as an English prisoner, if he was American, and supplying him with

Part I : Impressed

provisions and succoring him made us as good Englishmen as he was a Frenchman, and that was all the satisfaction that I could receive from him.

"At this time I kept a kind of a journal and had a great many remarks in the taking of the island of St. Christopher and the French and British fleet. The prisoners advised me to destroy it, for fear they should find it with me. As I was put into the prison, as supposed to support the British prisoners, they would take me for a spy, passing for a American, as one man had been hung for a spy about two month before. Therefore I burnt my book. I then wrote to the American counsel at St. Piers but never received any answer. The British prisoners that laid on the ground flore laid out a plan for making their escape in the night. They lifted a cuppel of boards so that one man could be employ'd digging under the foundation of the wall and upwards till they came to the pavement in the street where the sentry walked. When it was all completed they ware all to get out one by one, the hole not containing more, as the sentry walked to the other end of the jail. When they ware all fixed, the one broke down the stones, and seeing the sentry walking towards the other end, he started and got round the corner into the next street. The second, taking his opportunity, when half way up the soldier, turning suddenly and sooner than was expected, instantly fired and killed him out right in the hole. The rest had to retreat, and the alarm being given, the one that had got away was taken and confined in the dungeon for a long time before he was let out amongst the other prisoners.

"The jailor had a trustee Negro, which he put great depenance in, who brought the bread in every day and smugeld liquor in the bag and sell a ½ s wine glass for as much as you would get a quart bottle for. The prisoners were determined to fix him. In the morning when he came in with the bread, they seized the bag and took out the blather and gave it to the jailor. He was so enraged at the slave for spoiling his custom, he ordered him to be flogged and to encourage the prisoners, he made us all stand in ranks and served it all out to us in a wine glass. It went twice round the two ships companies. I remain'd in this prison as near as I can guess about 10 month

"A carteel was fitted out and all the youngest and the sickliest were sent in hur to St. Lucia, keeping the best of the seamen to be sent to France in the fleet, which sailed shortly after. We arrived and came to anchor at Pigeon Island and was sent to board the *Prudent,* 64 guns, and remained about three weeks, when we ware drafted on board the *St. Lucia* Brig,

6. Jacob Nagle

pink stern, had been taken from the Americans, and made a tender of, mounting 12 guns but pierced for 14 guns.

"I cannot describe the cruelty of this man a war, but I will endeavour to give a short sketch. Captain Brooklin commanded who was first lieutenant of the *Prudent* before mentioned, and six officers out of the same ship and seven of us that was draughted on board. The second day one man received two dozen upon suspicion of broaching a cask of rum. In a few days we pressed 5 more out of a transport, though it is not allowed in the service. When but seven men, we had to hoist a six oard boat in and out, night and morning, for fear of our running away with her. Nothing was to be done without nocking down and thrashing in every duty that was to be done. As soon as we had pressed hands sufficient to weigh the anchor, we run down to the Canash and came to an anchor at the entrance of it, and pressed every man, weather sailor or not, that came into the harbour. We pressed an old man from England, a house carpenter, and the merchant that was to employ him had to pay 30 Lb. sterling for a supernumery before he was let go. On shore we ware dreaded by all merchantmen.

"The purser one day finding a tin cup of mine that I had rought upon with a sail needle, he enquired of the men to know whoes cup that was. They all new but would not tell, for fear that I would get punished, I being away at the same time in the boat. When we came on board, as they came up he enquired whose cup that was. None of them would own that they new whose cup it was. I being in the boat as boatkeeper new nothing of it.

"The purser thought it strange, at last call'd me out of the boat, 'Is this your cup?'

"'Yes, Sir'

"'Come aft on the quarter deck.'

"I trimbled, though I new I got the cup honestly. I went aft, where the captain was sitting by a small table, and the purser giving him the cup. 'Is this your cup?'

"'Yes. Sir'

"'Is this your righting?'

"'Yes, Sir.'

"He called his steward and desired him to bring up pen, ink, and paper. When it was brought, he desired me to right. I asked him what I should right.

Part I : Impressed

"He made the answer. 'What was on the cup.'

"I rought, 'Jacob Nagle, Born in the Town of Reading, Berks County, Pennsylvania State. N. America.' With my fright and trimbeling I did not right it half so well, but he saw it was the same hand.

"'You must act a ships steward under the purser,' the captain replyed. I made answer that I did not know my own allowance.

"He replied, 'What is the pusser for, but to give you instructions and books.'

"It happened well for me, as I was then from under the lash of the boatswain, a meare tirent, and other officers.

"A few days after. What appeared strange to both men and officers was, though we weare dreaded as a man of war and cruel usage, a stout young sailor came to the captain on shore and told him he wanted to enter. He said he belonged to such a ship and the captain had fell out with him and would not pay him his wages.

"'Very well, my man,' said the captain, 'I will get your wages. There is my boat with 4 boys. You may go on board and tell the pusser to give you a bottle of rum to drink my health.'

"Accordingly, aboard he came, the officers and men staring to see a stout looking sailor coming on board by himself. When on board, he called out for the pusser, the boatswain and officers gathering round him enquiring who and what he was. The boatswain, more inquisitive than the rest, asked him how long he had been to see. He turned round and told him he had been two days to tomorrow. The officers all laughed at the joke and I was sent for the liqur. He would not except of it till I had drank and then he handed it round amongst all the sailors. In a few days the captain received 70 odd guineas for him and gave it to him and made a boatswain's mate of him, which he did not like.

"In a few days we went down to leeward to a watering place for a supply of water. We ware hoisting in the water as the cutter was rafting and towing it off. At noon they piped to dinner, and I served the grog. Luke Aarvour, which was his name, sat down on the comings of the main hatch way, where I was sitting and the captain on the quarter deck, and the boat was coming off to dinner. Luke said to me, 'I am now longanough on board this vessel, and you will not see me again, goodby.' I smiled as I was going below.

"In less that three minutes he was overboard like a fish. The captain hailed the boat that had an officer in her to ketch him and got a musket out of the arm chest and kept firing at him but whenever he pointed the musket he would dive and would not come up for 20 yard, and the boat after him. When they came near him, he told the young officer if he offered to lay holt of him, he would hall him overboard and drown'd him. Then he would go down again. The captain hailed the fort, and soldiers came down to receive him when he landed, but they war disappointed. He landed the opposite side of a creek and they could not cross. He made his escape from the whole in the noon day."[2]

Chapter 7
Joseph Bates

The story of Joseph Bates can be found in his autobiography, *The Early Life and Later Experience and Labors of Elder Joseph Bates.* In the book, he describes his impressment experience. In all the stories told by the impressed men, this one appeals to me as one of the most rebellious. He really is angry at his impressment, and schemes constantly at ways to secure his freedom. He writes of his experience as follows:

"Two of us crossed the Irish Channel to Liverpool to seek a voyage to America. A few days after our arrival, a 'press-gang' (an officer and twelve men) entered our boarding house in the evening and asked to what country we belonged.

"We produced our American protections, which proved us to be citizens of the United States. Protections and arguments would not satisfy them. They seized and dragged us to the 'rendezvous,' a place of close confinement. In the morning we were examined before a naval lieutenant, and ordered to join the British navy. To prevent our escape, four stout men seized us, and the lieutenant, with his drawn sword, going before, we were conducted through the middle of one of the principal streets of Liverpool like condemned criminals ordered to the gallows. When we reached the river side, a boat well manned with men was in readiness and conveyed us on board the Princess, of the royal navy. After a rigid scrutiny we were confined in the prison room on the lower deck, with about sixty others who claimed to be Americans, impressed in like manner to ourselves. This eventful epoch occurred April 27, 1810.

"On board of this ship one feeling seemed to pervade the minds of all who claimed to be Americans, viz. that we were unlawfully seized without any provocation on our part, hence, any way by which we could regain

7. Joseph Bates

our liberty would be justifiable. In a few days the greater portion of the officers and crew took one of their number on shore to be buried. It was then suggested by some that this was a favorable time for us to break the iron bars and bolts in the port hole and make our escape by swimming in the strong current that was rushing by us. In breaking the bars we succeeded beyond our expectation, and when all ready to cast ourselves overboard, one after another the boats came along side with the officers, and our open place was discovered. For this, they began by taking one after another and whipping them on their naked backs in a most inhuman manner. This dreadful work was in progress for several hours, and ceased bout nine o'clock at night, the officers intending to finish next day. But they did not have time to carry out their cruel work; for orders were given to transship us all on board a frigate near by that was weighing her anchors to put to sea.

"In a few days we came to Plymouth where we were reexamined, and all such as were pronounced in good condition for service in the British navy were transferred to one of their largest stationary ships, called the 'Saint Salvadore Del Mondo.' On this monstrous floating castle were fifteen hundred persons in the same condition as myself.

"Here, in conversation with a young man from Massachusetts, we agreed to try to make our escape if we perished in the attempt. We prepared us a rope and closely watched the soldiers and sailors on guard till they were being relieved from their posts at midnight. We then raised the 'hanging port,' about eighteen inches and put the 'tackle fall' into the hands of a friend in the secret, to lower it down when we were beyond the reach of the musket balls. Our rope and blanket, about thirty feet long, reached the water. Forbes, my companion whispered, 'Will you follow?' I replied, 'Yes.' By the time he reached the water I was slipping down after him, when the alarm ran through the ship. 'A man overboard.' Our friend dropped the 'port' for fear of being detected, which left me exposed to the fire of the sentinels. But I was soon in the water and swam to a hiding place under the 'accomodation ladder' by the time the boats were manned with lanterns to hunt us out.

"We watched for an opportunity to take an opposite direction from our pursuers, who were repeatedly hailed from the ship to know if they had found any one. We had about three miles to swim with our clothes on, except our jackets and shoes; these I had fastened on to the back of

PART I : IMPRESSED

my neck to screen me from a chance shot from the ship. An officer with men and lanterns descended the accommodation ladder and sliding his hand over the slat he touched my hand and immediately shouted, 'Here is one of them; Come out of that, you sir! Here is another! Come out, you sir!' We swam round to them, and were drawn upon the stage. 'Who are you?' Demanded the officer. 'An American' 'How dare you undertake to swim away from the ship? Did you not know that you were liable to be shot?' I answered that I was not a subject of King George and had done this to gain my liberty. 'Bring them up here!' was the order from the ship. After another examination we were put into close confinement with a number of criminals awaiting their punishment.

"After some thirty hours of close confinement, I was separated from my friend, and hurried away with about one hundred and fifty sailors (all strangers to me) to join His Majesty's ship, 'Rodney' of 74 guns, whose crew numbered about seven hundred men. soon as we had passed our muster on the quarter-deck of the Rodney, all were permitted to go below and get their dinners but Bates. Commander Bolton handed the first lieutenant a paper, on reading which he looked at me and muttered, 'Scoundrel.' All the boat's crew, amounting to more than one hundred men, were immediately assembled on the quarter deck. Said Capt. Bolton, 'Do you see that fellow?' 'Yes, sir,' 'If you ever allow him to get in one of your boats, I will flog every one of the boat's crew, Do you understand me?' 'Yes, sir, yes, sir' was the reply. 'then go down to your dinners, and you may, too, sir.'

"I now began to learn something of the nature of my punishment for attempting in a quiet and peaceable manner to quit his Majesty's service. In the commanding officer's view this seemed to amount to an unpardonable crime, and one never to be forgotten. In a few hours the Rodney under a cloud of sail was leaving old Plymouth in the distance, steering for the French coast to make war with the Frenchmen. 'Hope deferred makes the heart sick.' thus my hope of freedom from this oppressive state seemed to wane from my view like the land we were leaving in the distance.

"As our final destination was to join the British squadron in the Gulf of Lyons in the Mediterranean Sea, we made a stop at Cadiz, in Spain. Here the French troops of Napoleon Bonaparte were bombarding the city and British and Spanish ships of war in the harbor. These comprised a part of the Spanish fleet that finally escaped from the battle of Trafalgar, under Lord Nelson, in 1805 and were now to be refitted by their ally, the English, and sail for Port Mahon in the Mediterranean. Unexpectedly, I was one of fifty selected to refit and man one of them, the 'Apollo.' A few days after passing the Straits of Gibralter, we encountered a most violent gale of wind called a 'levanter,' common in those seas, which caused our ship to labor so excessively that it was with the utmost exertion at the pumps that we kept her from sinking. We were finally favored to return back to Gibraltar and refit.

"A number of Spanish officers with their families still belonged to the ship. It was wonderful and strange to us to see how tenaciously those people hung around their images, surrounded with burning wax candles, as though they could save them in this perilous hour, when nothing short of our continual labor at the pumps prevented the ship from sinking with us all.

"After refitting at Gibraltar, we sailed again and arrived safely at the island of Mahon. Here I made another attempt to regain my liberty with two others, by inducing a native to take us to land in his market load. After some two days and nights of fruitless labor to escape from the island by boats or otherwise, or from those who were well paid for apprehending deserters, we deemed it best to venture back. Our voluntary return to the ship was finally accepted as evidence that we did not design to desert from the service of King George III. Thus we escaped from being publicly whipped.

"Our crew was now taken back to Gibraltar to join the Rodney, our ship, which had just arrived in charge of another Spanish line of battle ship for Port Mahon, having a crew of fifty of the Rodney's men. In company with our Spanish consort, we sailed some eighty miles on our way to Malaga, where we discovered the combined armies of the English and Spanish in close engagement with the French army on the seaboard. Our ship was soon moored broadside to the shore. As the orders for furling the sails were not promptly obeyed, by reason of the Frenchmen's shot from the fort, all hands were ordered aloft and there remained exposed to the enemy's shot until the sails were furled. This was done out of anger. While in this condition, a single well-directed shot might have killed a score, but fortunately none were shot till all had reached the deck. Our thirty-two pound balls made dreadful havoc for a little while in the enemy's ranks.

PART I : IMPRESSED

Nevertheless, they soon managed to bring their enemies between us, and thereby check our firing. Then with a furious onset they drove them to their fortress; and many seeing our boats near the shore rushed into the sea, and were either shot by the French or drowned, except what the boats floated to our ship. This work commenced about 2 P.M. and closed with the setting sun. after disposing of the dead, and washing their blood from the docks, we sailed away with our Spanish consort for Port Mahon. Just before reaching there, another levanter came on so suddenly that it was with much difficulty that we could manage our newly built ship. Our Spanish consort unprepared for such a violent gale was dashed to pieces on the island of Sardinia, and nearly every one of the crew perished.

"After the gale we joined the British fleet, consisting of about thirty line-of-battle ships, carrying from eighty to one hundred and thirty guns apiece, besides frigates and sloops of war. Our work was to blockade a much larger fleet of French men-of-war, mostly in the harbor of Toulon. With these we occasionally had skirmishes or running fights. The French squadron was not prepared, neither disposed to meet the English Fleet in battle.

"To improve or mental faculties, when we had a few leisure moments from ship duty and naval tactics, we were furnished with a library of two choice books for every ten men. We had seventy of these libraries in all. The first book was an abridgement of the life of Lord Nelson, calculated to inspire the mind to deeds of valor, and to teach the most summary way of disposing of an unyielding enemy. This one of the ten men could read when he had leisure, during the last six days of each week. The second was a small Church of England prayer-book, for special use about one hour on the first day of the week."

Church Service on Board a King's Ship

"As a general thing a chaplain was allowed for every large ship. When the weather was pleasant, the quarter-deck was fitted with awnings, flags, benches, etc. for meeting. At 11 A.M. came the order from the officer of the deck. 'Strike six bells there!' These mates were required to carry a piece of rope in their pocket with which to start the sailors. Immediately their stentorian voices were heard sounding on the other decks, 'Away up to

7. Joseph Bates

church there — every soul of you — and take your prayer books with you!' If any felt disinclined to such a mode of worship and attempted to evade the loud call to church, then look out for the men with the rope! When I was asked, 'Of what religion are you?' I replied, 'A Presbyterian.' But I was now given to understand that there was no religious toleration on board the king's war ships. 'Only one denomination here — away with you to church.' The officers before taking their seats, unbuckled their swords and dirks, and piled them on the head of the capstan in the midst of the worshiping assembly, all ready To grasp them in a moment, if necessary, before the hour's service should. When the benediction was pronounced, the officers clinched their side arms, and buckled them on for active service. The quarter-deck was immediately cleared and the floating bethel again became the same old weekly war ship for six days and twenty three hours more.

"Respecting the church service, the chaplain, or in his absence, the captain reads from the prayer book, and the officers and the sailors respond. And when he read about the law of God, the loud response would fill the quarter-deck, '*O Lord incline our hearts to keep thy law.*' Poor wicked deluded souls! How little their hearts were inclined to keep the holy law of God, when almost every hour of the week their tongues were employed in blaspheming his holy name; and at the same time learning and practicing the best manner of shooting, slaying, and sinking to the bottom of the ocean all who refused to surrender and become their prisoners, or who dared to array themselves in opposition to a proclamation of war issued by their good old Christian king.

"King George III not only assumed the right to impress American seamen, to man his war ships and fight his unjust battles, but he also required them to attend his church, and learn to respond to his preachers. And whenever the band of musicians on shipboard commenced with '*God save the king!*' they, with all his loyal subjects, were also required to take off their hats in obeisance to his royal authority....[1]

"Ships belonging to the blockading squadron in the Mediterranean Sea were generally relieved and returned to England at the expiration of three years; then the sailors were paid their wages and twenty-four hours liberty given them to spend their money on shore.

"As the Rodney was now on her third year, my strong hope of freedom from the British yoke would often cheer me while looking forward

PART I : IMPRESSED

to that one day's liberty, in the which I was resolving to put forth every energy of my being to gain my freedom. About this time the fleet encountered a most dreadful storm in the Gulf of Lyons. For awhile it was doubted whether any of us would ever see the rising of another sun. These huge ships would rise like mountains on the top of the coming sea, and suddenly tumble again in the trough of the same, with such a dreadful crash that it seemed almost impossible they could ever rise again. They became unmanageable, and the mariners were at their wit's end....

"On our arrival at Fort Mahon, in the island of Minorca, ten ships were reported much damaged. The Rodney was so badly damaged that the commander was ordered to get her ready to proceed to England. Joyful sound to us all! Homeward bound! Twenty-four hours liberty! Was the joyous sound. All hearts were glad. One evening after dark, just before the Rodney's departure for England some fifty of us were called out by name and ordered to get our baggage ready and get into the boats. 'What's the matter' 'Where are we going?' On board the Swift shore 74. 'What that ship that has just arrived for a three years' station?' 'Yes,' A sad disappointment indeed; what was still worse I began to learn that I was doomed to drag out a miserable existence in the British navy. Once more I was among strangers, but well known as one who had attempted to escape from the service of King George III.

"The Swiftshore was soon under way for her station off Toulon. A few days after we sailed a friend of my father's arrived from the United States bringing documents to prove my citizenship, and a demand for my release from the British government.

"One of the most prominent causes of our last war with England in 1812 was her oppressive and unjust acts in impressing American seamen on sea or land, wherever they could be found. This was denied by one political party in the United States. The British government also continued to deny the fact, and regard the pass ports, or protection of American citizens of but little importance. Such proofs of American citizenship were required by them as were not very readily obtained. Hence their continued acts of aggression until the war. Another additional and grievous act was, that all letters to friends were required to be examined by the first lieutenant before leaving the ship. By accident, I found one of mine torn and thrown aside, hence the impossibility of my parents' learning even that I was among the living. With as genuine a protection as could be obtained

7. Joseph Bates

from the collector of the custom-house at New York, I nevertheless was passed off for an Irishman, because an Irish officer declared that my parents lived in Belfast, Ireland.

"Previous to the war of 1812, one of my letters reached my father. He wrote to the President of the United States (Mr. Madison) presenting him with the facts in my case, as for proof of his own citizenship referred him to the archives in the War Department for his commissions returned and deposited there after his service with the Revolutionary War. The President's reply and documents were satisfactory. Gen. Brooks, then governor of Massachusetts, who was intimately acquainted with my father as a captain under his immediate command in the Revolutionary War, added to the foregoing another strong document.

"Capt. C. Delano, townsman and friend of my father, preparing for a voyage to Minorca, in the Mediterranean, generously offered his services as bearer of the above-named documents, and so sanguine was he that no other proof would be required that he really expected to bring me with him on his return journey.

"On his arrival at Port Mahon, he was rejoiced to learn that the Rodney, 74, was in port. As he approached the R in his boat, he was asked what he wanted. He said he wished to see a young man by the name of Joseph Bates. The lieutenant forbade his coming alongside. Finally, one of the under-officers, a friend of mine, informed him that I had been transferred to the Swiftshore, 74, and that she had sailed to join the British fleet off Toulon. Capt. D. then presented my documents to the United States consul, who transmitted them to Sir Edward Pelew, the commander-in-chief of the squadron. On the arrival of the mail I received a letter from Capt. D. informing me of his arrival and visit to the R, his disappointment, and what he had done, and of the anxiety of my parents. I think this was the first intelligence from home for over three years.

"I was told that the captain had sent for me to see him on the quarter-deck. I saw that he was surrounded by signal men and officers, replying by signal flags to the admiral's ship, which was some distance from us. Said the captain, 'Is your name Joseph Bates?' 'Yes, sir.' 'Are you an American?' 'Yes, sir' 'To what part of America do you belong?' 'New Bedford, in Massachusetts, sir' Said he, 'The admiral is inquiring to know if you are on board this ship, He will probably send for you or something the like import.' 'You may go below.' The news spread throughout the ship that Bates was an American and his government had demanded his release, and the commander-in-chief was signaling our ship about it, etc. What a lucky fellow he was, etc.

"Weeks and months rolled away, however, bringing nothing but anxious suspense and uncertainty in my case, till at length I received another letter from Capt. D. informing me that my case was still hanging in uncertainty. It was probable that war had commenced, and as he was obliged to leave, he advised me, if I could not obtain an honorable discharge, to become a prisoner of war.

"It was now the fall of 1812. On our arrival at Fort Mahon to winter, the British consul sent me what money I then needed, saying that it was Capt. D's request that he should furnish me with money and clothing while I needed. Owing to sickness in the fleet, it was ordered that each ship's company should have 24 hours liberty on shore. I improved the opportunity to call at the offices of the British and American consuls. The former furnished me with some money. The latter said that the admiral had done nothing in my case, and now it was too late, for it was ascertained that war was declared between the United States and Great Britain.

"There were about two hundred Americans on board the ships in our squadron, and twenty-two on board the Swiftshore. We had ventured several times to say what we ought to do, but the result appeared very doubtful. At last some six of us united and walked to the quarterdeck with our hats in hand, and thus addressed the first lieutenant.—

"'We understand, sir that war has commenced between Great Britain and the United States, and we do not wish to be found fighting against our own country, therefore it is our wish to become prisoners of war.' 'Go below' said he. At dinner hour all the Americans were ordered between the pumps and were not permitted to associate with the crew. Our scanty allowance was ordered to be reduced one-third, and no strong drink. This we felt we could endure, and were not a little comforted that we had made one effectual change, and the next would most likely free us from the British navy.

"From our ship the word spread, until about all the Americans in the fleet became prisoners of war. During eight dreary months we were thus retained and frequently called upon the quarter-deck where we were harangued and urged to enter the British navy. I had already suffered for

7. Joseph Bates

The U.S. frigate Constitution *capturing His Britannic Majesty's frigate* Guerierre. Engraving by C. Taebaut after T. Birck, 1813 (Library of Congress, Washington, D.C.).

thirty months an unwilling subject. I was therefore fully decided not to listen to any proposal they might make.

"A few months after our becoming prisoners of war, our lookout ships appeared off the harbor and signalized that the French fleet (which we were attempting to blockade) were all out and making the best of their way down the Mediterranean. With this startling information orders were immediately issued for the squadron to be ready to proceed in pursuit of them at an early hour in the morning. The most of the night was spent preparing for this expected onset. The prisoners were invited to assist. I alone refused to aid or assist in any way whatever, it being unjustifiable except when forced to do so.

"In the morning the whole fleet was sailing out of the harbor in line of battle. Gunners were ordered to double-shot the guns, and clear way for action. The first lieutenant was passing by where I stood reading the

Part I : Impressed

Life of Nelson (one of the library books) 'Take up that hammock sir, and carry it on deck,' said he. I looked off from the book, and said, 'It is not mine, sir' 'Take it up' 'It is not mine, sir.' He cursed me for a scoundrel, snatched the book from me and dashed it out of the gun-port, and struck me down with his fist. As soon as I got up said he, 'Take that hammock (some one's bed and blankets lashed) on deck.' 'I shall no do it sir! I am a prisoner of war and hope that you will treat me as such.' 'Yes, you__ Yankee scoundrel, I will. Here,' said he to two under officers, 'take that hammock and lash it on to that fellow's back, and make him walk the poop deck twenty-four hours.' And because I put my hands on them to keep them from doing so, and requested them to let me alone, he became outrageous and cried out, 'Master-at-arms! Take this fellow to the gun-room and put him double legs in irons!' 'That you can do, sir' said I, 'but I shall not work.' 'When we come into action I'll have you lashed up to the main rigging for a target for the Frenchmen to aim at!' 'That you can do sir, but I hope you will remember that I am a prisoner of war.' Another volley of oaths and imprecations followed with an inquiry why the quarter-at-arms did not hurry up with the irons. The poor old man was so dismayed and gallied that he could not find them.

"The lieutenant then changed his mind, and ordered him to come up and make me a close prisoner in the gun-room, and not allow me to come near any one, nor even to speak with one of my countrymen. With this he hurried up on the upper gun-deck, where orders were given to throw all the hammocks and bags into the ship's hold, break down all cabin and berth partitions, break up and throw overboard all the cow and sheep pens, and clear the deck fore and aft for action, Every ship was now in its station for battle rushing across the Mediterranean for the Turkish shore, watching to see and grapple with their deadly foe.

"When all the preparations was made for battle, one of my countrymen, in the absence of the master-at-arms, ventured to speak with me through the musket gratings of the gun-room, to warn me of the perilous position I should be placed in when the French fleet hove in sight, unless I submitted and acknowledged myself ready to take my former station (second captain of one of the big guns in the fore-castle), and fight the Frenchmen, as he and the rest of my countrymen were about to do. I endeavored to show him how unjustifiable and inconsistent such a course would be for us as prisoners of war, and assured him that my mind was fully and clearly settled to adhere to our position as American prisoners of war, notwithstanding the perilous position I was to be placed in.

"In the course of a few hours, after the lieutenant had finished his arrangements for battle he came down to my prison room. 'Well sir,' said he, 'Will you take up a hammock when you are ordered again?' I replied that I would take one up for any gentleman in the ship. 'You would, ha?' 'Yes, sir.' Without inquiring who I considered gentlemen, he ordered me released. My countrymen were somewhat surprised to see me so soon a prisoner at large.

"The first lieutenant is next in command to the captain, and presides over all the duties of the ship during the day, and keeps no watch, where as all other officers do. As we had not yet seen the French fleet, the first lieutenant was aware that my case would have to be reported to the captain, in which case if I, as an acknowledged prisoner of war, belonging to the United States, were allowed to answer for myself, his unlawful, abusive, and ungentlemanly conduct would come to the captain's knowledge. Hence his willingness to release me.

"The British fleet continued their course across the Mediterranean for the Turkish coast, until they were satisfied that the French fleet was not to the west of them. They then steered north and east (to meet them) until we arrived off the harbor of Toulon, where we saw them all snugly moored and dismantled in their old winter quarters, their officers and crews undoubtedly highly gratified that the ruse they had practiced had so well effected their design, viz. to start the British squadron out of their snug winter quarters to hunt for them over the Mediterranean Sea. They had remantled, and sailed out of their harbor, and chased our few lookout ships down the Mediterranean, and, unperceived by them returned and dismantled again.

"After retaining us as prisoners of war about eight months, we, with others who continued to refuse all solicitation to rejoin the British service, were sent to Gibraltar, and from thence to England, and finally locked up on board an old sheer hulk, called the Crown Princess, formerly a Danish 74 gun ship, a few miles below the Chatham dock yard and seventy-miles from London. Here were many others of like description, many of them containing prisoners. Here about seven hundred prisoners were crowded between two decks and locked up every night, on a scanty allowance of food and in crowded quarters. Cut off from all intercourse except

PART I : IMPRESSED

floating news, a plan was devised to obtain a newspaper, which often relieved us in our anxious, desponding moments, although we had to feel the pressing claims of hunger for it. The plan was this, One day in each week we were allowed salt fish; this we sold to the contractor for cash, which we paid to one of our enemies to smuggle us in one of the weekly journals from London. This being common stock, good readers were chosen to stand in an elevated position and read aloud. It was often interesting and amusing to see the perfect rush to hear every word of American news, several voices crying out 'Read that over again, we could not hear it distinctly,' and the same from another and another quarters. Good news from home often cheered us more than our scanty allowance of food. If more had been required for the paper, I believe another portion of our daily allowance would have been freely offered rather than to give it up.

"Our daily allowance of bread consisted of course brown loaves from the bakery served out every morning. At the commencement of the severe cold weather, a quantity of sea biscuit was deposited on board in case the weather, or ice should prevent the soft bread from coming daily. In the spring, our first lieutenant or commander ordered the biscuit to be served out to the prisoners, and directed that one-quarter of the daily allowances should be deducted because nine ounces of biscuit were equal to twelve ounces of soft bread. We utterly refused to receive the biscuit, or hard bread, unless he would allow us as many ounces as he had of the soft. At the end of the day he wished to know again if we would receive the bread on his terms. 'No! no!' 'Then I will keep you below until you comply.' Hatchways unlocked in the morning again. 'Will you come up for your bread?' 'No!' At noon again. 'Will you have your meal that is cooked for you?' 'No!' 'Will you come up for your water?' 'No; we will have nothing from you until you serve us out our full allowance of bread.' To make us comply, the port-holes had been closed, thus depriving us of light and fresh air. Our president had also been called up and conferred with (we had a president and committee of twelve chosen, as we found it necessary to keep some kind of order.) he told the commander that the prisoners would not yield.

"By this time, hunger and the want of water, and especially fresh air, had thrown us into a state of feverish excitement. Some appeared almost savage, others endeavored to bear it as well as they could. The president was called for again. After awhile the port where he messed was thrown

7. Joseph Bates

open and two officers from the hatchway came down on the lower deck and passed to his table, inquiring for the president's trunk. 'What do you want with it?' said his friends. 'He is going to send him on board the next prison ship.' 'Do you drop it! He shall not have it!' By this time the officers became alarmed for their safety, and attempted to make their escape up the ladder to the hatchway. A number of prisoners, who seemed fired with desperation, stopped them, and declared on the peril of their lives that they should go no farther until the president was permitted to come down. Other port holes were now thrown open and the commandeer appeared at one of them, demanding the release of his officers. 'If you do not release them' said the commander, 'I will open these ports (all of them grated with heavy bars of iron) and fire in upon you.' 'Fire away!' was the cry from within, 'we may as well die this way as by famine; but, mark, if you kill one prisoner, we will have two for one as long as they last.' His officers now began to beg him most pitifully not to fire. 'for if you do,' said they, 'they will kill us; they stand here around us with their knives open, declaring if we stir one foot they will take our lives.'

"The president, being permitted to come to the port, begged his countrymen to shed no blood on board the ship any longer, and he entreated that for *his sake*, the officers be released.

"Double-plank bulk-heads at each end of out prison rooms, with musket holes in them to fire in upon us, if necessary, separated us from the officers, sailors, and soldiers. Again we were asked if we would receive our allowance of bread. 'No.' Some threats were thrown out by the prisoners that the commander would hear from us before morning. About ten o'clock at night, when all were quiet but the guard and watch on deck, a torchlight was got up by setting some soap grease on fire in tin pans. By the aid of this light, a heavy oak stanchion was taken down, which served us for a battering-ram. Then, with our large, empty tin water cans for drums, and tin pails, kettles, pans, pots, and spoons for drum sticks, and whatever would make a stunning noise, the torch-lights and battering-ram moved onward to the after bulk-head that separated us from the commander and his officers, soldiers and their families. For a few moments the ram was applied with power, and so successfully that consternation seized the sleepers, and they fled crying for help, declaring that the prisoners were breaking through upon them. Without stopping for them to rally and fire in upon us, a rush was made for the forward bulk-head, where a portion

Part I : Impressed

of the ship's company, with their families, lived. The application of the battering ram was quite as successful here, so that all our enemies were now as wide awake as their hungry, starving prisoners devising the best means for their defense. Here our torch-lights went out, leaving us in total darkness in the midst of our so-far-successful operation. We grouped together in huddles, to sleep if our enemies would allow us, until another day should dawn to enable to use our little remaining strength in obtaining if possible, our full allowance of bread and water.

"The welcome fresh air and morning light, came suddenly upon us by an order from the commander to open our port-holes, unbar the hatchways, and call the prisoners up to get their bread. In a few moments it was clearly understood that our enemies had capitulated by yielding to our terms and were now ready to make peace by serving us with our full allowance of bread.

"While one from each mess of ten was up getting their three days allowance of brown loaves, others were up to the tank, filling their tin cans, with water, so that in a short space of time, a great and wonderful change had taken place in our midst. On most amicable terms of peace, with all our keepers, grouped in messes of ten, with three days allowance of bread, and cans filled with water, we ate and drank, laughed and shouted immoderately over our great feast and vanquished foe. The wonder was that we did not kill ourselves with over-eating and drinking.

"The commissary on hearing the state of things in our midst, sent orders from the shore to the commander to serve out our bread forthwith.

"Our keepers were in the habit of examining the inside of our prison every evening before we were ordered up to be counted down, to ascertain whether we were cutting through the ship to gain our liberty. We observed that they seldom stopped at a certain place on the lower deck but passed it with a slight examination. On examining this place, a number of us decided to cut a hole here if we could effect it without detection by the soldier who was stationed but a few inches above where we must come out, and yet have room above water.

"Having nothing better than a common table knife fitted with teeth, after some time we sawed out a heavy three-inch oak plank, which afterward served us successfully for a cover when our keepers were approaching. We now began to demolish a very heavy oak timber, splinter by splinter. Even this had to be done with great caution that the soldier might not hear us on the outside. While one was at work in his turn, some others were watching, that our keepers might not approach and find the hole uncovered. About forty were engaged in this work. Before the heavy timber was splintered out, one of our number obtained the cook's iron poker. This was a great help to pry off small splinters around the heavy iron bolts. In this way, after laboring between thirty and forty days, we reached the copper on the ship's bottom, some two to three feet from thee top of our cover, on an angle of about 25' downward. By working the poker through the copper, on the upper side of the hole, we learned to our joy that it came out beneath the stage where the soldier stood. Then on opening the lower side of the hole, the water flowed in some, but not in sufficient quantities to sink the ship for some time, unless by change of wind and weather, she became more unsteady in her motion and rolled the hole under water, in which case we should doubtless have been left to share her fate. The commander had, before this stated that if by any means the ship caught fire from our lights in the night, he would throw the keys of our hatchways overboard, and leave the ship and us to burn and perish together. Hence we had chosen officers to extinguish every light at 10 P.M.

"Sunday afternoon, while I was at work in my turn, enlarging the hole in the copper, a shout of hundreds of voices from the outside, so alarmed me for fear that we were discovered, that in my hurry to cover up the hole, the poker slipped from my hands through the hole into the sea. The hole covered, we made our way with the rushing crowd, up the long stairway to the upper deck, to learn the cause of the shouting. The circumstances were these: Another ship like our own, containing American prisoners, was moored about one-eighth of a mile from us. People from the country, in their boats, were visiting the prison ships, as was their custom on Sundays, to see what looking creatures American prisoners were. Soldiers with loaded muskets, about twenty feet apart, on the lower and upper stages outside of the ship, were guarding the prisoners' escape. One of the countrymen's boats, rowed by one man, lay fastened to the lower stage, at the foot of the main gangway ladder, where also one of these soldiers was on guard. A tall, athletic Narragansett Indian, who like the rest of his countrymen, was ready to risk his life for liberty, caught sight of the boat, and watching the English officers who were walking the quarter deck, as they turned their backs to walk aft, he bolted down the gangway ladder, clinched the soldier, musket and all, and crowded him under the thwarts, cleared the boat, grasped the two oars, and with the man (who most likely would have shot him before he could clear himself) under his feet, he shaped his course for the opposite, unguarded shore, about two miles distant.

"The soldiers, seeing their comrade, with all his ammunition, snatched from his post, and stowed away in such a summary manner, and moving out of their sight like a streak over the water by the giant power of this North-American Indian, were either so stunned with amazement at the scene before them, or it may be with fear of another Indian after them, that they failed to hit him with their shot. Well-manned boats, with sailors and soldiers, were soon dashing after him, firing and hallooing to bring him to; all of which seemed only to animate and nerve him to ply his oars with herculean strength.

"When his fellow-prisoners saw him moving away from his pursuers in such a giant-like manner, they shouted, and gave him three cheers. The prisoners on board followed with three more. This was the noise which I had heard while working at the hole. The officers were so exasperated at that that they declared if we did not cease this cheering and noise they would lock us down below. We therefore stifled our voices, that we might be permitted to see the poor Indian make his escape.

"Before reaching the shore, his pursuers gained on him so that they shot him in his arm (as we were told) which made it difficult to ply the oar; nevertheless he reached the shore, sprang from the boat and cleared himself from all his pursuers, and was soon out of reach of all their musket balls. Rising to our sight upon an inclined plain, he rushed on, bounding over hedges and ditches, like a chased deer, and, without doubt, would have been out of sight of his pursuers in a few hours, and gained his liberty, had not the people in the country rushed upon him from various quarters, and delivered him up to his pursuers, who brought him back, and for some days locked him up in the dungeon. Poor Indian! He deserved a better fate.

"The prisoners now understood that the hole was completed, and a great many were preparing to make their escape. The committeemen decided that those who had labored to cut the hole should have the privilege of going first. They also selected four judicious and careful men, who could not swim, to take charge of the hole, and help all out that wished to go.

7. Joseph Bates

"With some difficulty we at length obtained some tarred canvas, with which we made ourselves small bags, just large enough to pack our jacket, shirt, and shoes in, then we fastened a stout string, about ten feet long, to the end, and in the other end made a loop to pass around the neck. With hat and pants on, and bag in one hand, and the other fast hold of our fellow, we took our rank and file for a desperate effort for liberty. At the given signal (10 P.M.), every light was extinguished, and the men bound for liberty were in their stations.

"Soldiers with loaded muskets, as already described, were on guard all around the ship, above and below. Our landing place, if we reached it, was about half a mile distant, with a continued line of soldiers just above high water mark. The heads of those who passed out, came only a few inches from the soldiers' feet, i.e. a grating stage between.

"A company of good singers stationed themselves at the after port-hole where the soldier stood that was next to the one over the hole. Their interesting sailor and war songs took the attention of the two soldiers some, and a glass of strong drink now and then drew them to the port-hole, while those inside made believe drink. While this was working, the committee were putting the prisoners through, feet foremost, and as their bag string began to draw, they slipped that out also, being thus assured that they were shaping their course for the shore. In the mean time, when the ship's bell was struck, denoting the lapse of another half hour, the soldier's loud cry would resound, 'All's well!' The soldier that troubled us the most would take his station over the hole and shout, 'All's well!' Then when he stepped forward to hear the sailor's song the committee would put a few more through, and he would step back and cry again, 'All's well!' It surely was most cheering to our friends while struggling for liberty in the watery element, to hear behind and before them the peace-and-safety cry, 'All's well!'

"Midnight came; the watch was changed, the cheering music had ceased. the stillness that reigned without and within retarded our work. At length it was whispered along the ranks that the few that had passed out during the stillness had caused great uneasiness with the soldiers and they judged it best for no more to attempt to leave for fear of detection. It was also near daylight, and we might better retire quietly to our hammocks.

"Edmond Allen and myself, of New Bedford covenanted to go and keep together. We had kept hold of each other during the night, and had advanced near the hole when it was thought best for no more to go. In the morning the cover was off, and E.A. was among the missing.

"The committee reported seventeen, and E.A. made eighteen that had passed out during the night.

"The prisoners were greatly elated at the last night's successful movement and took measures to keep the hole undiscovered for another attempt at 10 P.M.

"We were confined between two decks, with no communication after we were counted down at night and locked up. During the day some tools were obtained, and a scuttle was cut through the upper deck, and covered up undiscovered. Word was then circulated among the prisoners to go up from the upper deck as soon as the soldiers ordered the prisoners up to be counted down for the night. But those on the lower deck were to move tardily, so that those on the upper deck might be counted down before the lower deck was cleared. This was done and eighteen that had just been counted, slipped through the scuttle unperceived by the soldiers, mingled with the crowd up the lower deck ladder, and were counted over again. At 10 P.M. the lights were again extinguished for another attempt to escape.

"On taking our station at 10 P.M. it was whispered along our ranks that two men not of our number were waiting at the hole, insisting that they would go first, or they would raise a cry and prevent any one from going. They had been drinking, and would not be reasoned with. It was finally settled to let them go. The first was put through very quietly, saying to his drunken companion, 'I will hold on to the ship's rudder rings until you come.' The second man, not being much of a swimmer, sank like a log, and rose up under the stage, splashing and struggling for life. Said the soldier to his next companion, 'here's a porpoise.' 'Put your bayonet into him,' replied he. 'I will,' said the first, 'if he comes up again.' We were by this time all listening with almost breathless attention, fearing our chance for liberty was about gone. Up he came again. We heard the rush and then the cry, 'Don't kill me! I'm a prisoner.' 'Prisoner? Prisoner where did you come from?' 'Out of a hole in the ship!' 'Prisoners are getting out of the ship!' was the quick response of all the watchmen. All hands came rushing on the deck.

"In a few moments our vigilant commander came running from his bed, frantically inquiring, 'Where?' and hearing the second outside, he rushed down the accomodation ladder, crying out, 'How many have gone?' One of the prisoners, who felt disposed to quicken our chief captain's speed, put his face in the grating hole and cried out, 'About forty I *guess*.'

"In quick succession, the night signals of distress brought well-manned boats to pick them up. 'Where shall we pull?' 'Here, there, all around.' 'Do you find any?' 'No, sir, no, sir.'

"Orders were given to land a body of men, and surround Gelingham forest, where they supposed the 'forty' must have escaped, explore it in the morning and take them on board. We were much amused to see what full credit the commander gave to the prisoner's guess.

"After making these arrangements, they got the drowning man on deck and demanded of him to state the facts, but he was too far gone with the large draughts of salt water which he had swallowed, somewhat mixed up with his rum, and the dreadful fear of being harpooned with a soldier's bayonet, that he failed to satisfy them, only that there was a hole in the ship, from which he passed out. One of the boats at length found it, pushed a long iron rod inside, and remained there watching until morning.

"When we were permitted to come on deck in the morning, poor Johnson was lying tied to a stake, floating in the water near the beach. All that we could learn was that the string of his bag was fast around his left wrist, below which his hand was nearly cut off. Some of his friends knew that he had a sharp knife in the pocket of his pants, which was missing when he was found near shore. Fastening his bag on his wrist instead of his neck, was doubtless a great hindrance to his getting away from the boats. In attempting to cut this string, we supposed he cut his wrist, and thus bled to death by the time he reached the shore.

"We were kept on deck all day without food, mustered by name, and strictly examined to see if we answered by our original descriptions. When it was clearly ascertained that eighteen living men has escaped the night previous to the discovery of the hole, and the full number of prisoners still reported on board, the British officers were arrested for making a false report, but released again on our president's declaring how the affair was managed.

"The following day the king's carpenters, from Chatham, were sent on board with their tools and a heavy stick of timber to plug up the hole.

Part I : Impressed

While they were busy cutting and pounding in our midst, some of the prisoners picked up a few of their loose tools and began to cut another, equally good on the opposite side of the ship, and finished it before the carpenters had closed up the other. The soldiers outside ascribed the noise to the king's carpenters.

"That night a number of us stationed ourselves at this hole to watch for an opportunity to escape and remained there until about four in the morning. The copper being cut off in a great hurry, ragged and sharp points were left. To prevent these points from mangling our flesh, we fastened a wooden blanket to the lower side to slip out on. Besides the vigilant guard a boat was pulling around the ship during the night with one man in the center, sounding the side of the ship, under the lower stage, with a long iron rod. The rod continued to strike on each side of the hole during the night but failed to find the place they were punching for.

"Before daylight one of our number ventured to slip out, just after the boat passed, to ascertain whether the night was light, or dark enough to escape detection by swimming astern of this ship before the boat could get round. After pulling him in, he said the night was clear, and he could see a great distance on the water. We therefore concluded to wait until the following night. By negligence of our committee, the blanket was left with the end floating in the water. This was discovered by the boatmen soon after daylight. 'Here's another hole on this side of the ship!' and in came the iron rod, blasting all our hopes of escape from this quarter. To repair these damages, a portion of food was deducted from our daily allowance and continued for some time.

"Our boasting commander began to be sorely troubled for the safety of himself and family. It seemed almost certain that these audacious, daring Yankees would yet sink their prison-ships or gain their liberty. I was told that he declared he would sooner take charge of six thousand French prisoners than six hundred Yankees.

"After all their search for the eighteen who had escaped, a letter came from London, directed to the commander of the Crown Princess prison-ship, informing him of the happy escape of every one of them and of their safe travel, seventy miles to the city of London, and that it would be useless for him to trouble himself about them, for they were on the eve of sailing on a foreign voyage. They gave him to understand that they should remember his unkind treatment.

7. Joseph Bates

"From this the British government began to talk of sending us all to Dartmoor prison, a dreary waste, some fifteen miles inland from old Plymouth harbor, where we should find some trouble in getting outside the massy stone walls and dungeons that were so strongly fortified."[2]

Chapter 8
Dartmoor Prison

Sometime during the War of 1812 many of the Americans impressed aboard British ships were sent to Dartmoor Prison in England. A number of accounts of Dartmoor Prison during the days when it was occupied by American prisoners have been written. These accounts include those written by Joseph Bates, James Durand, and Nathaniel Pierce.

Durand in his account, *The Life and Adventures of James R. Durand,* tells of a delegation of impressed men going to the captain of the ship and stating they were prisoners of war and asking to be treated as such. The captain had replied by knocking their spokesman down and threatening to send him up the straits or to the East-Indies. Durand he kept because he was a member of the musical band. Some he retained to "show further proofs of their citizenship." Still others were sent away to Dartmoor Prison.[1] Although Durand was not sent to Dartmoor he describes his impressment experience and relates some incidents he learned from others about Dartmoor Prison.

Dartmoor Prison was located in Devonshire, England, about 17 miles north of Plymouth. It was a sturdy prison, with high walls arranged in a circle enclosing seven separate prison buildings; each prison was about twenty feet high and the walls were fifteen feet. There were also a hospital and barracks, there were sentry boxes along the walls. A river, the Dart, ran through it. Outside the prison were grassy hills: "This view to the prisoners was dreary enough" for there were no trees or shrubs. There was one little farm in sight, and a small village of about 12 houses was located two miles from the prison. Most of the people who lived there worked in the prison.[2]

Joshua Bates writes, "The prisons were three story, with a flight of

8. Dartmoor Prison

stone steps at each end, open in the center. There was one iron-grated porthole on each gable end. We were guarded by a barrack of six hundred soldiers, counted out in the morning, and driven in at sunset. It was quite a sight when the sun shone, to see those who desired to keep themselves decent, seated in groups about the yard, clearing their blankets and beds from vermin."[3]

One of the prisoners, Nathaniel Pierce, kept a journal. Pierce had been born in Newburyport, Massachusetts, in 1795. He probably sailed from Portsmouth, New Hampshire, and was captured in November of 1814 by the HMS *Bulwark* and then transferred to a prison ship. He begins his account by describing the prison ship: "When I was taken on board this ship I found to my great surprise one hundred and thirty seven unfortunate Americans." They were the crews of the privateer *Harlequin* of Portsmouth, New Hampshire, and two prize crews belonging to the privateer *Harpey,* also from New Hampshire.

Pierce recognized many of the men as former shipmates and acquaintances. They were poorly fed and shut down belowdecks. Sometimes they were without light or fresh air. At times they were not allowed to "go up to do what nature required, but like the swine obliged to drop [their] filth on deck, which was very unpleasant and unhealthy." Nor were they allowed to wash themselves, so the vermin grew thick.[4] On the 27th of December, 120 of the group were dispatched in three boats to go ashore. There they were received by about 80 soldiers who took them to Dartmoor Prison. Pierce estimated that there were about 6000 inmates there. They were cold, wet and hungry when they arrived at the prison and received no help that night. But in the morning they were measured, and received a bed, blanket and hammock. They also were put in the yard and allowed to choose a prison for themselves. In the yard, Pierce met an old acquaintance who led him to prison #7, where he joined a group of his townsmen.

Bates also describes the greeting of new prisoners: "On hearing of a fresh arrival, the prisoners would crowd up to the gates and make a lane for all to pass through; and as they passed through, some of them would recognize their friends. 'Haloo, Sam! Where did you come from?' 'Marblehead.' 'Any more left?' 'No, I was the last one.' And in this way all were recognized. It was often stated that nearly all the Marblehead sailors were prisoners."[5]

PART I : IMPRESSED

During the winter, Beasley, the American consul living in London, sent his men to supply the prisoners with warm clothing. Also, "religious meetings were held in the colored prison every Sunday and some professed to be converted and were baptized in the small pool of water in the yard, supplied from a reservoir on the hill, which was generally used by the prisoners in washing their clothes."[6]

Sometime later, the prisoners learned that peace had been declared. There was general rejoicing and every prisoner contrived to display an American flag and the motto "Free Trade and Sailor's Rights." They even formed a band and played all day with a large crowd following them. They all expected to be released soon. According to Bates, "Those who were never doomed to imprisonment in this dark and most dreary spot can appreciate nothing respecting our feelings. Yet we were held in suspense while a frigate was dispatched across the ocean to obtain President Madison's signature. In February 1815, she returned with the treaty ratified. Shoutings of rapturous joy rang though out gloomy dungeons, such as most likely will never be heard there again. What! About to be liberated, go to our native country, and gather around the paternal fireside once more? Yes, this hope was in us, and it seemed sometimes as though we were almost there."[7] But the days continued, and no release came. Sometimes it was cold and rainy. Pierce became sick with aches and a cough. Others, about five a day, were dying with smallpox and other disorders.

Bates writes of the attempt of a group of prisoners to escape:

About this time the prisoners in one of the prisons had commenced the Herculean task of opening a subterranean passage to the outside of the prison walls, to obtain their liberty. To accomplish this, one of the large, heavy flagging stones on the ground floor was raised, and the work began of scratching the dirt into small bags and packing it snugly away under the flight of stone steps which reached up to the third loft, planked up on the back side. To effect this, one of the planks had to be removed, but carefully replaced, and also the flagging stone before morning, subject to the critical inspection of the turnkeys after all the prisoners were counted out.

The length of the passage from under the foundation of the prison to the first wall across the prison-yard (as near as I can remember) was about one hundred feet; from thence to the outer wall about twenty feet more. These walls, we were told, were fourteen feet high, and two feet below the surface of the earth, broad enough for the soldiers on guard to pass and repass on top.

8. Dartmoor Prison

A friend of mine, Capt. L. Wood of Fairhaven, Mass. who lived in this prison, with whom I had frequent intercourse, informed me about the work, and how difficult it was to enter that stifled hole after they had progressed some distance, and return with a small bag of dirt. Said he "Their faces are almost black and they are nearly exhausted for want of breath," but still another would rush onward and presently return with a full bag. In this manner they continued their night work, undiscovered, until they reached and dug under the foundations of the first, and the second, or outer wall. Many now prepared themselves with knives and such deadly weapons as they could defend themselves with, determined to fight their way at the risk of their lives, to the sea coast, and seize on the first vessel or boats and steer for the coast of France.

Before they broke the ground outside of the outer wall for as many as desired to pass out, one following the other in the darkness of the night, one of the prisoners, being acquainted with their proceedings informed on them. Suddenly armed soldiers and officers came into the prison yard with their informer in their midst who pointed to the place over the dark passage which they soon broke in, and thus in a few moments it was filled with stones and dirt from the stone-paved yard, and the traitor carefully conveyed out under guard for fear the prisoners would seize him and tear him to pieces. "What is his name? Who is he? What State does he belong to?" was the inquiry. Those who knew him replied that he belonged to New Hampshire. The governor gave him his liberty and we heard no more about him.[8]

On the arrival of the frigate from the United States, bringing the ratified treaty of peace between us and Great Britain, we learned that Mr. Beasley had resumed his functions as United States consul in London, and was instructed by our government to procure suitable ships to convey the American prisoners from England to the United States. After waiting a suitable time, Mr. B. was addressed in behalf of the Dartmoor prisoners, to know why the ships did not come. His reply was very unsatisfactory. Again we expressed our surprise at his seeming neglect of us, when nearly two months had expired since the treaty of peace was ratified, and no relaxation of our sufferings. His reply was far from relieving us. At length the prisoners became so exasperated at his willful neglect of them, they erected a gallows in the prison-yard, and hung, and then burned Mr. B. in effigy. As the English periodicals began to herald this matter, Mr. B. began to wake up and expostulate with us for daring to take such liberties with his character. We gave him to understand that he was instructed to relieve and release us from imprisonment and we were still waiting for the event.[9]

One day a prisoner exercising in the yard, leapt over the picket fence into

PART I : IMPRESSED

another enclosure. There he was seized by several guards but his fellow prisoners rushed in to rescue him and took him to #7 prison where he was received with applause by his fellow prisoners. He was supposed to be confined in the dungeon until release because he was suspected of attempting to blow up a British ship. But he declared that there was not a pound of powder on the ship.

When Captain Shortland, the commander in charge of the prison demanded that the escaped prisoner be returned to him, the prisoners voted unanimously not to give him up. The Captain responded by stopping their indulgences such as being able to buy goods from the country people or visiting other prisons. The prisoners then retaliated by refusing to allow lamp trimmers or other workmen into the areas where they were enclosed. When the captain sent 800 or 900 soldiers to force the prisoners into their separate prisons before the usual time, the prisoners resisted and surrounded the soldiers and pressed them against the wall. When the captain came down and made threats, they would not listen to him. But when the doctor and the clerk came, the prisoners said they would go in at their usual time if the soldiers were removed. Which they did. This was on the thirteenth of February.[10]

Things continued calm for some time after this, although Pierce mentions that some soldiers upset the prisoners' kettles of tea and coffee. Pierce comments that they are "new recrew & have not learn'd how to treat American Prisoners." The days go by with scarcely any employment for the prisoners, except Pierce mentions that he occasionally does some laundering or mending or that it is his day to cook for the mess. They hear all sorts of rumors concerning boats coming to take them home to America. Beasley, the American agent in England, has not written to let the inmates know anything about ships to return them or the peace process. A committee writes somewhat sarcastically to Beasley: "Sir we have the pleasure to inform you that the *Favorite* has arrived & the Peace is ratifid by the President, you living in the City of London and in an out of the way place we don't think it likely that you have heard of it & that we are very sorry we have treated you so ill since our captivity but as soon as we can make it convenient we shall send you some show."[11] A few days later a letter was received from Beasley reassuring the prisoners; he promised them there would not be a man in prison in twelve months.

But to Pierce and others it was very tedious lying in prison after peace has been declared. Looking out from on top of one of the buildings, Pierce

8. Dartmoor Prison

**Constitution*'s Escape from the British Squadron after a chase of sixty hours, July 17, 1812.* Engraving by W. Hoagland 1885 after M. Come (Library of Congress, Washington, D.C.).

could see people enjoying more liberty than the poor prisoners: "[T]hey [the people outside] are walking about as they please ... but the prisoners are shut in at night and let out in the morning."

On April fourth, the prisoners were angry because they were given 8 pounds of hard bread instead of the 12 pounds of soft bread to which they had become accustomed. Bates wrote about the situation:

> This was what the commander of the prison-ship attempted to do with us the year before, and failed.... We unhesitatingly objected to Governor S.' proposals. He said we should have that or none. We claimed our full allowance or none. We continued thus two days without bread, with a threat, that if we did not yield, our water would be withheld also.
>
> It was now the 4th of April 1815. Governor S. left the depot that day on a visit for a few days, thinking that probably by the time he returned we should be hungry enough to accede to his terms. But before sunset, or the time came for turning us in to be locked up for another dismal night, a great portion of the prisoners were becoming so exasperated with their down-trodden and starving condition that when the soldiers and turnkeys came to order us in to be locked up, we refused to obey until they gave us our bread. "Go into your prisons!" they cried. "No, we will not until we get our bread!" Soldiers were called to arms, and with their colonel and second

in command, arranged above the great iron gate-way, above the great public square containing the hospital and storehouses where our bread was stored. On the lower side of this square was another iron fence and locked-up gate-way, which was the line of demarcation between us and our keepers. Here was a narrow pass-way of about ten feet wide and thirty long, where all the prisoners, when out of their prisons were continually passing and re-passing into yards Nos. 1, 4 and 7 containing the seven prison houses prepared to accommodate about ten thousand prisoners.

About dark the excitement had become general on both sides, and the narrow pass-way became so crowded that it was difficult to pass. The pressure at length became so heavy that the lock of the great folding gate-way broke, and the gates flew open. In a few moments the prisoners, unarmed and without any reconverted plan, were treading on forbidden ground, filling up the public square and crowding up to the great iron gate-way On the opposite side of which stood the colonel in command with this regiment of armed soldiers, commanding the prisoners to retire or he should fire upon them. "Fire away!" cried the prisoners, as they crowded in front of the soldiers, "we would as lief die by sword as by famine." The colonel still more unwilling to fire, wished to know what we wanted. "We want our bread, sir." "Well, retire quietly to your respective prisons, and something shall be done about it." "No, sir, we shall not leave until we get our full allowance of bread." The colonel ordered the contractor to serve the prisoners with their full allowance of soft bread. About nine in the evening the various messes had all received their bread. The prisoners then quietly entered their respective prisons, and commenced satiating their appetites on the coarse brown loaves and cold water, commending in the highest terms the cool courageous, and gentlemanly manner in which the colonel received us and granted out request.[12]

Pierce tells a similar story but adds that the prisoners were so angry that they threatened to burst open the store and take what they liked. The soldiers and officers promised that they should have their bread, but the prisoners would not leave before the bread was handed out. By that time, according to Pierce, it was nearly 11:00 P.M.[13]

Bates reports that when Captain Shortland, or Governor S. as he called him, returned to the prison, "On learning what had transpired on the evening of the 4th he declared (as we were told) that he would be revenged on us."[14]

April 6, the prisoners were gathered out in the yard, gambling, walk-

8. Dartmoor Prison

ing around, talking with each other and playing ball. Bates writes of his observations: "Several times the ball was knocked over the wall and was as often thrown back by the soldiers when kindly asked to do so. Presently one of the prisoners cried out in quite an authoritative manner, 'Soldier throw back that ball!' And because it failed to come, some of the ball-players said, 'We will make a hole in the wall and get it.' Two or three of them began by pecking out the mortar with small stones. A sentinel on the wall ordered them to desist. This they did not do until spoken to again. I was walking back and forth by the place during the time, with others, but did not suppose they could make a hole with the stones they were using, or that anything touching that matter was of much or any importance. Aside from this trifling affair, the prisoners were as orderly and as obedient[15] as at any time in the past."

About 300 prisoners gathered on a grassy plot and tore up turfs of grass, which they were throwing at each other. When the soldiers ordered them to leave the plot, they complied. About 6:00 P.M. some soldiers gathered in the square and others were stationing themselves on the walls. One of them observed that the prisoners should go in, for they would soon be charged up.[16] Now comes the often confusing accounts of what has been called the Dartmoor Prison Massacre. The various observers reported different aspects of this tragedy.

Bates writes:

At sunset the turnkeys, as usual ordered the prisoners to turn in. To effect this, and get to their respective prisons, the narrow pass-way was so densely crowded that the folding gate-way, which had not been repaired since the 4th, and was very slightly fastened, burst open, and some few were necessarily and without design crowded into the square. It appeared that Governor S. with a regiment of armed soldiers, had stationed himself above the square, watching for a pretext to come upon us. The bursting open of the folding gates, though unintentional, seemed sufficient for his purpose; for he advanced with his soldiers and ordered them to fire. His orders were promptly obeyed, the soldiers rushing in among the fleeing prisoners and firing among them in all directions. One poor fellow fell wounded and a number of soldiers surrounded him. He got on his knees and begged them to spare his life, but their answer was, 'No mercy here!' They then discharged the contents of their muskets into him and left him a mangled corpse. Others, fleeing for the doors of their respective prison, that always before had been left open at turning-in time, found them shut, and while endeavoring to gain the opposite door, found themselves subject to the crossfire of the soldiers. This was further proof that this work was premeditated.[17]

As I was crowding my way down the flight of stone steps to ascertain respecting the uproar and report of muskets, a number of soldiers came rushing to the doorway (while the remnant outside were wedging themselves in), and discharged their musket-shot upon us. One man fell dead, another fell just before me with the loss of his leg and one English soldier, against his will, was crowded in, and the door shut against those most cowardly murderous soldiers, who discharged their muskets on those who had not been outside their prison.[18]

About this time Captain Shortland, who was reported to be drunk, ordered the soldiers to charge the prisoners. And then he ordered the soldiers to fire. Some of them were reluctant to do this because the prisoners were "using no violence." They kept up this fire as the prisoners were running for the doors of the prisons. The guards were sent to lock up all but one of the doors of the prisons and thus the fleeing prisoners had to run through gunfire to attempt to get to safety. A great number (approximately 50) were killed or wounded at the entrances of the prisons.

Some men hid in a corner, hoping to be out of the way of the fire. But Captain Shortland ordered his men to fire on them, killing or wounding all of them. He even ordered the soldiers to fire upon a man who was carrying a wounded man upon his shoulders, and when he laid the man down, Captain Shortland stamped upon him.[19] Shortland even opened the gates and ordered his soldiers to fire into the prisons. When the soldiers hesitated, Shortland seized one of their guns and commenced firing. So parties of soldiers went to the windows and doors of prisons #3 and #4 and in each prison one man was killed and several were severely wounded.[20]

Bates then relates a curious incident:

> The greatest confusion and excitement now prevailed throughout the different prisons. The most we could learn was that some, while fleeing from these murderers, said they passed the dead and dying all along in their way to the prison. We hailed the next prison to our own, and they said about two hundred of their number were missing. We thought this was about the number missing in ours. Judging thus, we supposed a great many must have been massacred. Fathers, sons, and brothers were missing, and a most intense excitement prevailed in our prison. Suddenly we heard the boatswain's whistle from the daily crier. All was silent in the upper floor. He now began to read the following: "There is an English soldier found among us on the

lower floor, and a number of prisoners have a rope around his neck, and the other end over the beam, urging him to say his prayers, for they are about to hang him. Two of the committee have prevailed on them to hold on until they get the mind of the prisoners. *What shall be done with him?* "Hang him! Hang him! Hang him!" cried some; others, "No, no, let him go!" Second loft and lower floor about the same. The crier reported the majority for hanging him. The committee, with others, begged them to hold on until they tried the vote once more. The prisoners were too much excited and therefore judged too hastily. The poor soldier was still begging for his life, expecting to be swung up the next moment. When the crier passed around the second time, it was difficult to decide, but many more were in favor of sparing the life of their enemy. This opened the way for a third trial which was decidedly in favor of releasing him. The frightened soldier was told "Americans never murder their prisoners: rest easy, your life shall be preserved to distinguish between the humanity of a British soldier and that of an American sailor."[21]

During this interval, the dead and dying had been gathered out of the yards, and conveyed to the hospital. A guard of soldiers then came to our door for the dead and wounded prisoners, "Have you any here?" "Yes, here are two; and here also is also one of your own soldiers, take him along with you."[22]

Pierce relates that when the prisoners were all back in their buildings, the doctor sent for the wounded. He is said to have wept as they were brought into the hospital. Captain Shortland appeared and threatened to run his sword through the arm of a wounded man. But the doctor prevented him and put the captain outside, even though the captain protested and struck the doctor several blows. The next day, the prisoners were let out into the yard where they could still see blood and brains scattered about.

Bates' experience was different: "It was late in the morning before the doors of our prison were opened; for it required some time to wash away the blood of our murdered companions, which our enemies were very unwilling for us to see. When we got out into the yard, many found their lost friends, for during the massacre, to escape the fire of the soldiers, several fled to the nearest prisons and remained in them until the morning, while others sought and found theirs in the hospital, among the murdered and wounded. After much inquiry, we learned that seven were killed and sixty wounded."[23]

PART I : IMPRESSED

Captain Shortland appeared and told the prisoners it was not his fault. He said that he did not order the soldiers to fire. But Pierce interjects that this was a lie because he had heard the captain order the soldiers to fire.[24] Later that day two admirals and a number of militia arrived and questioned the prisoners concerning the matter. They said that it was a very serious matter and that Captain Shortland and all the soldiers were under arrest and were being sent to Plymouth. And for a time the prisoners hoped that Shortland would be punished for his crimes.

Bates goes on to describe a court of inquiry which was instituted to investigate the massacre. Bates must have attended the court because he describes the scene in some detail:

> A court of inquiry was now instituted to investigate this matter — John Quincy Adams, late Secretary of the American Legation at Ghent, on the part of the United States, and one of the experienced admirals from Plymouth, on the part of Great Britain, with their retinue were part of the court.
>
> A place was fitted for the court on top of the walls over the narrow passage and place of demarcation between the prisoners and their keepers, so that the court could be addressed by the prisoners on the left, and by their keepers on the right, the walls being between us. The statement of Governor Shortland and his party with respect to the attempt to make a hole in the wall, and the bursting open of the broken locked gates, to justify his attack upon in the manner already described, seemed to have but little weight. It was settled with us at the time of the massacre, that his plan was preconcerted. The British admiral seemed intent on questioning the prisoners with regard to their allowance of food, and whether they had not had all that was allowed them, etc. The reply was, that our grievance was not then about our allowance of food but the inhumane manner in which our countrymen had been massacred. Finally, in the settlement of this grievous question, the massacre at Dartmoor was *disavowed* by the British government, and compensation was made to the widows of the sufferers.[25]

Rumors continued as to when ships would arrive to take the prisoners back to America. But Pierce in his despair writes in his journal: "The wind is yet favorable for ships from London, but I don't believe the timber is cut to build them with nor the men born to build them."[26]

But then men begin to be called out to leave. And once more there is hope. Apparently, the men are called out according to when they arrived at the prison — those who came in 1812 leave first and so on. Bates was in one of the first groups to leave the prison: "As I was among the first on the

8. Dartmoor Prison

prisoner's list at this time, I was called out and mustered with a draft of two hundred and fifty. Many of this number, as we were mustered before Governor S. and his armed soldiery, bore white flags on long poles, with mottoes like the following in large black letters. '*Massacre of American prisoners in Dartmoor prison, April 6th, 1815,*' '*The bloody 6th of April!*' and others had flags with Shortland's name as the murderer of American prisoners. Some of the prisoners openly declared that they would kill him if they could get near him. He seemed to be aware of these threats, and kept himself at a safe distance while we were being mustered in the upper yard near his and his officers' dwellings preparatory to our final departure. We also expected that he would command us to strike our flags while we remained under his immediate inspection, or his armed regiment of soldiers that guarded us from thence to Plymouth harbor, (a distance of fifteen miles), but he did not, for they continued to wave them until we passed through Plymouth to our place of embarkation."[27]

Some of the departing groups give three cheers as they leave. This was answered by the remaining prisoners.

The days go by. Sometimes Pierce loses heart. At one time he writes, "I don't see as ever I shall get liberated again as it is nearly 3 months now since the Peace." There are reports that the war had started up again. There also came a letter from Beasley enclosing a copy of a letter from the Lords Commissioners of the Admiralty which justified Captain Shortland. It stated that the prisoners had disarmed the soldiers. This, Pierce says, was a lie. The prisoners were enjoying themselves in the yard and knew nothing of it before the soldiers began firing.[28]

Then on the 18th of May there came the glad news that more ships had arrived. On every face there were smiles as they awaited their departure. Pierce begins to knit a pair of shoes to wear to walk down to Plymouth when his time comes. Still they wait. Some 30 men bribe the guards to let them over the wall at five pounds per man. Later, other prisoners were caught attempting to scale the walls and were confined in the dungeon. But others continued to escape. Pierce was very angry at Beasley, writing, "Dam Beasley & all who are concerned in getting us away."

On the 21st of June more men were called out to leave. The militia came to relieve the regulars who were to join an expedition to Spain. There was also a report that Captain Shortland, who had been returned to his post, was to make the prisons ready for 5000 French prisoners.

Part I : Impressed

On the 2nd of July Pierce wrote: "Begins pleasant wind. N.E. At 12 noon, it was cry'd round that 360 men would be called out tomorrow & this draft takes me there are now (2 P.M.) 2000 Frenchmen entering the gates mostly soldiers end pleasant & ends this journal for want of paper."[29]

Finally, Pierce is able to leave "this cursed Depot" on July 3, six months after peace was signed.

Chapter 9
Stephen Cabot

Stephen Cabot wrote this account of his experiences:
"Monday 18 Oct 1814 — Left Boston in the Brig Principe Real.... 19th were boarded by the M.L. Junon, treated well.... Nothing occurred till the 25th saw a ship close a board of us. Constant headwinds & bad weather until the 10th Nov — Saw two Frigates just to windward of us coming down under full sail — Had just time to get our dinner before they brought us to. After hoisting our colors, they hoisted the French Flag & sent a boat board of us. Blowing a gale & heavy Sea running, we were under close reefed fore top sail & main sail, The Boat was scarcely along side before we were all *sans ceremonie* tumbled headlong into it, with the greater part of our Baggage, that which happened to be in our trunks; the residue was soon upon the backs of the sailors, all out boots, shoes, hats, &c were lost in the squabble. As soon as I got on board the Frigate I spoke to the Captain & asked him if he would ransom the vessel, I told him it was American property which I would prove to his satisfaction, He replied the Commodore was on board the other Frigate & he would ask him — signals were exchanged, & we were ordered to board the Com's Vessel, ie the Portuguese Captain, Singleton, & myself at the expense of a wet jacket. As soon as we got on board here, I renewed my application & even offered to pay the actual cost of vessel & cargo, give up all the Portuguese on board as they were prisoners of War, And navigate ourselves into port, but he sternly replied to me in the negative & after asking particularly what our cargo consisted of, & if there was any money on board, ordered her to be burnt, it blew so hard they could not take any thing from her of consequence, at about six o'clock they made a *petit feu de joi* of her & we had the pleasure of witnessing it, They immediately shaped their course

Part I : Impressed

to the southward & kept us ignorant of their destination, we were however treated with the utmost attention on board the Commodore's vessel. W Staymaker & March on board the other were treated like dogs, they messed with the doctor's mates in the cock pit, Singleton & myself had our hammocks slung in the mendroom & messed with the Commodore & his officers, his first Lieutenant & indeed all the officers spoke English & seemed one & all to take unvaried pains to make our situation as comfortable as possible. We remained on board till the 21st Nov. Lat 23.2 Saw a sail dead to windward of us, gave chase to her & gained but very slo[w]ly when just at night she bore down to us & proved to be a vessel from Malaga loaded with fruit & wine, the cry of "Bon Pris" reechoed from every quarter & joy beamed in every countenance, the weather was delightful & the sea smooth as a bowling alley, she laid by us till day light when all the boats from both vessels were employed in pillaging her, the confusion this occasioned is not to be dissembled, for a moment, 800 French sailors, nine tenths of them drunk, endeavoring who should cabbage the most, in every boat that came from the schooner two or three were so drunk, they were obliged to hoist them into the vessel & in one instance, one fell over board & no notice was taken of it, During this confusion, we were, as the sailors say, working a traverse to get the Commodore to let us have the vessel to get home in, with a little intrigue we succeeded and everything was settled with all the impetuosity of a Frenchman.

"The Commodore ceded to Cpt. Singleton the vessel and the residue of the cargo, which consisted of a very light set of ballast, of pipes of wine & brandy, upon his giving an obligation to remit to his friends in France the sum of 1000 dollars, it being presumed that the vessel & cargo would produce that in America.... The command of her was given to our Portuguese Captain & we were ordered to St Michaels. The original crew of the schooner 16 in number, our Brig's crew, & 4 Germans, making all 34 souls — no person on board knew the nature of this transaction except Singleton & myself, nor who had the best right to the vessel on arrival. Our Portuguese captain thought she was given to him & his crew as an indemnity for the loss of the Brig. This belief we encouraged, & he remained in it till we arrived in this place. All was confusion we embarked just at night jumbled up together like poultry in a coop. Nobody knew who was Captain, or where we were going. There were scarcely any provisions. The

9. Stephen Cabot

Cabin was stripped of every thing, not a utensil of any description on board, & every thing in horrible uproar, we were so anxious to get away from the Frigate that we did not reflect upon the consequences of the step we had taken, our situation did not strike us until we had been on board a few hours, The first token we had of it was one our crew an American, calling to us for help, he came running to us cover'd with blood, one of the Portuguese sailors having stabbed him very badly, we dressed his wounds and were laughed at by the perpetrators of the deed, who intimated that our turn would come next. This, was the first night, I cannot say I slept much, I was glad when the morning came that I might see what sort of beings were my fellow passengers; just as the day dawned there was a general muster and just such a one I believe never was before seen. Singleton and myself went on deck, & found them on the verge of a general battle, their knives drawn & every thing prepared. On casting our eyes round we immediately saw how things would operate, The Spaniards had prepared to repossess themselves of the vessel. Our Captain was afraid to make any resistance, & expected instant death, we endeavored to impress upon them the truth that we were all fellow sufferers & that we should endeavour to adopt that plan which would be most advantageous to all, instead of adding to our sufferings, reason had no weight with them, the helm was taken by the Spaniards, and they shaped their course for the West Indies. Some resistance was made by a gallant little Portuguese Sailor, but he was immediately silenced by the mate who brought a musket on deck, & swore he would shoot the first man who attempted to alter the course of the vessel.

"The next serious inquiry was, what provisions were on hand, there being 34 souls, it was an important question. We found we had not at the extent more than ten days provisions, upon very short allowance, & the distance of more than 2500 miles to run, fortunately however there was an abundance of garlic & oil, & a quantity of peas enough to keep us alive, but for fear we should starve, they had determined to give us an easier death, & cut our throats the first opportunity that offered. The third night everything was prepared, indeed we had expected it before, for they were constantly sharpening their knives & did not even hesitate to avow it. Singleton overheard one of them say 'put him out of the way, he has a pair of pistols.' They had the impertinence to ask us if we were Christians. The night came & as we thought, our last. We mustered as strong as we could

Part I : Impressed

in the cabin, 5 in number, we determined to sell our lives as dear as possible. Our situation at that moment was not an enviable one, for we had been so strictly watched that we had no time to load our pistols, so we had no weapons, we remained an hour or two in this horrible suspense, till it became unsupportable and we called the Spanish Captain & told him we were aware of the designs of his crew, and prepared to meet them like men if they persisted. In consequence of this declaration we got a lease for a few days, mean time they were endeavoring to put us off our guard, we however knew their characters too well, & improved the opportunity of exciting a jealousy between the Portuguese & Spaniards, we succeeded in a great measure, tho our Captain was such a coward & had such a dread of The Spaniards, that a child of two years old might frighten him out of his senses. We have since learnt that the Spaniards made a proposition to the Portuguese, that if they would assist, or even remain neutral they should share the booty. They knew he had considerable gold and money, valuable clothes, but the gallant little Portuguese, I have before mentioned refused, & said, instead of assisting them, he would defend us, to the last drop of his blood; We had unfortunately in our Brig two Spaniards who were the ring leaders, & the cause of our sufferings. We never went to sleep, all at a time, one half watched the others, often we caught them stealing down the companion way, with their knives drawn, as it happened, there was only 3 or 4 butchers among them, the others were willing to participate in the booty, but were not so hardened as to perpetrate the deed, in this sort of way we got along for eleven days; were I to attempt to tell all that happened in this eternity I would fill a small volume, we never for a moment during this time thought of our other sufferings, such as being confined in a little cabin not big enough for a mouse trap, filled with vermin of every description, on short allowance & very hot weather between the tropics & many other inconveniences such as being obliged to eat out of a tub with these miserable wretches there not being a knife, fork, spoon, plate or dish of any description, nothing but peas, oil & garlick, morning noon & night, twas a variety to be sure, tho not a very pleasing one, what would I not have given to be seated round one of our great Indian puddings or what would I not have given to have taken even my peas &c with you at the Fort.

"On the first December as I was sitting on deck just before night musing on our unpleasant situation, I discovered a sail, from its singular appearance we were at a loss to know what it was, but had determined to make an exertion to speak her, the Spaniards were for shearing off, but while they were disputing what was best to be done, we discovered it was a boat making for us, We immediately hauled out wind & in a few moments she was so near that we could see a man waving a handkerchief, & even then the Spaniards said it was only a lure, that she was certainly a Yankee Privateer & should not come along side we however told them, it was doubtless some of their own countrymen, probably from South America in distress & that they could not be so cruel as to see them perish before their eyes, what alarm'd them was one of the sailors saying it was an English boat, we gained our point, & and had the inexpressible pleasure of saving the lives of 16 Americans; they had been 18 days in a little boat, upon half a biscuit & 2 gills of water per day. What is remarkable the ship they belong'd to, foundered within a few miles of the spot where ours was burnt, & only two days after, the gale of wind I well recollect while on board the Frigate, & of my saying to Singleton some poor fellows are worse off than we are in this storm & perhaps it is fortunate as we are not in the old Brig, we might not have weather'd it.

"It was some time before they recovered, so as to assist us, the sailors would get drunk & we were fearful would kill themselves from excess, as there was constantly a cask of wine on broach & they could get at it when they pleased. This was the intention of the Spaniards, who finding how they were to be managed, still entertained hopes of accomplishing their plan, indeed they had new reasons as such an increase of number would soon diminish our small stock of provisions, we kept a good watch over them & began to assume a little command ourselves, insisted upon having an equal allowance of water & bread, we made an unsuccessful attempt to take the water from them, we determined if they behaved properly not to take the vessel, only to watch them, as we fear'd, some blood might be shed on the occasion, & wished if possible to avoid it, in consequence of this, they thought we were afraid of them & became outrageous, they formed several plans which we defeated, & we at last found that the only way to secure peace was to commence hostilities, before we made the attack, we called the Spanish Captain into the cabin & asked him if he knew what were the intentions of his crew, & if he would suffer them to behave so, he said he had not control over them & was not responsible for their actions, as we knew that something unpleasant would take place that

Part I : Impressed

night, we lost no time in mustering our forces, & armed ourselves with such weapons as we could get, Singleton & myself headed the party with a pair of pistols each, & took the rascals by surprise & without the least difficulty possess'd ourselves of the vessel, we pinioned them for a little & deprived them of their knives, one of which I have preserved as a curiosity, it is about the size of a carving knife we then confined in the fore scuttle & gave them an equal allowance of every thing. We took the precaution to place a guard over them night & day, another on the quarter deck, we had four muskets on board, we found it necessary to keep very strict discipline, we made out Portuguese Capt. Commodore, Singleton Sailing master, Stay mate & March Stewards, & myself Captain of Marines. We all stood our watch & immediately shaped our course for the U.S. We were then in the Lat. of St. Burts & not far to the eastward of it. Nothing important occurred untill the 18th when we made land which we supposed to be Cape Fear, we were close in Shore & anchor'd, the wind blowing fresh from N.E. could not fetch, we had not been at Anchor two hours before we saw a sail standing to S.E. supposed her a coaster bound to Charleston, determined to follow & get some assistance if possible, finding it difficult to heave up our anchor, cut the cable, & gave chase to her, but unfortunately there blew up a thick fog & we lost sight of her & were forced to give up the chase. The wind still blew most violently from N.E. we put her under close reefed fore sail & stood off & on during the night, in the morning finding we did not gain to windward, determined to put her before it and get into the first inlet we could, we stood to S.E. long shore several hours & saw a sail a head, gave chase & after firing several shots over her head, brought her to, she proved the schooner Howard from Newbury Port & informed us of our mistake, that the bluff of land we took for Cape Fear was Cape Look Out, & that New Inlet Bar, bore ___ distance ___ which did not know, tho in sight in consequence of the Light &c having been washed away; we got provisions eno from her for two meals, & beat all that day & came to anchor that night close to the entrance of New Inlet & expected Pilots would be off in the morning for we could see their houses on shore; In heaving up at day light next morning we broke our second & last anchor, & fired guns repeatedly, hoisted a white flag, finding no Pilots coming & fearing we might be blown off in our distress'd condition, having no provisions, anchors, or charts determined to attempt going over the Bar ourselves & struck on the shoalest part of it, about 10

9. Stephen Cabot

o'clock, at which Pilots came off to our assistance, she thumped very hard & the breakers broke over her. Singleton went on shore in a ferry boat, thinking she would not go to pieces & we might save her cargo, we kept her free 5 or 6 hours with both pumps, found it useless after that time, she gain'd upon us fast, & indeed before we left her, she was 2 feet of water in her Lee Gang Way, we all got ashore with the greater part of our baggage, & in the course of the night were safely moored in Mr Cellar's kitchen, eating sweet potatoes. In the morning nothing more of the Schooner was to be seen, her cargo was floating in various directions about the beach, we rolled up that day 20 pipes, 10 of which were stolen by the Pilots in the night, the next day Singleton came over with Captain T's sloop & took what wine there was left on the beach, we bade adieu to Federal Point, went over to the Fort at Smithville & refreshed ourselves where there is a very comfortable house, the same where Fos was left Hostage. In consequence of very bad weather we could not get up to Wilmington for a week, I at last was obliged to go up on horse-back, Singleton followed me a week afterwards with the wine he had pick'd up, which was immediately claimed by the Spanish Captain, & a compromise took place, agreeing to divide what was saved, we had much difficulty in soothing the Portuguese Captain, who presuming the property was his, thought it hard he could not even get a share of it, & refused to give up the papers, but we persuaded him into it, and had just settled our business & taken our passage on the stage when the unfortunate accident happened to Singleton, so ends the acount of my voyage, I have written it at intervals while watching with Singleton, while I write this, he is breathing his last.
"Wilmington, Feb. 20"

"The following is intended as a continuation of my journal from Wilmington.

"After settling our business with the Spanish Captain, we prepared to leave W... where we had been detained nearly a month, seats were taken in the stage & our trunks packed, the morning previous Singleton was invited to a Fox Chase, which he reluctantly accepted, & it was with great difficulty he was persuaded to join them in the morning, he tried to excuse himself but they would not let him off & fairly pulled him out of bed. I knew nothing of the excursion till I was sent for in the morning by Singleton, who had been thrown from his horse against a tree, he was struck just

Part I : Impressed

in the small of the back & tho it did not break it, injured the spinal marrow, & caused his body below the injury to be perfectly senseless & deprived him of the use of his arms; when I saw him he was in the greatest agony & I expected immediate dissolution in him, who was only a few hours before in perfect health, & with whom I was anticipating the pleasure of meeting our families & friends; on seeing me, he was much affected, & said 'Cabot 'tis all over with me.' I tried to encourage him as much as I could and promised to remain with him till he got better. We boarded at different houses & I immediately sent for my clothes & did every thing in my power to sooth him. I had not been with him an hour before he told me he had no hopes whatever that a few nights before he had had a very singular dream, which impressed him in an unusual manner & had made him thoughtful ever since, he dreamed that he saw his sister who died several years before, who spoke to him in a very affectionate way and bade him be good & prepare for death; he spoke of it repeatedly during his illness, on the second day he made his will, & requested to see a minister, I immediately sent for one, who remained with him for some hours, he frequently called by Singleton's request & assisted greatly toward tranquilising him, he constantly convers'd with me about the state he expected soon to enter & prayed most fervently for forgiveness; I watched with him 30 days & nights, during which time I never took off my clothes to go to bed, my presence seemed to be necessary to his existence & he would often weep when I only went out of the room for a few moments, he was as helpless as an infant; he preserved his senses till within a few hours of his death & appeared to approach it with a confidence that his sins would be forgiven him, he frequently said to me that he calculated upon my closing his eyes; this painful task I performed & followed him to his grave on the 23 of February. From this period till the 5th March I was employed in fitting away a Schooner which I bought in company with Mr Winslow; when I sailed for Havannah having to contend with many difficulties in getting off, for having no passport from government I was obliged to conceal myself on board & was fortunate enough not be discovered after rather an unpleasant confinement for 20 hours; we pursued our voyage without any accident or occurrence of any importance till the 13 when we struck on a reef off the S.E. extremity of the coast of Florida at about 10 o clock in the morning; we immediately threw all our ballast over board, stove our water, & in fact threw over everything that could lighten her, got an

9. Stephen Cabot

anchor out to windward & caught upon it waiting for the tide. She did not thump very hard, but we despaired of getting her off, got our boat in readiness, made a memo of what we should take with us, & prepared ourselves as well as we could for a land cruise, we judged ourselves about 9 miles from the first Island & about 20 from the main land, our prospect was rather gloomy, for that part of the country is only inhabited by Indians & it was 500 miles to the first town, in the hope of getting the vessel off we worked all that night, the wind increased & the breakers were seen in every direction & almost stunned us with their howling, after heaving the anchor close home we perceived she started a little and discovered she floated, we immediately made sail having previously sounded in every direction to find the deepest water, the current however drifted us, so she would mind the helm, & we struck a second time, which I thought would have started her floor timbers, she however struck only a few times & we got over, at this time we had a foot of water in the hole & kept our pumps going 4 hours without gaining an inch, we therefore gave this up & went below to see if we could discover where the water came in & I, to my great satisfaction found the hole. We arrived at H... without further accident, and finding my vessel rather unruly, having parted her cable while at anchor in the bason, I left her & took passage in a Swedish Brig & arrived at New Port on the 3rd of April, & Boston on the 4th where I found to my inexpressible delight all well.

"Boston, April 30, 1814."[1]

Chapter 10
James R. Durand

James Durand's account of his life comes from a book entitled *James R. Durand, an Able Seaman of 1818*. He begins his account:

> I was born December 1, 1786 in the town of Milford, County of New Haven, State of Connecticut, where I lived until I was six years old. My parents having a large family, my elder brother and I were bound apprentices to a farmer for a term of five years. We stayed there in the town of Washington for the term of our apprenticeship without any occurrence of remark.
> We then returned to Milford resolved to go to sea.
> On our return, we found our relations all in good health and tarried with them a few days. Then we went to New Haven, a town eight miles distant from Milford. There we took a packet and arrived at New York. After tarrying seven days without an offer to our satisfaction, we put back to New Haven. My brother here shipped for sea. I, however, found employ in a packet for nearly three months.

Durand then continues to describe his various voyages. At one point he tells of a voyage to France in 1807 (this was during the years when France and Great Britain were at war): "On the morning after our arrival at Bellisle, we hired a pilot to conduct us to Nantz, forty miles away. We got under way about 9 o'clock in the morning and as it was very foggy it was a fine time to escape. The British were blockading the ports of France.

"However, in spite of the fog, we had not sailed far when we saw a British 74 in chase of us. She cut us off from the land, so that we could not get into Nantz, but were forced to anchor at a place called Goree, about 60 miles from Nantz. Therefore we discharged our cargo there and sent it to Nantz in wagons. This was a considerable trouble as our cargo was sugar, molasses, cotton, boxwood &c.

10. James R. Durand

"While we were lying at Goree, two men-of-war were launched there and General Napoleon himself came to the launching.

"He had on a snuff-colored coat and breeches, very indifferent hat and epauletts and I could observe no marks of haughtiness about his person. The most I can say of him is that he is small in stature, dark complexion, but has a sharp and expressive countenance.

"We all attended meeting or service in the forepart of the day on Sundays, while we were in this place and danced in the latter part, for Sunday is the greatest day for amusement of any day in the whole week. Provisions in Goree were very cheap. A man may go on shore and have as good an entertainment as he might wish for one French crown, or five shillings, lawful money.

"When we had unladen our ship, we took in ballast, which was brought to our ship's side as small pebbles. It was carried by women in baskets, which they balanced on their heads. They emptied it down the hatchway. The Captain sold his cargo for money, and, at the time, it was unlawful to take money out of the country. Accordingly it was smuggled on board in small quantities at night. Each man brought his share on board in a belt that was strapped around his middle. Each belt held about 100 crowns.

"Our design was, as soon as we got ready, we would go to the West Indies for a cargo of salt, but the English prevented us. We came out of the harbor about 5 o'clock, leaving Bellisle about 7 o'clock P.M. On the following morning about daylight, we found a British ship astern of us with all sail set. We advised Captain Pick to also set all his sail but he would not follow our judgment. So the British ship Shannon soon came up to us. They gave us a shot and we hove to. They sent their boat with a lieutenant on board. He overhauled us, then told us to make sail.

"However we had not sailed far before they fired at us again. They came on board a second time and ordered us to make ready to go on board the Shannon as prisoners. Every man had his belt full of gold and silver and the money for the cargo which we could not put into our belts, we secreted, so that it would not be found if searched for.

"We packed up our things and boarded them. They did not leave one man from our crew on board the brig. They took us to Plymouth in England, where we remained as prisoners for six weeks. We were on a very short food allowance, scarcely sufficient to sustain life. The first sustenance I received on board them was some boiled oat-meal without salt or butter or other seasoning. In America, we ordinarily feed our swine better than this but I was obliged to eat it to preserve life.

"At Plymouth, we were finally allowanced. This allowance consisted of nine pounds of pork, half a pint of pease, one pound of bread (fourteen ounces to the pound) for six men for two days. Six of our men were allowed no more than four of theirs. We lived in this manner for six weeks.[1]

"I made myself as happy as I could and used to sport with the ship's company, because in this way I got more to eat. I had seventy crowns upon me, which was not discovered. At the end of six weeks, we fell in with the Channel Fleet and were put on board the Ville-de-Paris of 110 guns and sent to Torbay at the town of Bricksom. I considered myself happy to get there. We then got passage to Plymouth, to join our brig once more.

"On our arrival, we found that the English had eaten all the provisions on the brig. We procured some through the assistance of the Consul. Our Captain Pick left us to go to London to try to clear the brig. He was absent for near three months, before we heard from him. In fact, he never returned to the brig, when he found he could not clear her for she had been condemned as a runner.

"So we were turned out on shore, having spent our money and sold our clothes for our support during the time we waited on the brig. We applied to the Consul, but he would allow us only a shilling a day each, which was enough to buy one meal.

"As no American vessels were going out of port, I shipped on a Swedish vessel to go to Portsmouth, thinking that I could get passage from there to America. I hired for 15 $ per month. The Swedish captain died of a sickness before we reached Portsmouth.

"Now lying in this harbor was a brig belonging to New York. I applied to the Captain for a passage but was refused. I then informed the Consul of this circumstance, who wrote a letter to the brig's Captain which made the latter very indignant against me. However he told me to bring my things on board Friday. This was a Wednesday. The Captain informed me he would come to anchor at Spithead. On my arrival there, I found that they had put off without me. I was obliged to put back to the town and pay the waterman 10 s.

"You may judge if my feelings were very pleasant when I found that

10. James R. Durand

I was stranded again with very little money and no employment. I put up for the night at Mr. Turner's and there I met an English transport officer, who had heard good reports from the pilot of the Swedish vessel. He was in want of a mate and offered me a situation.

"'I am afraid of being impressed by the British,' I told him.

"'I can protect you from capture by the press gang,' he replied.

"I knew nothing else to do for a livelyhood, so I shipped as mate with him for seven pounds per month.

"In the month of March 1809 we took a hundred and forty-nine prisoners on board and sailed for Spain under convoy of two gun brigs from Plymouth. Then we joined other sail to the number of forty. After the fifth day out, thick fogs caused the fleet to separate and some of the vessels put in at one place and some at another. However, after being out eighteen days we made land and found that we were 30 miles to leeward of Corunna, our intended harbor.

"The wind and currents were so unfavorable that we were forced to beat on and off for three days. At last, the prisoners got discouraged, took the brig from us, and put into Vevarrow Bay. They hoisted themselves a boat or boats, put themselves and what they wished into them and took themselves and our property off. It would have been folly for us to tempt resistance as we were seven in number and they were 149 against us.

"As I was mate of the brig, I was forced to make an accounting of all the blankets, sheets and pillows that were in her before the prisoners decamped. After the prisoners left us, we put things in order on board and in three days came to Corunna. The greatest part of the fleet, under convoy, lay in the harbor. We remained here for three months with little to do.

"I had saved some money, over and above our wages, by supplying the cook with a morning bitter each day. Accordingly the cook gave me all the slush or fat that remained after cooking. This thing is allowed all cooks on shipboard for themselves. So on our passage I secured 95 pounds and sold it very high in Corunna.

"We waited as I said for three months to take on board some British troops and sailed July 10th, 1809 for Plymouth where we arrived after passage of 21 days. As soon as we came to anchor, I went on shore for a short time and then returned on board.

Part I : Impressed

"At length we were ordered out to sea. The men wished for a little pleasure on shore before we sailed and asked the Captain for permission

"'I have no objections,' he said, 'but there is a very hot press on shore and you'll all do better to stay on board.'

"This caution had no effect on the plans of the men and they accordingly went. I was afraid of the press and stayed on board.

"While they were away, about 11 o'clock at night, there came along side a boat belonging to the Narcissus frigate. They boarded our brig and they came below where I was asleep. With much abuse, they hauled me out of my bed, not suffering me to even put on or take anything except my trousers.

"In this miserable condition, I was taken on board their ship but did not think to be detained there for a term of seven years. Had I known my destiny that night, I would have instantly committed the horrid crime of self-murder. In this sorrowful condition I spent the night. At day light, I found my way on deck and soon after heard the word given to unmoor the ship and get her ready for sea.

"At this I was overcome by grief. I ran below and tried to procure some paper, pen and ink from the members of the crew, offering any price. I was able to offer money, as I had concealed some of my savings by tying the coins in a handkerchief about my neck. The robbers who took my money from my belt did not find this horde. However, no member of the crew durst sell me pen ink, nor paper, as they guessed my intention of writing for aid to escape from a hateful service.

"There came along side a boat with stuff to sell. For a shilling, I procured a sheet of paper on which I wrote a letter to the Captain of the brig. I desired him to break open my chest and take out my protection and indenture and send them on board as quickly as possible. I hired the boat to take this message to him immediately. The message boat made all possible speed; she had a mile and one-half to go, yet she went with such rapidity that in one hour and one-half after, the Captain was on board with my indenture and protection.

"The Lieutenant of the Narcissus said he could do nothing about clearing me, but told the Captain of the brig that if he (the Captain) would go ashore and see the Captain of the frigate, he would direct him where to find him.

"There is an island to pass, between the spot where we lay on the frigate and the town. It is called Drake's Island. It was my bad fortune that the Captain of the brig carrying my protection and indenture passed on one side of this isle in the message boat, while the Captain of the Narcissus passed it on the other side. Therefore they missed each other and my last chance of regaining my liberty was gone. As soon as our Captain arrived on the Narcissus, he weighed anchor and put out to sea. I never saw the Captain of the brig again.

"I lost, as I left behind me on the brig, more than 50 pounds sterling, a chest full of excellent and well-chosen clothes. Only lately I had quitted the service of the U. States after enduring everything. The thought of serving with the British fleet touched every nerve with distress and almost deprived me of reason. I had been eight years from home and I began to despair of ever seeing that place again.

"After I had been on board a few days, the Captain called me to the quarter deck and asked me if I would enter. He said that if I would, he would give me 5 pounds.

"I utterly refused, telling him I was an American. I also said I would not do duty if I could help it.

"'If you will not work I'll flog you until you're glad to set about it,' said the Captain. 'Go below for I won't hear another word out of you.'

"Below decks I found twelve more Americans who had been previously impressed. One of them told me that, when he refused to obey an order, the Captain had given him four dozen lashes. 'Therefore,' he said to me, 'I advise you to do as you are bid.'

"I thought this excellent advice and I went to work and made myself as contented as possible. I concluded I would write to the American consul when we came to port again.

"We voyaged to France and lay to off the port of Nantz. Near us lay the Shannon, on which I was detained a prisoner when they took the American brig as a prize. Some of the Shannon's crew told me I had better have stayed with them

"'Our captain is twice as clever as the Captain of the Narcissus,' they said.

"'Yes,' I replied, 'I'd give the devil one if he'd take the other.'

"At length, I was noticed by our Captain and put in the gig boat. Our allowance for food was so small that I began to lose flesh. One night the gig boat was ordered to go thirty miles from the ship under cover of

PART I : IMPRESSED

the darkness, to a place called Horse Island. This lies about 4 miles from the main land. A great many small boats come out there to pass it by, and our purpose was to capture them.

"The island was uninhabited except for five wild horses we saw there. We had only two days provisions with us, and, as we stayed there five days, we were forced to shoot one of the horses for food. Neither did we durst make much fire, through fear of being seen from the main land and being surprised and captured. However we made a little fire that just scorched the outside of the meat, which we ate with a great relish, notwithstanding that we had no salt to put on it.[2]

"We returned to the frigate after the fifth day on the island. We were not put on duty the morning we returned, which we considered a great favor. The next day again, we were sent off in the same boat, to try if our luck would be better.

"This time we took five prizes and brought them to the frigate. They were full of stores and supplies for General Napoleon. They were small craft called 'chamois,' of five to 25 tons burden.

"Our Captain, considering my forwardness in taking and securing these boats, gave me better usage than I had previously received. We lay off Nantz for six months, then returned to Plymouth.

"At once I wrote to our Consul at London, but I have since been informed that my letters as well of those of other impressed Americans, were intercepted. Even the petitions which the Consul made were little noticed and many a sailor brought himself to an untimely end through despair, in consequence of this cruelty and oppression which is called British courage and justice."

Durand continues to write of his shipboard experiences for several years, then when the United States declared war on Great Britain, he and several other Americans onboard his ship asked to be released: "I informed the ship's Captain that I would not fight until the opponents were more to my liking to fight against. I said, 'I would rather be hung than fight against the flag of my own country, in the very view of my native shores.' Two other Americans said the same. Then he ordered the boatswain to make three halters. 'I will hang these damned rascals,' he said.

"The halters were accordingly made and put about our necks. Then he gave us fifteen minutes to change our minds and agree to fight. We would not change our minds.

10. James R. Durand

"So then he ordered the master to put us in irons and keep us on maggoty bread and water until we complied with his commands. So we were put in irons.

"Commodore Hardy now put the Vengeance under way as a bomb ship, together with a dispatch brig. They came to anchor direct before the battery at Stonington and sent a lieutenant on shore with a flag of truce. He demanded the surrender of the town. He told them that if they did not surrender, the civilian inhabitants had only four hours in which to retire, before the British should open fire.

"The inhabitants paid no attention to this demand. So the British opened fire and kept it up for a space of 14 hours, without doing any particular damage to the town.

"On the other hand, the British received a most destructive fire from the battery, which contained a double fortified 18 pounder and a 12 pounder. These pieces kept us such a continuous fire of well-directed shot that our vessels were forced to retire after sustaining much loss and damage.

"Some of the American shot went through the brig from stern to stem, dismounting 5 guns, killing 7 men and wounding 17 others. Her spars were so cut that she was about disabled. The Spencer, a 74, now got under way to assist the brig, but she was grounded on a sand bar and only got off by lightening ship. Her crew were forced to throw overboard her shot racks and other heavy stores. She was afraid of a flotilla of gun boats under command of Commodore Lewis.

"Our frigate received a shot from the American artillery which was so well directed that we were obliged to wear out with the tide, to get out of range.

"The barges now attempted to land some soldiers at a point beyond the reach of the battery. They were repulsed by the militia, who had the use of a light piece of ordinance. In fact, one barge was taken with 8 or 10 men. The British loss was considerable; a single shot killed a doctor aboard the brig, completely severed the arm from the body of a woman near him, and broke several crates of wine bottles.

"We were obliged to retreat and it was lucky for the English that we did. The next morning the Americans received more troops and guns from New London. They were hoping we would return to the attack, as they had plenty of Yankee trouble waiting for us.

PART I : IMPRESSED

"Our Captain stated that this attack cost the British not less than 10,000 P. as every rocket that was thrown cost 5 P.

"After repairs, we cruised up and down the sound off Milford and Bridgeport without any capture except one boat. She lowered her sails at the command but the British gave her a volley of musket bullets just the same, breaking a man's leg. The injured man was brought on board. His name was Brainard and he hailed from Brantford. He was given good care and, after his recovery, we sent him on shore.

"After this cruise, we sailed to Philadelphia and captured a brig which had once been a British privateer. She was ordered to Halifax. We also took the Lady Washington, a sloop bound for Charlestown from New York. Then we returned to our former station at New London.

"It was customary with us to send our boats out in the night to capture small craft. We would permit these small craft to ransom themselves at a price that best suited our disposition. When the ransom was so high that they refused it, our officers would burn the craft.

"We captured the Armistice from New York. We ordered her to lower her sail, she obeyed; but our commander ordered a full discharge of musketry poured into her quarter, killing some of her crew and wounding others.

"We manned her and sent her for Bermuda, but before she reached there she was captured back again by an American privateer and consequently lost to the British prize master and crew.

"About this time, news of peace was in circulation. Accordingly we repaired to Bermudas, took dispatches and returned to New London, February 25th, 1815. On our arrival there all the ships were dressed in their colors. A grand salute was fired by the ships and complemented by the forts in return. Our officers went on shore by invitation of the American officers, to attend a ball, the most superb that had been exhibited since the Revolution. Both parties were in full military uniform and attended by their guards. They convened at the hotel, with bells ringing and everything illuminate. I now expected to be put on shore but was disappointed.

"So I made the resolve that none of my relatives who had not seen me for 14 years, should meet me as an English sailor. However, I was not able to carry out this plan as a boat came along side with articles for sale. One of the boatmen partly recognized me and inquired my name.

"He offered to take a letter to my uncle, who was in Milford. I wrote

10. James R. Durand

Nelson's Flagships at Anchor, Nicholas Pocock (National Maritime Museum, Greenwich, London).

to my relative and received an answer four days later, with an enclosure to my Captain, demanding my release.

"He put me off by saying he had no orders to discharge me in New London. I would not leave without my discharge and my wages which I had labored so hard for.

"However, my uncle next wrote to Lyman Law, Esq. an attorney at New London and also a Member of Congress. Lyman Law came on board to see me and asked me about the usage, within the hearing of our Captain. I told him a small part of what they had done to me and other Americans.

"Mr. Law then turned to the Captain and said, 'I want you to give me your word before witnesses that this man will suffer no more ill-usage from you or your officers and that he will be discharged immediately upon your return to Plymouth.'

"The Admiral as well as the Captain gave him their word, although they were quick enough to break it afterwards. I have heard much about

PART I : IMPRESSED

English officers and gentlemen and what their word is worth, but I never met one whom I would believe under the most solemn oath. They are and always will be perjured, lying, scottish brutal creatures arrogant in victory and sullen in defeat. I know something of them, for as I have indicated, I spent many years in their service.

"I might here mention an altercation which took place between Mr. Law and this British officer. Mr. Law positively knew me for an American illegally detained and the other asserted me to be an Englishman, with all the effrontery of which a press gang officer is capable.

"We made a quick sail from Montaug Point to Plymouth England, namely sixteen days, although we rode out a gale in the bargain. I now expected my discharge, but the Admiral and the Captain had forgot all the promises they made to Mr. Law. Our ship was sent up for repair and I was as tight in their service as ever. I called the Captain's attention to the promise he had made, but he flogged me for it.

"At this time we heard that Napoleon had escaped from Elba and had arrived in France. Our ship was hastily refitted and sent to Bordeaux.

"This order made me very uneasy and I earnestly prayed the Captain to secure me my discharge. He only answered that the ship was in a hurry to put to sea; therefore it could not be attended to.

"So I wrote to our Consul in London, enclosing a petition for my discharge. Many others who had been impressed were doing likewise. I received a kind letter from the Consul saying he would do all in his power in my behalf. That was all the satisfaction I obtained.

"We set sail for France, having two of the French king's generals on board. Our intention was to put into Bordeaux.

"Next we heard of the battle at Waterloo and that Napoleon had made his escape to Rochford. We now found our way into the Bordeaux river. We lay there some time, during which term Napoleon got into a small island near the mouth of the river with about a thousand troops. He was completely surrounded by the British forces. Then he attempted to escape in a small boat, but seeing the impossibility of managing it, he made for the Bellerophon, a 74 gun ship, where he delivered himself up as a prisoner of war. Then the ship sailed for Plymouth with the illustrious prisoner on board. After he tarried at Plymouth for five or six weeks he went on board the Northumberland to sail for his place of exile, an island called St. Helena.

10. James R. Durand

"The presence of this hero excited much curiosity while he was at Plymouth and brought together a great concourse of people. He usually exposed himself to view for two hours a day, to gratify their wishes to see him. He is said to have chosen a retreat or banishment to this solitary island rather than to be delivered up to the Russians.

"Orders were now given for all the ships to return to England, so that the crews could be paid off and discharged. Our Captain, fearful of losing his authority over us, stayed out as long as he dared but at length he sailed for Portsmouth. We arrived there September 14th, 1815 and just a week later I received my discharge.

"The long wished for happy hour had arrived when I again enjoyed my freedom. I received from the Captain the following:

THESE ARE TO CERTIFY

That James R. Durand has served on board His majesty's ships, the Narcissus and Pactolus from the 19th day of October 1809 to September the 21st, 1815; during which time he conducted himself with sobriety and attention and was always obedient to commands.

Given under my hand, John Pancher, late master of the above ships.

"After I got my discharge, I proceeded to London to secure my pay in full and, if possible, to obtain a pension for the wounds I received while in the British service. I accordingly took coach and called on the Consul in London, to whom I had formerly sent my protection. I learned there the former consul had sent my protection to the British admiralty years before, in an attempt to procure my release from bondage. The admiralty had destroyed it, the Consul supposed.

"To protect me against further abuses, I received the following:

AMERICAN CONSULATE AT LONDON

I, Ruben G. Beasley, consul of the United States of America, for London and the dependencies thereof, do hereby make known and certify to whom it may concern that JAMES R. DURAND of the town of Milford, State of Connecticut, United States aforesaid, mariner, is a citizen of the United States as appear proofs produced, to be in force while on his way to the United States.

The said JAMES R. DURAND is twenty-nine years of age, is five feet, three and one half inches high, has a high forehead, hazel eyes, small nose, common mouth,; he has a pointed chin, round face, dark hair, dark complexion and is marked with a scar on his right leg.

PART I : IMPRESSED

Given under my hand and official seal in London aforesaid, this twenty-seventh day of September, in the year of our Lord, one thousand, eight hundred and fifteen and of the Independence of the United States, the 40th.

"Having called at the Board of the Admiralty and received nothing, not even promises of which the English are usually most liberal, I returned to Plymouth. I found no good employment and my money was growing short.

"Then I learned that I was in danger of being impressed a second time, as the press gangs were working busily. Therefore I hastened back to London dock and found a ship clearing for New York. I asked the Captain if he would give me passage to the U. States, but he refused, unless I came with an order from the Consul. I procured the order and delivered it to Captain Day of New London, who commanded the ship Nabby of that port.

"I now set sail, losing me effects in Plymouth to the value of 20 P. or more as I dared not go back there for them lest I be marked by a press gang. I paid my last respects to London on January 18, 1816 and arrived in New York on the 19th day of March following....[3]

"The only accident of our passage from London to New York was that the ship took fire. Some bottles of Aqua Fortis were broken. Before the flames could be extinguished several of the passengers were badly burned. However, we put a stop to the danger by throwing the Aqua Fortis overboard.

"I landed at Milford from the new Haven packet. I received a hearty welcome from all my friends and relations whom I found in good health.

"It is my wish that the foregoing pages will be a sufficient admonition to all youths to avoid the snares and usages of the English men-of-wars-men.

"Yours Most Resp.
James R. Durand

"Rochester, N.Y. 1820."[4]

Chapter 11

Thomas Urquhart

Thomas Urquhart, a mercantile seaman in London, began a lifelong crusade to end the practice of impressment after a narrow escape from a press gang. In a letter to Wilberforce, the well known reformer who worked tirelessly to end the evils of the slave trade and slavery in the British islands of the Caribbean, he wrote the following:

"To give you some idea of the impress, I shall mention a circumstance which occurred to myself. While walking in a street in the East of London in the year, 1808 in the month of July, about nine o'clock in the evening, with my wife holding by one of my arms, and her sister by the other, I was stopped by a man who demanded who I was; on which I desired to be informed by what authority he dared to ask me that question. I had hardly uttered the words when I was brutally seized by him and two or three more. My wife received a violent blow on the breast, which compelled her to quit her hold; and which was struck with such force that symptoms of cancer appeared in a short time afterwards; those symptoms continued for several months, and only the first medical attention could have prevented the consequences that were apprehended. The ruffians struck me on the head, tore my coat from my back, and afterwards [dragged] me by the neck for fifty yards, until life was nearly exhausted. At this critical moment some people who had collected from curiosity, fortunately happened to recognize me, interfered, and probably by this means saved my life. The fellows who had been guilty of this daring outrage upon a British subject, ran off to save themselves from the indignation which their violence had excited in the crowd. Having been informed that they belonged to a gang on the impress service, I applied to Lieut. Crawford for their names, which he refused to comply with; and

PART I : IMPRESSED

requested me to compromise the outrage: of course I rejected the proposal. I next applied to the Lord Mayor, represented my case to Lord Howick, then first Lord of the Admiralty; his Lordship, after instituting an enquiry, transmitted the report he received from Capt. Richbell, with an affidavit of the gang; and the report of Lieut. C___; all of whom according to their own testimony, were the most harmless of men. At the same time Lord Howick represented that it was not in his power to punish the man, but that he should not be protected by government if I chose to enforce the civil law against him. A most gracious boon! Such were the feelings of sensibility expressed by Lord Howick, on an injury done to a British seaman, and to the females of his family: compare them with the ostentatious sympathy he always manifested on the subject of negro slavery, and inform me if he desires that a mercantile seaman should risk his life to protect him and his family from a foreign enemy. It was the bounden duty of his Lordship to have discharged this man from the service and to have publicly expressed the most marked disapprobation of the conduct of the officers under whom he acted, in order to offer a salutary example to others. This man was continued in the service during the war.

"Upon application to my solicitor I was advised, if I wished to inflict punishment on the delinquent, to sue him in the Court of King's Bench for damages (although he was not worth a shilling) in preference to an indictment, as the plea of necessity might be set up as an excuse for his conduct, and be perhaps accepted by the magistrates.

"At the expiration of four months of trouble and expense, and having no positive evidence to prove the first part of the assault, I received from the jury a verdict for fifty* pounds damages.

"The compensation appears trivial for such an act of outrage, but it produced the effect I desired: the fellow absconded for some months, when he found means to offer me security for payment in the course of two years, by installments which I accepted. This sum did not pay my law expenses, not to speak of the medical and other incidental expenses incurred by this act of violence.

"But what would have been the situation of a man differently circumstanced to what I was, with regard to property, and who would not

---

*"This was fully more than I expected; as pecuniary satisfaction was not to be obtained; neither was it my aim; Unfortunately I could not prove the person who struck my wife; this prevented me from instituting a criminal prosecution against them."

11. Thomas Urquhart

have had the means of suing for redress. He would have been dragged on board the tender. Perhaps sent off to a foreign station; his wife without money and protection, would have been exposed to the effects of the violence, she had sustained, to which she must inevitably have fallen a victim, whilst her distress and agony would be inexpressibly sharpened from the despair of never again seeing her husband; had she a family depending on her exertions for their subsistence, her misery would be intolerable.

"Had a negro slave sustained a similar outrage and the circumstances had come to your knowledge, would it not have awakened all your indignation and called for the strongest powers of your eloquence...."[1]

Urquhart returned to this theme in a letter to Lord Melville:

Had the friends of humanity taken up the interests of our mercantile seamen, with the same zeal that they manifested on questions of much less importance, and compared their situation with that of the French conscripts or negro slaves, they would have found the condition of the latter almost enviable, when contrasted with that of the former. The conscript law was a general law of the land, and acted equally on all men; and as to the West Indian slaves, the master has a particular interest in his welfare; whereas, the abuses of impressments, and arbitrary conduct of many naval officers, with the refuse of mankind acting under them accompanied by the stern wants of the public service, expose our mercantile seamen in time of war, to such oppression and insult, that the suffering of the two former classes of persons, may by considered comparatively light. The masters of merchant ships and their officers, are not exempt in their persons or property, from this system of abuse, contrary as it is to express regulations.[2]

Later Urquhart proposes a series of questions which he believes ought to be among the subjects for a Committee of the Legislature:

1st, What has been the general conduct of the impress service during the late war?
2nd, What is the present state of naval discipline and if it is founded on principles adapted to the command of regularly bred seaman?
3rd, Are the present articles of war for seamen suited to the enlightened minds of men of the present day?
4th, What has been the general conduct of officers toward men?
5th, What is the cause of the rooted aversion in the minds of our mercantile seamen to the naval service?
6th, What is the best method to raise a sufficient number of seamen in time of war, to man our navy and mercantile service without foreigners?

PART I : IMPRESSED

> 7th, What would be the most efficacious mode of training men and boys in the merchants' service which is the only good school, to make them effective seamen, and form their minds for the navy, when the country may require their service?
> 8th, What mode of training is best adapted for officers to enable them to command mercantile seamen, render them effective, and prevent desertion?
> 9th, What privilege and rights ought to be granted to seamen so as to place them upon an equality with other men, when the country requires their particular services, and exacts sacrifices from them beyond those which are imposed upon any other class of his Majesty's subjects?
> 10th, How far is it necessary to blend the two services together for general and individual good?
> 11th, What would be the best methods to give employment to our seamen after the conclusion of a war, until their numbers were reduced to answer the peace establishment of the navy and the merchant service?
> 12th, What would be the best plan for gradual extinction of impressments, without depriving the executive altogether of the right of such power on great and suddenly emergencies?
> 13th, Whether a serious injury, does not arise to the naval service, by holding it up as a place of punishment for those who commit petty crimes, when it ought to be held up as a service of honor and interest?
> 14th, What is the cause that men taken from the merchants' service with a good moral character, after having been in the navy, though for a short time, become more or less corrupted; so much so, that they have great difficulty in again obtaining employment in the mercantile service when any other can be obtained.
> 15th, What would be the best plan, during peace of ascertaining as nearly as possible the number of seamen that might be obtained for the naval service, in case of war; and what would be the best means, should their numbers be insufficient, of obtaining the requisite supply in the shortest space of time?
> 16th, How far would it tend to the general good, to cause all ships, in those trades that particularly belong to this country, to carry a certain number of people according to tonnage, and to do away with direct taxation as a means of indemnifying the owners for the increase of expense?[3]

In another letter Urquhart continues the discussion:

> I mention this because I conceive you are fully acquainted with the circumstances, through the communication I had with you at the time, and

11. Thomas Urquhart

the manner in which I acted on the occasion. As the country was engaged in hostilities at the time, I communicated my ideas to the Board and yourself privately; and I adopted, as long as the war lasted, the same precaution with Impressment; though I suffered in my own person from its effects. But the restoration of Peace has rendered this delicacy superfluous; and I have therefore made a public appeal as likely to prove the most efficacious, as well as prompt mode of removing an evil, which outrages humanity and the laws of the country.

The perseverance I showed in correcting the abuses in the transport service, I am determined to manifest on the subject of impressments; until men of my profession are restored to their civil rights, and I become at least as worthy of public sympathy as the negro slave; in a word until a British seaman can walk upon British ground without the dread of being dragged away from his family and friends as I was myself.[4]

Part II
Afterward

The reader may be wondering what happened to these men after they escaped or were released from their impressment. For some of the men whose accounts are given here, the rest of the story is unknown. That is all we have. For others, they continued in their accounts to relate other events in which they participated. Some of those events were as exciting as those they related in the time of their impressments. For some of the men, we have accounts in other sources to tell us what happened to them.

Chapter 12

William Molyneux Afterward

After his escape from the British ship of war, William found employment with a surveying team assigned to survey lands in the northeastern mountains of Pennsylvania. While traveling with the crew he fell in love with the beautiful mountains and streams of the area and decided to settle there. It certainly would be a long way from the ocean and press gangs of the British Navy.

He cleared some land and built a cabin, yet he still remembered his wife and children back in England. William was the first white settler in this area, which is now called Sullivan County, and he may have been a little lonely. Besides, he may have also been concerned for their welfare.

So he decided to make the risky step of returning to England and bringing them back with him to America. All went well on the return voyage. But he was saddened to learn that his wife and baby had died in his absence. However, he went about the village and surrounding farms and found his older children. One child, Edward, was indentured and so could not leave at this time. The others William brought to Liverpool to seek passage back to the United States.

But as they were getting on the boat, William caught a glimpse of the press gang. He feared he might be captured and impressed a second time. The accounts vary as to his next step. Some say he put soap in his mouth, others say it was crumpled paper. Whatever it was, he pretended to be foaming at the mouth and mad. The gang left him alone and he and his family were able to continue on their voyage. Edward was able to join his family later.

William Molyneux never remarried. But the Molyneux children married and farmed in Sullivan County for several generations. One of

PART II : AFTERWARD

Battle of the Nile, Thomas Whitcombe, 1798 (National Maritime Museum, Greenwich, London).

William's grandsons fought in the Civil War and returned home to farm and teach school in the mountains.[1] Some Molyneux descendents still live near the old homestead. Others have scattered across the United States. Descendents include teachers, doctors, farmers, businessmen and other professions.

Every four years the Molyneux clan have gathered in the mountains of northeastern Pennsylvania for a family reunion. I think William would have been proud of them.

Chapter 13

John Newton Afterward

Following his stormy voyage and religious experience, Newton shipped aboard a slave ship transporting African slaves from the west coast of Africa to the islands of the Caribbean. Within a few years, he became a captain of a slave ship and made several voyages transporting slaves. After suffering a severe stroke, he left off being a ship captain and became a tide surveyor for the port of Liverpool.

Sometime during these years Newton married his sweetheart, Mary Cathart. He had first fallen in love with her when she was quite young. He wrote: "Almost at the first sight of this girl (for she was then under fourteen) I was impressed with an affection for her, which never abated or lost its influence a single moment in my heart from that hour." According to his account, he carried this affection for seven years before he was able to finally claim her as his bride.[1]

While making a living as a surveyor, Newton began to study Greek and Hebrew so that he could read the words of the Bible in the original. He also became a lay minister and became quite well known. He applied for ordination but was turned down a number of times. Finally, after seven years, he was ordained a minister in the Church of England. He was appointed to serve the church of Olney in June of 1764.

While in Olney, he and the poet William Cowper wrote a number of hymns. Cowper had moved to Olney in 1767 and worshipped in the church Newton served. The hymns were printed in the *Olney Hymns* in 1779. Among the hymns is one of Newton's hymns that came to be known as "Amazing Grace" and is a retelling of Newton's life:

> Amazing Grace! how sweet the sound
> That saved a wretch like me!

Part II : Afterward

I once was lost but now am found,
Was blind, but now I see.

'Twas grace that taught my heart to fear,
And grace my fear relieved;
How precious did that grace appear,
The hour I first believed!

Through many dangers, toils, and snares,
I have already come;
'Tis grace has brought me safe thus far,
And grace will bring me home.

The Lord has promised good to me,
His word my hope secures;
He will my shield and portion be,
As long as life endures.[2]

The hymns of Newton and Cowper were to become beloved and used by Christians of many denominations.

In 1779 Newton was invited to become the rector of a church in London. He became a very popular evangelical preacher and many people visited him there to seek his counsel. Among his visitors was the writer and philanthropist Hannah Moore and a young Member of Parliament, William Wilberforce. From his correspondence with William Wilberforce, it is apparent that Newton was an important figure in Wilberforce's life. He appears to have been one of the people that Wilberforce discussed his life's direction with. Newton wrote to Wilberforce: "You were pleased to make me the first acquainted with the Lord's goodness to you. The joy that I felt and the hopes I conceived when you called on me in the vestry at St. Mary's I shall never forget."[3]

Despite his having served on slave ships, Newton came to abhor the slave trade and regret his part in it. He encouraged Wilberforce to stay in Parliament and "serve God where he was" rather than to become a minister. Wilberforce followed Newton's advice and was an influential member of Parliament. He is especially noted for his lengthy (twenty years) and eventually successful campaign to abolish the slave trade in the British Empire. He was aided by Newton, who wrote "Thoughts Upon the African Slave Trade" to support the abolitionist's position in 1787.

13. John Newton Afterward

During his ministry at St. Mary's, Newton's wife died. In one of his letters to Wilberforce he tells of his sorrow at her passing. He begins by discussing the time before she died: "Then my dear Mrs. Newton was living, and my regard for her tied me too closely to this life and the concerns of it by a thousand invisible strings. These are now broken. Now I seem to feel myself a stranger and a pilgrim indeed."[4]

Newton died December 21, 1807.

Chapter 14

Joseph Bates Afterward

As Joseph leaves Dartmoor Prison he looks back at "that dark and massy pile of stone buildings where we had suffered so many privations, and then forward to the western horizon, which could now for the first time since our confinement be seen stretching away in the distance toward our native country, where were our paternal homes and dear friends." He continues, describing the experience:

"Our mingled emotions of oppressive bondage on the one hand, and unbounded liberty on the other, were more easily felt than described. With an old pair of worn out shoes. I stooped to relash them on my feet, and felt myself competent to perform what was to us, in our weak state, a tedious journey. But the joyful feelings of liberty and the pleasant anticipation of soon greeting our dear friends, though an ocean of three thousand miles in width divided us, cheered us onward to the city of old Plymouth. The people stared at us, and no marvel, for I presume they had never seen so motley a company of men, with such singular flags flying pass through their city before.

"Boats were waiting, and before night we were embarked on board the cartel. This was an English merchant ship of four hundred tons burden, called the Mary Ann of London, commanded by Capt. Carr, with temporary berths between decks to accommodate bout two hundred and eighty persons. Some officers that had been paroled joined us at P., which swelled our number to two hundred and eighty....

"Our berths on board the cartel were much crowded together, and were prepared for both sleeping and eating, with a narrow pass-way, just wide enough to admit of our passing up on deck and down, rank and file. The next morning we weighed our anchor and passed out of the harbor under a cloud of sail, with a fair wind. Very soon we took our departure from old England, and were glad enough to find ourselves on the wide ocean steering westward. Nothing worthy of note occurred on board until we reached the eastern edge of the celebrated banks of Newfoundland....

"When a few days out, we learned from the captain that Mr. Beasley, our consul at London, had chartered this ship to land us at City Point (a long distance up the James River, Va.), and load with tobacco for London. We considered this a cruel and unwarrantable act of Mr. B.'s for only about six of our number would be accommodated while the rest would have to travel hundreds of miles to reach their homes in New York and New England, if they could beg their way. We expostulated with the captain, but he declared he would not deviate from his charter to land us at any other place. The prisoners declared on the other hand, that his ship should never carry us to City Point; whereupon arrangements were soon made among us in a private manner, in case of a revolution in our floating castle, who the captain and officers should be.

"As we approached the eastern edge of the banks of Newfoundland, about two-thirds of the distance across the Atlantic Ocean, I found we were in the place where I was shipwrecked by the ice several years before.... As this perilous place became the topic of conversation we learned that a number of us had experienced like difficulties in passing over these banks in the spring season of the year. Capt. Carr said he had made fifteen voyages to Newfoundland and never had seen any. He did not believe there was any in our way. In the afternoon we saw a large patch of sheet-ice. We asked the captain what he called that. He acknowledged that it was ice. As the night set in the wind increased to a gale from the east. Capt. Carr unmindful of all that had been said to him respecting the danger of ice in our track, still kept the ship scudding before the gale under a close-reefed main-top-sail and foresails, determined to have his own way rather than lay by until morning as suggested by some of the prisoners. Some thirty of us, unwilling to trust to the captain's judgment, took our position on the bow and bowsprit of the ship to look for ice. At midnight the ship was driving furiously before the gale and storm, evidently without any hope of our having time to avoid ice if we should see it, and in danger of being dashed to pieces without a moment's warning. We also felt a marked change in the air. In this dilemma we decided to take the ship from the captain and heave her to. We found him at the quarter deck con-

PART II : AFTERWARD

Mr. B.—Seeking the Bubble Reputation. The Byron poem at the bottom reads: "The pulses' maddening play / That thrills the wanderer of the trackless way / That itself can woo the approaching fight / and turn what some deem danger to delight / No dread of death, if with us die our foes / save that it seem e'en duller than repose." George Cruikshank: Thomas McLean (National Maritime Museum, Greenwich, London).

ning* the ship. We briefly stated our dangerous position, and told him that about three hundred souls were at the mercy of his will; and now, if he did not round his ship to, *we would do it for him.* Seeing our determination to act in this matter immediately he cried out to his crew, 'Round in the larboard main brace! Put the helm a-starboard!' This laid the main-top-sail to the mast, and let the ship come by the wind.

"This being done, the onward progress of the ship was stayed until the dawn of the morning, which showed us how narrowly we had escaped with our lives. Large islands of ice lay right in our track, and if we had continued to run before the gale we should have been in the midst of them, in imminent danger of being dashed to pieces. The willfulness of

*"*Conning*: In seamen's language, guiding or directing a vessel by orders to the steersman."

14. Joseph Bates Afterward

Capt. Carr was now evident to all, and the course we pursued in requiring him to heave the ship to was also justified. And after the ship was again turned on her onward course, and passing these huge islands of ice, we were all stirred to watch until we had passed the banks and were again safe in the fathomless ocean. These bodies of ice had the appearance of large cities in the distance, and had it not been for our forethought, would in all probability have been the cause of our immediate destruction.

"Moreover, a large majority of us were satisfied that this was the best time to take the ship from the captain and proceed to New York or Boston, from whence we could more readily reach our homes; for we had decided and declared, as before stated to Capt. Carr, that his ship should never take us to City Point, Va. where his charter party required him to land us. Having passed beyond all danger from ice, the most difficult point to decide was, which of the two ports we should steer for, if we took the ship. Suddenly and unexpectedly, one of our company placed himself amidship upon the main hatchway, and with a stentorian voice cried out, 'All you that are for New York go on the starboard side of the ship, and all that are for Boston go on the larboard side!' Sides were immediately taken, when it was declared that the greatest number were on the starboard side; hence the ship was bound for New York. Capt. Carr stood in our midst, near by the man at the wheel, gazing at this unlooked-for and strange movement, when suddenly one of our number took the wheel from the helmsman. Capt. Carr demanded that he should leave it immediately, and ordered his man to take the helm again. A number of us also urged our friend to take the helm, assuring him that we would protect him. At this Capt. C. became very much enraged, saying what he would do with us if he had a crew able to cope with us. But he saw that resistance was vain; we had taken possession of the helm, the ship therefore would no longer be steered by his direction. Seeing what was done, he called us a 'rabble,' 'roughally,' etc for taking his ship from him on the high seas, and wished to know what we were going to do with her, and who was to be the captain. Capt. Conner of Philadelphia, was lifted up [by] those who stood near him, and placed with his feet on the head of the capstan, (a cylinder four feet high, with levers to weigh the anchors, etc.) 'there is our captain!' cried the multitude. Said Capt Carr, 'Are you going to take charge of my ship, Capt. Conner?' 'No, sir,' was the reply. 'yes you shall!' was the unanimous cry. 'I don't want anything to do with her,' said Capt. Con-

Part II : Afterward

ner. 'You shall,' was the loud cry, 'or we will throw you overboard!' 'You hear what they say, Capt. Carr. What shall I do?' 'take her, take her, Capt. Conner,' said the English commander. This being settled, Capt Carr began to call us hard names again.

"Some that stood near him advised him to cease and get down into his cabin as soon as possible out of the way of danger. He did so and order was soon restored. Capt. Conner took charge of the ship and named three officers for mates. A number of us volunteered as sailors to man the ship, and we were divided into three watches, that every advantage might be taken to urge our ship onward for the port of New York under all the sail she could bear.

"Capt. Carr and crew had their liberty and were treated kindly; but they were not allowed to interfere with the sailing of the ship. He declared that if the vessel ever arrived in the States he would have us all arraigned before the United States Court for taking his ship from him on the high seas. The idea of being deprived of our liberty and arraigned before our country for trial in this case, on our arrival, troubled us some; nevertheless, we were resolved to keep charge until we arrived.

"A ship was seen bearing toward us with American colors flying. We hoisted English colors. It was a rare sight to see one of our own country's ships, with the stars and stripes floated at her peak. As she came riding triumphantly within speaking distance by our side, the cry was given, 'What ship is that?' 'Where are your from?' and 'Where bound to?' Answers: 'From the United States, bound to Europe.' 'What ship is that?' etc. Answer: 'The Mary Ann of London, a cartel with American prisoners from Dartmoor, England, bound to the United States.' A few more inquiries, and as each ship filed away on its onward voyage, we gave them three loud cheers, so glad were we to see the face of some one from our native country afloat on the wide ocean.

"About ten days after the revolution, or time we took the ship, we saw the land looming in the distance before us. As we drew near the coast, we learned to our great joy that it was Block Island, R.I. about forty miles from our home. Sailboats were now pushing out from the land to get the first opportunity to pilot us in. Some of our number thought it would be a rare chance for them to get on shore in their boats and so got up their hammocks and bags, waiting to jump aboard when they should come along. A heavy squall was now rising out of the northwest, so the top-sails

14. Joseph Bates Afterward

were clewed down and many hands were on the yards reefing them. As the boats came sheering up to our side, the men on the top-sails cried out, 'Don't you come here! For we have got the plague on board!' The men that were waiting for them declared that we had nothing of the kind, and bade them come alongside. A multitude of voices from the top-sails were again saying, 'Yes we have got the plague on board, too! Don't come here!' The boats immediately hauled their wind and steered for the land. Nothing that we had would induce one of them to come on board, for they knew that a bare report of their doing so, would subject them to a tedious quarantine. The plague we had on boards was this: We were expecting that Capt. Carr would (as he had threatened) have us arraigned before the United State Circuit Court for piracy on the high seas. Therefore we were unwilling to part with them until we learned more about the matter.

"The wind died away during the night, and the next morning we perceived that a heavy swell and current was setting us in between the east end of Long Island and Block Island into Long Island Sound. We now concluded if we could get a pilot we would pass up the Sound to New York. From some of the many fishing smacks in sight we hoped to find one. At length one of the smacks was induced to come alongside. In less than five minutes she was taken possession of, while the captain and the crew retreated away to the stern in amazement at the strange work that was going on. We judged that nearly one hundred of our company began throwing their bags and hammocks on board of her, and themselves after in quick succession. They then cast off from the ship gave us three cheers, and bore away for Newport, R.I. before we could learn their object. They had no idea of being brought to trial for piracy on the high seas by Capt. Carr.

"As the wind was now unfavorable to proceed to New York, we concluded to go to New London, Ct. at which port we arrived the next forenoon, and anchored off the wharf before the town, six weeks from Plymouth, in England. A great number of us now crowded aloft for the purpose of furling all the sails at the same time. We then stood on our feet at the yards, and gave three cheers to the gazing multitude on the wharfs in New London. In a few moments more, boat loads of our joyous company, with their bags and hammocks, were crowding for the shore, leaving their captured ship and Capt. Carr to find his way from thence for his load of tobacco at City Point, Va., as best he could, or even to find us the next

Part II : Afterward

twenty-four hours, if he still felt disposed to prosecute us for our so-called piratical proceedings on the ocean. Doubtless, he was so wonderfully relieved at the departure of such a rebellious crew that he had no particular desire to come in collision with them again.

"The good people on the land seemed about as glad to see and welcome us on shore as Capt. Carr was to get rid of us. But neither party was half as glad as we were. It seemed almost too much to believe that were actually on our own native soil once more as freemen, from British warships and their gloomy dismal prisons. After our joyful feelings in a measure subsided, we were inquiring our ways home. Within twenty-four hours a great portion of our company took passage in a packet for New York city. Four of us, by fair promises, without money, chartered a fishing smack at two dollars per head, to carry twenty-two of us around Cape Cod to Boston, Mass. This placed us beyond the reach of Capt. Carr, or ever hearing from him again."[1]

Chapter 15
Jacob Nagle Afterward

Following his experiences in the Caribbean, Jacob Nagle served on board the British warship *St. Lucia*. He served on the *St. Lucia* and two other ships of the Royal Navy. Then, when the war was over and he was discharged in London, he stayed there until he signed on as a seaman on another ship bound for Gibraltar. When he returned to London the fleet bound for Australia came into port and Nagle jumped at the opportunity of serving aboard. Later he traveled to South America and then to Portugal. At times he suffered from ill health and at the age of sixty-two decided that his naval career was done. The last pages of his journal tell of his experiences as an old man:

"Left Canton bound for Washington at 8 o'clock A.M. weather warm. I received a litter from Mr Shorb in Canton to Major A.J. Hook in Washington as a recommendation. Arriving in Lisbon, I went to Mr. Thompson, Member of Congress. He backed my papers, I went on. I wish to make short. I only mention the chief of the villages I went through from Lisbon: FullTown, or West Union, Little Beaver, come to Ohio, crossed to Geore Town, came to Hooks Town, Frankfort Hill, Williams Port. Being in the rong road, went to Brownsvill and crossed, then Bridgeport, Monegehele, Union Town, Munrow, went over to Lorrel Hill, past Braddocks Run, Smithfield, Cumberland land, Boonsbury, Middle Town Fredericks, Town, Willms Port, Mariland, Boonsbury, MiddleTown, Fredericks Town, George Town, Cockvile, Kenly Town.

"Arrived in Washington City on the 24 July. I went to Mr. Laskeys where I had been before. The next day I went to Major Hook and delivered the letter from Mr. Shorb and my papers. He sent his secretary with me and my papers was approved and I was examined by the Board of War,

Part II : Afterward

or by J.L Edwards, Commissioner of pensions in Washington City, but by the neglect of my loyer, Mr. Brice, not sending my dockerment with me, it could not be settled. Therefore I was in a bad situation and without money. Having no way to remain there while I sent to Canton, and not informing Majer Hook where I was gon, I started for Baltimore in hopes I could get work till I sent to Canton. It came on to rain heavy, which wet me to the skin, and having no money for a bed, I laid down in the porch, but the landlord taking a fancy to my staff and perhaps seeing I was in distress, I gave it to him. He gave me a good brandy sling going to bed and my bitters with a good warm breakfast and a half dollar in cash. His name was Mr. Gibbs, capt the state house.

"I started on the road, and being tierd, I steped into a porch at Mr. Rummons, an open house. While sitting there, a Catholic Priest came out, and having a little conversation, asked me if there was any Catholiks about Canton. I tild there was, and as he step'd into his coach, he clap'd a half dollar into my hand and started for Baltimore.

"I then travel'd on and laid all night in the woods. This day I was very unwell. I travel'd on for Baltimore. Came to a stage house, Though I had part of the money I received, I had to be careful, and being unwell, I did not wish to lay out all night. Seeing the hosier in the stable, I spoke to him. He gave me a good hayloft to lay down. I remain'd till morning. He came early and let me out. I travied on.

"I must say this of the country, they have no respet or humanity for a person in poverty. At 8 o'clock A.M., coming a long on the turnpike, passing a few houses, a stout able man came out of a house, running at me with a white shirt in his hand, tearing it all to peaces and running at me. I took him to be a lunateck. I having a good stick in my hand, I put myself on a gard and told him to stand off or I would nock him down. He steped back and picked up three or four stones of about 1 lb. weight and made offers to heave them at me, but I still remained on my gard and closed in with him till I observed some men and wimen behind a corner of a house laughing. I then slapped him on the sholder. He then laughed, otherwise I should have laid him lower than he then was. I told them I was an Old Revolutioner and was not be skared in so simpel a maner. They all laughed hartily at him and told him he had met his match, thoug I was an old man. They gave me a treat. I bid them good by and went on and arrived in Baltimore and went to[1] Smiths Point."

15. Jacob Nagle Afterward

Strachan's Action After Trafalgar, 4 November 1805, Francis Sartorius (National Maritime Museum, Greenwich, London).

Here, the old sailor continues to tell of his journey. He stays with one relative or friend for a few months and then moves on. He dies in Canton, Ohio, at the age of eighty. One of the last of the Revolutionary War veterans, he is buried with military honors.

Chapter 16
Joshua Penny Afterward

Joshua Penny had sailed to many ports and tried in many ways to make his fortune, all of which had been unsuccessful. Now after a number of years he determines to go home, at least for a visit. He had been gone more than 11 years.

"I had been long waiting for an opportunity to return home, though my fortune had not been made; when the sloop Hero, of Stonington: capt, Bathan Fellows, arrived. In her I took my passage, much pleased with the captain's behaviour towards me. We had a very pleasant time, until we made Montock — the eastend of my native island; which I had not seen in so many years before. This was the most agreeable sight my eyes ever beheld, and in a paroxism of joy I wept; but my eyes dwelt upon the green hill, crowned now by its lofty elegant light-house. Language is inadequate to the expression of my feelings, and would be lost on the cold heart that has worn out its action in one monotonous course at home.

"We closed the voyage at Stonington in 21 days from St. Domingo. Here I waited two days for a conveyance to Long-Island — procured a passage in a lighter, captain Clark of Rocky point. It was Sunday morning in June 1805. A violent thunder storm drove us on shore at Oyster Pond Point, where the lighter, by a surge was suddenly thrown on me, and fastened me to the stones and sand. I cried murder, and captain Clark extricated me; but finding me much hurt, carried me on his back half a mile to a house, and then took me in a carriage to his own dwelling. My knee was fractured and much swelled, but captain Clark and his wife did every thing in their power for my relief, during my stay; and their kindness shall never be forgotten while I exist. How happy would be the condition of mortal man, if all were like captain Clark and his charitable companion.

16. Joshua Penny Afterward

A carriage was dispatched to my father's house, only eight miles from me. I learned that my father yet lived; and I told the messenger to inform him that his lost son was living and that was all he could boast of— that if any of my young friends were living, also, they must come and see me. My youngest sister, whom I had left a child, came into the room where I was lying and walked the room without my knowing her. Mrs. Clark asked me if I knew that woman? I told her that I was too much distressed with pain to notice her; particularly as she was a woman. However the discovery was made, and my sister returned home with me.

"I found my parents rejoiced to see me, as may be well imagined, when it is known that *I had been absent eleven years and six months.*

"I had written to them from the Cape of Good Hope, from St. Helena and elsewhere, but they had received no letters from me in nine years, except one dated at Cape Francois, which they received shortly previous to my arrival. This letter they conjectured was a forgery, because it was not in my junior hand writing. In short, they had long since buried me. Two of my sisters and one brother had died in my absence.

"Here I hobbled on crutches until my recovery, and spent the residue of the summer in visiting my friends. In December I was married. My employments were from this period, either coasting or going to the West Indies.

"I was in my own coasting vessel at New-York, when war was declared against Great Britain. I immediately sold my vessel, and resolved to put myself in an attitude to annoy the enemy of my country, and the scourge of the terrestrial globe. I returned to my home at Three-Mile-Harbour, in the township of East Hampton, determined to avail myself of the first opportunity of doing mischief to those who had so long tortured me.

"The British landed frequently on Gardiner's Island, in sight of my house, on the opposite side of Gardiner's Bay. Commodore Decatur being blockaded in New London. I crossed the Sound in my boat, and informed him there was an opportunity to apprehend some of those men. He ordered four boats to proceed under my direction as pilot, and crossed the Sound in the night of the 26th of July 1813; It being very dark, we missed one boat on our arrival at three Mile Harbour. The militia of East Hampton were alarmed at our approach and repaired to attack their invaders; but on finding we were not British, they let us sleep that day: and when the night was nearly spent we crossed to Gardiner's Island, where we landed

PART II : AFTERWARD

at daylight and concealed ourselves on shore. The Ramilies 74, sir Thomas Hardy, and the Orpheus frigate, captain Pigot, were lying in the bay.

"We perceived by our glasses that they were fitting out nine of their boats; viz: two launches, four cutters, two barges, and a gig; which last contained captain Pigot, who commanded the squadron of boats. They had one 18 pounder on the bow of a launch belonging to the Ramilies; and a carriage gun in the frigate's launch. They were manned by 160 marines and sailors, whom we counted as they went down the ship's side. Lieutenant Gallagher, our commander told me that 'if they do not attack us with more than twice our number, I am determined to meet them.' We had calculated to take them by surprise. They rowed to the opposite side of the island where lay our boats. We had every reason now to think they had been informed of our expedition, and instantly went to hurry off our boats from great Pond to the Fire-Place, while the British aimed to cut us off. They fired on us for about half an hour and threw shot in all directions about us, while we were rowing in our whaleboats. Their last 18 pound shot struck about six feet from the boat's stern and threw water all over us, when the lieutenant ordered us to 'avast oars and give the British three cheers for that shot.' It was calm and we could hear captain Pigot give orders to 'elevate that gun — the shot fell short.' The next shot would strike half a mile beyond us. We felt ourselves safe and put into Three Mile Harbour. Our enemy returned to Gardiner's Island, to abuse Mr. Gardiner for suffering us to come there; as if he could help it. Our arrival, and this connonade alarmed the town of East-Hampton once more — but the militia came too late to capture the enemy's boats, which had grounded but got off again.

"Captain Pigot could securely insult Mr. Gardiner for permitting Yankees to come on his island, when every body knows that he could not have been apprised of it in season to prevent them, and wanted the power if he had known it. He is very critically situated — in the power of the British, and consequently censured by both parties.

"We refreshed ourselves and found, the next day, the crew of the missing boat under the command of midshipman Ten Eyck, who joined us and related their proceeding. They found themselves at Gardiner's Island, and left the boat on the beach at sunrise. When they had retired into the woods, they observed a British boat to land — take possession of their boat and take her off; leaving behind them seven men and officers, whom they

16. Joshua Penny Afterward

took prisoners without resistance—One of the enemy attempted to run; when one of the men under Ten Eyck put a ball through his hat and brought him to the ground unhurt. The prisoners were the 1st and 2nd lieutenants, the sailing-master and four men of the Ramilies, who submitted themselves to our midshipman and five or six men.

"The lieutenant, on being told that he had his choice to be paroled or go to the American squadron, at first hesitated; but being obliged to answer immediately, concluded to be paroled. They were paroled, and our men went from Mr. Gardiner's house to his whale boat, which they immediately took into possession, and crossed the bay to the Fire-Place. The next day we started for Sag-Harbour, and thence to New London; after an absence of five days.

"I returned home in my boat alone, as I went. Lieutenant Gallagher recommended me for my conduct in that affair; and besides my compensation for this service, the commodore approved of what I had done.

"A short time after this, a stranger from New-York came to me and said, that he had been advised to make application for my assistance in a *torpedo*, to explode the craft which infested our bays and harbors. I agreed without hesitation to embark on the enterprize, and conducted him to places where we might unobserved watch the motions of the enemy. Unsuitable weather for several days, prevented the execution of our designs. The ships shifted their anchorage every night, so that we found the object impracticable, and abandoned a project which might have succeeded any where but in a *blue-light region*. I again left New London and returned to my house—open to the bay, and in sight of the British ships.

"I expected a commission, and it became necessary for me to go properly recommended to Commodore Decatur for the purpose of getting me into the service. A recommendation of me, as suitable person to command a row-galley, was subscribed by some persons of respectability in East-Hampton, and the officers of the garrison at Sag-Harbour—backed by a certificate of the collector of that port. I left Sag-Harbour with the intention of crossing the Sound from my own house, as soon as I should have an opportunity.

"The next morning, Sunday, August 20, 1813, a boat was discovered taking sounding near my house. I hastened to my nearest neighbour, who lived at some distance, and both of us advanced to attack the boat. We were armed—the boat made off and went along side the Ramilies. I sus-

Part II : Afterward

pected their design, for I saw them viewing with a glass and pointing to my house. In consequence of discovering that boat, I concluded to desist from crossing the Sound until the next day when I could remove my family to a safer place and have a guard here that night. I had made application for a guard and expected it; but thought to take a short nap before it should arrive. I had been sleeping about half an hour, when the house was surrounded by people who had lain in ambush among my corn, growing near it. My wife, three little boys, old Robert Gray, and a female Indian, composed, with myself, the family. The eldest of my children was nine years old; the youngest three, and were all in bed.

"The first salutation was three spiteful raps with the fist, at the door. Being awakened I rose up in bed, and demanded, 'Who's there?' 'Decatur's People' was their answer—'Mr. Penny, we want you to get up immediately.' I was satisfied, however, that they were the Prince Regent's people—sprang out of my bed, and in my shirt ran for my gun. I had to pass through two doors before I reached the kitchen, where my gun was hanging. They heard me, as they afterwards said, both when I went to bed, and when I left it. They saw me through the window as I opened the kitchen door, and I observed the heads were very thick there. My gun lay on hooks, so near the floor overhead, that in my hurry I was baulked in getting it down. When they perceived me aiming for the gun, they burst in the door, and surrounded me. I was seized with one hand on the gun, and expected no quarters. They took me, with my arms extended by two men, who held them, to the door, where stood Lieut. Lawrence, 1st of the Ramilies. He presented a pistol to my nose, and attempted to shoot me. I never saw more fire issue from a lock in my life—it flew into my eyes—it rolled on the floor; but as luck would have it, missed fire!

"I then addressed him, not at that time knowing his name—'officer,' said I 'you are determined, I see to murder me. I hope you will be gentleman enough to take me out of the sight of my wife and children first.' He then, with a tremulous voice, said 'It is presumption in you, Mr. Penny, to make any resistance—I have 500 men around you.' I told him, 'I did not make any resistance—was stark naked, and as many had hold of me as could touch me.' 'It is Sir Thomas Hardy's orders to blow your brains out if you should make the smallest resistance.' My wife followed us to the door and shrieked; upon which a sergeant of marines struck her with the breech of a gun, the point of which he thrust at her left breast,

16. Joshua Penny Afterward

with so much violence, that she is unwell from that cause to the present time.

"They led me about ten rods to their boat — one officer before and another behind me; and two others marched with their naked cutlasses on each of my shoulders. As soon as we had entered into the boat, the lieutenant threw on shore a bag of shavings; and ordered the only man on shore to 'burn that d — d rascal's house.' I spoke to the lieutenant — 'Sir, you are not surely going to burn my wife and children!' The man who received the lieutenant's order, told him the 'match was out; and he could not make fire.' It appeared they had come prepared to burn the house, but were afraid of the militia; and thus hurried off.

"The lieutenant said — 'From the appearance of that woman, she is not in a situation to take off her children to the woods — we'll let it stand. Never mind the house men, let us go and burn his boat.' My boat was about twenty rods from us, at anchor in the creek near a thicket; we proceeded about half way to it when I laid down in the bottom of the boat. The lieutenant asked why I did so? I answered that since his pistol had not killed me, I did not wish to be killed by the militia of my own country, who might throw a shower of balls from the bushes. 'Aye,' said he, 'is that the case?' then stamping with his foot on the bottom of the boat, he cried 'about with the boat! Pull around men: pull round men!' He was much agitated and left my boat uninjured. They hurried the boat out of the creek, nearly half a mile, as fast as possible; and getting fairly out he ordered the men to lay on their oars: 'Hurra!' said he 'we've got *Tom Pedro* safe enough now — let's drink some gin': The lieutenant handed some to me first, but I told him that 'after him was manners.' All drank and a dialogue commenced which lasted 'till we reached the ship. He began — "'Where are your documents which you obtained yesterday at Sag-Harbour, to carry to Decatur?' 'They are in my pocket; and if you had been gentleman enough to have let me got my clothes, you could have had my papers.' I knew he dared not go back; besides I could not avoid this language after the usage I had received. The servant girl had gone of the house with my coat, in a pocket of which these papers were; and on her exclaiming, 'you are not going to take Mr. Penny without his coat or other clothes!' He said 'd — the clothes, we've got him, that's enough.' He continued — 'Well, *your* papers will never do you any good, or any one else. You'll get disappointed in obtaining a commission in a row galley. Your character has been

PART II : AFTERWARD

given me by a fellow in that boat which you saw taking soundings, and a d — d good description of your house he gave us; with woods on one side and a corn-field on another. He told me there was nothing to be seen of your house until you come within three rods of it; and could then see three poplar trees. He perceiving my teeth to chatter with the cold, gave me a boat-cloak to put around me. 'You have some d — d good friends' continued he, 'who live close by you, or you would not have met with this misfortune. I have been informed by one of your countrymen, that you deserted from a British ship of war; and are the most inveterate enemy of the British within five hundred miles of here. You have been assisting in Decatur's expeditions; and also concerned in conducting those d — d torpedoes!' I am a true-born American, sir, said I, that I will not deny. I have never been employed by my government, but am ever ready to engage in her service against her enemies; whenever and wherever called. He told me that I should undoubtedly suffer death; because I had been concerned in torpedoes, which was contrary to the law of nations.

"I then asked him if it was not contrary to the law of nations to blow up a number of their men, in Canada, for the sake of destroying a greater number of our men? 'Yes (he said) and if you Americans could have caught the one who communicated fire to the magazine, they would have hung him, as we shall you.' I told him I was a prisoner, and they dared not hang me on the word of a *traitor*! He inquired if Decatur was concerned in torpedoes? I told him 'such questions were very improper.' Between 11 and 12 o'clock we reached Ramilies, with her boats about her to guard against torpedoes.

"I was conducted up the ship's side as naked as when they put me into the boat; and had to wait on the quarter-deck, until the officer had reported his expedition to Sir Thomas. All the other officers came up to gaze at me, while my shirt in tatters was hanging by the wristbands. They afterwards took me below and put me in irons, to lie without clothes on the bare deck, alongside of old Robert, whom they had also brought with them.

"Early next morning the master of arms brought us a pot of cocoa and some bread, and told us he could get nothing else for us until after 12 o'clock. He then went off, but came running back before our cocoa had cooled so that we could drink a drop of it. He took off the pot, saying it is the order of Sir Thomas that 'you have nothing but bread and water.'

16. Joshua Penny Afterward

And nothing else did I have until we arrived in Halifax eighteen days after they had kidnapped me.

"The second day, they crammed me into a hold which is in the after part of the ship. They let me through a narrow scuttle down to her sternpost, where I remained nine days, and found it difficult to breathe in this dark place. It was so cramped that I could neither lie strait nor stand up (The British refused me a Bible and I, according to my Custom was singing Psalms, when a midshipman overhearing me said 'he is a damn Psalm singing Yankee').

"Leaving me in this dungeon, let us hear what passed on shore relative to my case. I do not know that we can do better here, than to transcribe the following correspondence and introduction to it, from the Columbian, a newspaper printed in New-York.

CASE OF JOSHUA PENNY

The seizure of Mr. Penny (mentioned in our paper of yesterday) having excited Considerable interest in the public mind, we have obtained copies of the correspondence Which took place on the subject, between commodore Hardy and Major Case, commanding officer at Sag Harbor, and present them to our readers. The grounds of the prisoners seizure are made quite plausible by the commodore's statement, though the reason for his detention and refusal of exchange, supposing him to be a legal prisoner of war, is evidently bad; and we should be pleased to hear of two British officers being put in close confinement in retaliation. The commodore appears informed of the most private and confidential transactions in our ports and vessels — what dependance he has a right to place on his informants, and by what means he procures his intelligence, the public will judge.

(COPY)

Sir Thomas Hardy, Commander of H.B.M. squadron off Gardiner's Island

Sir — The inhabitants of the town of East-Hampton have requested of me a flag, which I now authorize, for the purpose of demanding Joshua Penny, a native-born citizen of the township of Southold, on this Island, and a resident of the town of East-Hampton.

He is demanded as a non-combatant, being attached to no vessel as a mariner or corps military whatever, but was taken by force by your men from his own home unarmed.

The bearer of this flag is lieu Hedges, an officer under my command, in government service. You will have the goodness to deliver Mr. Penny to lieut. Hedges, as he cannot be consistently be retained as a prisoner of war

PART II : AFTERWARD

by any article in the cartel agreed on, ratified and confirmed by the agents of each of our governments for the exchange of prisoners.

Given under my hand, at the garrison of Sag-Harbor, this 23rd day of August, 1813.

BENJ. CASE major commanding the
Troops in the U.S. service
at Sag-Harbor.

(COPY)

His Britannic Majesty's ship
Ramilies in Gardiner's Bay
August 23, 1813

Sir, I have the honor to acknowledge the receipt of your letter of this day's date, and as I do not wish to detain lieutenant Hedges, the bearer of your flag, I will do myself the honor of replying to your letter to-morrow by a flag of truce. I have the honor to be sir, your very humble servant.

THOMAS M. HARDY, captain

To major Case, commanding the troops in the
U.S. service at Sag. Harbor

(COPY)

His Britannic Majesty's ship Ramillies
Gardiner's Bay, 24th Aug. 1813

Sir — As it was late yesterday afternoon when I had the honor of receiving your letter of the 23rd instant, requesting the release of Joshua Penny, I did not judge it proper to detain lieut. Hedges for my reply.

I now beg leave to inform you, I had received certain information that this man conducted a detachment of boats sent from the United States squadron under the command of commodore Decatur, now lying in New-London, from that port to Gardiner's Island, on the 26th of July last, for the express purpose of surprising and capturing the captain of his Britannic majesty's frigate Orpheus and myself, and having failed in the undertaking, but making prisoners of some officers and men belonging to the Orpheus, he went with the remaining boats to Three Mile harbor. The next account I had of him was his being employed in a boat contrived for this purpose, under the command of Thomas Welling, prepared with a torpedo to destroy this ship, and that he was in her at Napeug Beach, when this ship and the Orpheus were in Fort Pond Bay, last week. He has also had a certificate given him on the 18th of this month, by some of the respectable inhabitants of Easthampton, recommending him to commodore Decatur, as a fit person to be employed on a particular service by him, and that he

16. Joshua Penny Afterward

has for some time entered on the books of one of the frigates, at forty dollars per month, add to which, this notorious character has been recognized by some of the officers and men of this ship, as having been on board here two or three times, with clams and fruit, of course, as a spy, to collect information of our movements. Having been made so well acquainted with the conduct of this man for the last six weeks, and the purpose for which he has been so actively employed in hostilities against his Britannic Majesty I cannot avoid expressing my surprise that the inhabitants of Easthampton, should have attempted to enforce on you a statement so contrary to fact, I therefore cannot think of permitting such an avowed enemy to be out of my power, when I know so much of him as I do. He will therefore, be detained as a prisoner of war, until the pleasure of the commander in chief is known. Robert Gray, an inoffensive old man who was taken with Penny, I have landed; as it does not appear that he is one of his accomplices in the transactions I have alluded to. I think proper to enclose a copy of my letter to justice Terry, to warn the inhabitants of the coast against permitting the torpedoes to remain any where near them.

I have the honor to be, sir, your most obedient humble servant.

THOMAS M. HARDY, captain
H.B.M. ship Ramilies

Major Benj. Case, commanding the troops in the
U.S. service at Sag-Harbor

(COPY)

His majesty's ship Ramilies, off New London
Aug. 23 1813

Sir — Having received positive information that a whale boat, the property of Thomas Welling and others, prepared with a torpedo, for the avowed purpose of destroying this ship, a mode of warfare practiced by individuals from mercenary motives, and more novel than honorable, is kept in your neighborhood; and as from the very good information I obtain from various sources there is no doubt these persons will soon be in my power, I beg you to warn the inhabitants of the towns along the coast of Long-Island, that wherever I hear the boat or any other of her description, has been allowed to remain after this date, I will order every house near the shore to be destroyed.

I have the honor to be, sir, your obedient servant.

THOMAS M.HARDY, capt.

Terry, esq. justice of the peace
Southold, Long Island.

Part II : Afterward

"This letter to esquire Terry is a proof that the writer was a bitter enemy to the torpedo; but a paragraph in the editorial department of the *Long-Island Star* will further illustrate this topic:

Wednesday, Sept. 8, 1813

By our attentive correspondent at Sag-Harbor, it appears that com. Hardy's persecution of Joshua Penny is principally on account of his having piloted a torpedo boat, commanded by Thomas Welden, which boat was discovered by the guard boats, and made its escape only by frequent diving. The commodore threatens to lay waste the towns and show no mercy to the inhabitants that harbor torpedoes, which as he informed lieutenant Hedges, has given him so much inquietude that it had taken almost all the hair from his head!

Penny comments and completes his account: "Why there should be a complaint against this species of warfare as being dishonorable, I cannot understand, unless it proceeds from a man subject to the horrors. It is our enemy's power to avoid American torpedoes, by keeping out of our harbors, and I cannot for my life, see any difference between killing your enemy with balls, bombshells, rockets, &c. and blowing them up by torpedoes. In both ways ships may sink, or some body get hurt; and it is no objection that it is a 'novel' mode of warfare.

"The objection never ought to come from those, who hire savages to destroy indiscriminately, the man in arms and the helpless innocent female with her infant in the cradle — or, what is too horrid to name — can tamely listen to such an enemy or to its partisans in this country, when he had heard of their Vandalism at Washington and of the violation of female chastity on our coast! An American who would hesitate to blow up such infernal monsters as Cockburn and his myrmidons, deserves no country to own him; he is worse than savage, who deals out this hypocritical whining at the novel mode of using torpedoes, to drive the invading Goths and Vandals from our sacred soil. I know I displeased Sir Thomas Hardy, by aiding in the attempt to blow him to the moon; but I am also out of humour, that I was prevented from teaching a useful lesson to the invaders. Had there been no treachery in my country, we should have succeeded; as it is we have caused them uneasiness; and perhaps have kept them more from our harbors than otherwise could have happened.

"I am now returned to my dungeon! We were on our passage and shipped a sea which poured through the stern-port and filled my prison nearly full. The sentinel who stood over me sung out, 'Tom Pedro is drowned! Tom Pedro is drowned!' then I was taken out almost dead — put in irons and confined between two guns on the hard deck, during the voyage. On our arrival I was sent to Melville prison, under an escort of one serjeant, one corporal and nine men, to conduct me only. There were about thirty other prisoners in the Ramilies, taken out of coasters, &c. whom commodore Hardy detained until he sailed, as hostages to protect him against torpedoes, with which he was haunted on the station of New-London.

"A few days after my imprisonment in the hole, lieut. Lawrence came to ask me questions which I did not think proper to answer. He said, 'it was by order of Sir Thomas,' I told him that 'if Sir Thomas wished to know, he might send for me, and ask his questions himself.' He said, 'Your character is so heinous to him that he cannot endure you in his presence.' I told him 'it was not in character for a friend to his country to answer his interrorogatories: I should not.'

"Another time, the master-at-arms told me 'it is Sir Thomas Hardy's opinion that you will be hung; but if not, you will be taken to England and detained until the close of the war, and be at last tried as the laws of nations direct. Should I have to hang you, I should be sorry to have you suspect an innocent person of having betrayed you. Whom do you suspect to be your betrayer?' I told him I did not know. I had observed a number of boats were often trading the ships in the day time and it might be a trader. I thought it would come to light sooner or later.* (*I think now, I know the man, but his name shall not disgrace this publication. Besides, I am too poor to litigate.) He told me who had sold me; and added, 'but no one in the ship except Sir Thomas Hardy knows how much he got, but I suppose he got a large sum. If you wish to be liberated, you can. Sir Thomas has ordered me to ask you if you will discover to him that torpedo? If you will, he says you shall be liberated and have 3000 dollars.' I felt too much insulted to answer him.

"While I lay in Melville prison, 400 prisoners arrived from Bermuda; some of whom had been masters of vessels, mates, or supercargoes. They told me that on their passage they heard Sir Thomas talk of me and my betrayer. He said, 'he had seen in a yankee newspaper an account of his having given the man 1000 dollars for his services in apprehending me;

Part II : Afterward

but it was not so — he had only given him 200 dollars.' Afterwards he said, 'I gave him up his vessel, which, perhaps *might make 1000 dollars.*'

"While I remained here, a stranger in the habit of a citizen came to inspect my legs for scars, and examine me for the purpose of identifying me as the husband of a woman in town, who said she had lost a husband, and from the description given her, I must be the missing husband. I told this man that my wife was on Long-Island. Not long after, I was summoned to a house where this woman and my former examiner were sitting, with a table covered with decanters and glasses. This man, after having led me into the room, asked the woman if she could swear that I was her husband. She answered that 'she could not but that I looked much like him,' then turning to me, asked, 'if that was my wife?' No, I answered, I would not give my wife for ten thousand of her. This created a laugh and ended in drinking.

"I satisfied myself that this woman was a common prostitute, and my examiner a justice of the peace. But they were unable to make a British subject of me by this or any other stratagem. She requested the company to leave the room to herself and me; but I refused and retired with the others — one of whom laughing said, 'I believe you don't like our English women very well.'

"While I was in prison I was visited by many people and teazed with many questions relative to torpedoes which I generally found means to avoid. An officer of an Irish regiment called one day and wished to speak to me, and asked me within hearing of a number of the prisoners, if I was the inventor of torpedoes? I was tired of being quizzed on this subject, and therefore told him I knew as little of torpedoes as one of his countrymen, who having put up at a tavern in America, was asked by the landlord, if he would have a warming pan to take up to his bed. '*Yes, by J—s*' says he, *and 'I'll eat a bit of it at any rate.*' The Hibernian swelled, and retired amid the shouts of the prisoners.

"I was taken sick of a fever and accounted dangerous. The attending physician said 'there were more inquiries after my health than there was about any other man's in prison; and when he told them I should not live till 10 o'clock that night there was more lamentation than he had ever known in a prison,' this was told me when I was recovered from danger — I found the principal cause of this unusual interest they had taken, was that I had been barbarously kidnapped. I was released in consequence of

16. Joshua Penny Afterward

my having been taken contrary to the stipulations referred to in major Case's letter to the commodore dated the 23rd August 1813.

"I was landed at Salem from the cartel. The marshal of that place told me, that I should be provided with everything necessary to make me comfortable. I was bare-foot and bare headed; but the inhabitants of that town supplied me with what I needed, and treated me with great kindness. I was enabled to go on in the stage to New-London. At Providence, a printer was kind enough to take his hat about the streets; and procured a handsome collection of money from the inhabitants, to defray my expenses on the way. In short, I was very kindly treated by my generous countrymen, and offer them my tribute of acknowledgement.

"From New-London I crossed the Sound to my own house, where I had the satisfaction of finding my family in good health, after my absence of nine months and nine days. I had not been long at home before I was invited to engage in another torpedo enterprize, but this failed in consequence of bad weather — and I removed my family — as advised to Sag-Harbour.

"It was never my good fortune to command a torpedo; and perhaps I might then have been unsuccessful; but I should be pleased to have the privilege of terrifying John Bull and avenging myself while I was engaged in the service of my beloved country. Like poor Hall, '*I shall not give this business up for one bad job.*'

"JOSHUA PENNY
"Sag-Harbor, Jan. 1815."

Conclusion

In looking over these accounts of impressments, I have noticed a few similarities and differences. These impressed men came from a variety of places, but many were impressed during a relatively narrow period of time. Joshua Davis came from Boston. He was born in 1760 and impressed in 1779. Joshua Penny was born in 1773 on Long Island and impressed around 1790. William Molyneux was born in England and impressed sometime around 1792. The various pirate ships recruited and impressed men in Newfoundland, along the Atlantic coast and also in the Caribbean. The time period when the pirates were most active in impressing seems to have been between 1750 and 1825. John Stradley was born in London in 1757 and impressed in 1781. Joseph Bates was a native of Boston and impressed around 1770. Jacob Nagle was born in Pennsylvania and impressed in 1810. Pierce came from Newberry Port, Massachusetts, and was impressed in 1814. Stephen Cabot from Boston was impressed by the French in 1814; James Durand of Connecticut was impressed in 1807; and Thomas Urquhart of London was almost impressed in 1808.

It is noteworthy that most of the accounts of impressed men seem to have been written by Americans, although surely the number of men impressed into the British navy (the main impressor) tended much more proportionately toward British citizens. Perhaps the fact that there was a greater number of American accounts was the result of a variety of factors. One of these factors might have been the higher proportion of American men who had learned to read and write. New England communities were required to provide some sort of elementary schooling for their children even in colonial times.

Another factor could be the greater resentment felt by Americans at

Conclusion

being forced by a country not their own to serve aboard foreign ships of war. After all, impressment was in essence a crude form of the draft, which many nations have used, especially in time of war. And a nation's right to impress or draft its own was generally not opposed. But this was different. Americans, not only the impressed but also their fellow citizens, were concerned about the practice of forcing Americans to serve on British ships. Thus the American accounts of impressments probably found a sympathetic audience.

The time of impressments listed in the accounts is also significant. Most of these men were impressed at a time when the British were fighting the French. Desperate measures may seem more justified when the nation is threatened, and the British navy was the main defense against invasion of the British homeland. The writing of the accounts mostly came soon after the War of 1812, in which British impressments of Americans was often given as one of the causes of our engagement in the war.

The impressed were of varying ages: Joshua Davis was 19, and William Molyneux's age was not recorded (but since he was married and the father of four children, one would suspect he might have been in his late twenties or even thirty). Joshua Penny was 17 when he was impressed. John Stradley was 33. James Durand was 24. Thomas Urquhart may have been middle-aged. He writes as though he was an experienced merchant seaman, perhaps a captain, when the press gang attempted to carry him off. Those impressed were mostly sailors, but some were landsmen. William Molyneux was a weaver; John Stradley was a blacksmith. Pirates tended to impress men who had particular skills, such as carpenters, doctors, pilots and the like; but, according to the advertisements, many sailors were also impressed.

The reactions to the impressment experience varied. Joshua Davis tells of getting away from the British ship and finding an American ship bound for Boston. He is able to help recruit a crew of men who had been "hiding themselves from the press-gang." Joshua Penny escapes from his impressments by leaving his ship and going into the interior and staying there for a year. On a later tour he climbs Table Mountain near Cape Town and survives alone on wild game and honey for a year before returning to Cape Town after he believes the British fleet had left. John Newton attempts to get away, but is caught and punished. He then is very angry and takes the next available means to leave the ship, binding himself to work in Africa, with disastrous consequences. John Stradley is released from his ship and then becomes ill and experiences a religious conversion.

Joseph Bates serves aboard several British war ships, then is imprisoned in Dartmoor Prison, and after the war participates in a rebellion aboard a ship sailing for Virginia rather than the New York/New England area the returning ex-prisoners prefer. But then he goes back to the sea as a merchant seaman and eventually becomes a captain. He also becomes very religious and participates in the formation of the 7th Day Adventist Church.

Jacob Nagle serves aboard British and American ships the rest of his life as an ordinary sailor and never seems to have acquired any roots. He finally returns to the U.S. in his old age and lives with various friends and relatives until his death. William Molyneux builds himself a home in the Pennsylvania wilderness, returns to England for his family and brings the remnants to his cabin in the mountains and lives out his life there.

John Newton returns home after a number of adventures, including a violent storm which nearly destroys the ship he is sailing back on. He also experiences a religious conversion on the voyage. Hoping to see his father, he barely misses him as his father leaves for a post with Hudson Bay in Canada. He does contact the woman of his dreams and some sort of understanding seems to have existed from then on. He makes a number of further voyages, some as mate and later as captain of a ship bringing Africans to slavery in the Caribbean. He then takes a position as a tide inspector at the docks at Newcastle. In his spare time he studies Hebrew and Greek and applies for a position as a minister in the Church of England. Thus, several of the impressed men (Stradley, Bates, and Newton) seem to have turned to religion.

Those who wrote accounts seem to have fiercely resented the impressment experience. They write of themselves and others trying a variety of methods to avoid impressments. And when opportunity offered, they often tried to escape. It may be that their impressment experience led them to work for freeing others. Urquhart certainly campaigned against impressments. And Newton, even though he served for a time as a captain of a slave ship, eventually became a leading advocate of the abolition of the British slave trade. After the defeat of Napoleon, British impressments decreased. The British no longer needed a large navy to protect the homeland. But another form of involuntary naval servitude sprang up on the

Conclusion

West Coast of the United States. This time it was not a function of government; instead it was very much private enterprise. This new type of enforced labor aboard ships was called shanghaiing, after the Chinese port to which many of these ships were bound.

The ships built in these years were beautiful clippers with larger hulls and high sails. But the ships did not provide more comfortable spaces for the crew. Instead, the sleeping quarters were crowded and the men were underfed and overworked in an effort to achieve speedier voyages and more profits for the captains who brought their vessels in to port in ever shorter times.[1] Because many sailors were not interested in working on these ships, a variety of tricks were played to catch men. Some of these tricks were similar to those used in the older impressment days, such as getting a man drunk or drugged and then hauling him on board; using the wiles of prostitutes; enticing a man to run up huge bills at taverns and then demanding payment or jail or shipping aboard a clipper ship. These practices continued, especially in the West Coast ports, until the late 1890s and sometimes even into 1900.

Sadly, impressment in a variety of forms still exists today. Children and young men and women are forced into bondage. And perhaps someday we may read other accounts — of the survivors of modern impressments.

Chapter Notes

Introduction

1. J.R. Hutchinson, *The Press-Gang Afloat and Ashore* (London: Eveleigh Nash, 1913), 54.
2. John Lehman, *On Seas of Glory, Heroic Men, Great Ships and the Battles of the American Navy* (New York: Simon and Schuster, 1995), 105. Lehman writes of a 1000-man crew, but other authorities suggest that the *Victory* had 820 men, approximately 100 officers, and a detachment of 146 Marines.
3. N.A.M Roger, *The Wooden World: An Anatomy of the British Navy* (New York: W.W. Norton, 1986), 153–154.
4. David McCullough, *John Adams* (New York: Simon & Schuster, 2001), 66.
5. Ray Raphael, *A People's History of the American Revolution: How Common People Shaped the Fight for Independence* (New York, New Press, 2001), 11.
6. John J. Campbell, "The Havana Incident," *American Neptune* (October 22, 1962): 264.
7. *Ibid.*, 273.
8. *Ibid.*, 275.
9. Anthony Steel, "Impressment in the Monroe-Pinkney Negotiations," *The American Historical Review* 57, no. 2 (January 1952): 355.
10. *Ibid.*, 356.
11. *Ibid.*, 361.
12. Thomas Barclay (Private) to Sir Robert Barclay March 10, 1807, quoted in Steel, "Impressment in the Monroe-Pinkney Negotiations," 363.
13. Samuel Eliot Morison, *The Growth of the American Republic* (New York: Oxford University Press, 1953), 403.
14. Robert Cray, "Remembering the USS *Chesapeake:* The Politics of Maritime Death and Impressment," *Journal of the Early Republic* 25 (Fall 2005): 455.
15. Thomas Jefferson, quoted in Nathan Miller, *Broadsides: The Age of Fighting Sail, 1775–1815* (New York: Wiley, 2000), 303.
16. Cray, "Remembering," 466.
17. *Ibid.*
18. McCullough, *Adams*, 598.
19. *Eastern Argus*, May 16, 1811.
20. *New York Evening Post*, May 4, 1811, quoted in Cray, "Remembering," 470.

21. *Boston Patriot*, May 18, 1811, quoted in Cray.
22. *Essex Register* (MA), 1811, quoted in Cray, "Remembering."
23. Quoted in Cray, "Remembering," 471.
24. *Ibid.*
25. James R. Durand, *The Life and Adventures of James R. Durand, During a Period of Fifteen Years from 1801 to 1816, in Which He Was Impressed on Board the British Fleet and Held in Detestable Bondage for More Than Seven Years* (Rochester, NY: Massachusetts Historical Society Archives, 1820), 64.
26. *Ibid.*, 67.
27. Louis P. Jervey, "Thomas Hall Jervey, Man of God and the Sea," *South Carolina Historical Magazine* (April 1995): 147–148.

Chapter 1. John Newton

1. John Newton, *An Authentic Narrative of Some Remarkable and Interesting Particulars in the Life of W.J. Newton Communicated in a Series of Letters to the Reverend Mr. Hawlis*. 3rd edition (London: S. Drapier, T. Hilsh and P. Hett, 1765), letter 3, pp. 42–48.
2. *Ibid.*, letter 4, pp. 52–59.
3. *Ibid.*, letter 5, pp. 60–70.
4. *Ibid.*, letter 6, pp. 71–81.
5. *Ibid.*, letter 7, pp. 82–93.
6. *Ibid.*, letter 8, pp. 94–104.
7. *Ibid.*, letter 9, pp. 105–116.

Chapter 2. Joshua Davis

1. See N.A.M. Rodger, *The Wooden World: An Anatomy of the Georgian Navy* (New York: W.W. Norton, 1986), 103,105, for a discussion of sickness in the navy.
2. Joshua Davis, *A Narrative of Joshua Davis, an Impressed American Citizen Who Was Pressed and Served on Board Six Ships of the British Navy* (Boston: B. Trudo, 1811), 19–20.
3. *Ibid.*, 51–52.
4. *Ibid.*, 54–55.
5. *Ibid.*, 56–58.

Chapter 3. Joshua Penny

1. For a discussion of children at sea, see N.A.M. Roger, *The Wooden World* (New York: W.W. Norton, 1996), 27–28, 68–69.
2. For an older book which gives a fascinating picture of the press gang, see J.R. Hutchinson, *The Press-Gang Afloat and Ashore* (London: Eveleigh Nash, 1913).
3. Joshua Penny, *Adventures of Joshua Penny* (Brooklyn, NY: Spooner, 1815), 1–39.

Chapter 4. Pirates!

1. *Boston Newsletter,* Oct. 17, 1720.
2. *Boston Newsletter,* June 8, 1721.
3. *Boston Newsletter,* August 14, 1721.
4. *Boston Newsletter,* October 10, 1723.
5. *Ibid.*
6. John Richard Stephens, ed., *Captured by Pirates: 22 Firsthand Accounts of Murder and Mayhem on the High Seas* (Cambria Pines by the Sea, CA: Fern Canyon, 1966), 171–172.
7. *Ibid.,* 26–27.
8. *Ibid.,* 48.
9. *Ibid.,* 49.
10. *Ibid.,* 185–243.
11. Marcus Rediker, *Between the Devil and the Deep Blue Sea: Merchant Seamen, Pirates, and the Anglo-American Maritime World,* paperback ed. (Cambridge and New York: Cambridge University Press, 1987), 261, note 16.
12. David Cordingly, *Under the Black Flag: The Romance and Reality of Life Among the Pirates* (San Diego: Harcourt Brace, 1995), 70.
13. *Ibid.*
14. George Francis Dow and John Henry Edmonds, *The Pirates of the New England Coast 1630–1730* (Salem, MA: Marine Research Society, 1923), 227.
15. Edward Lucie-Smith, *Outcasts of the Sea, Pirates and Piracy* (New York: Paddington, 1978), 200.
16. *Ibid.,* 203–205.
17. Dow and Edmonds, *The Pirates,* 300.
18. *Ibid.*
19. *Ibid.,* 302–305.
20. Ibid, 305–307.
21. Walter J. Fraser, *Charleston! Charleston!: The History of a Southern City* (Columbia: University of South Carolina Press, 1989), 33.
22. *Ibid.,* 33.
23. *The Trials of Major Steve Bonnet and Others for Piracy,* South Carolina Historical Society Archives, 167.
24. *Ibid.,* 169.
25. *Ibid.*
26. *Ibid.*
27. *Ibid.*
28. *Ibid.,* 180.
29. Fraser, *Charleston!,* 36.
30. Hugh R. Rankin, *The Golden Age of Piracy* (New York: Holt, Rinehart and Winston, 1969), 91–101.
31. *Ibid.,* 102–103.
32. Dow and Edmonds, *The Pirates,* 310.
33. Stephens, *Captured by Pirates,* 51–57.
34. Rankin, *The Golden Age of Piracy,* 151–158.
35. *Ibid.,* 157–158.

CHAPTER NOTES

Chapter 5. John Stradley

1. For a thorough description of naval clothing see N.A.M. Roger, *The Wooden World* (New York: W.W. Norton, 1986), 64–65.
2. Memoirs of John Stradley, 1757–1825, National Maritime Museum Archives, 1–30.

Chapter 6. Jacob Nagle

1. Jacob Nagle, *Voyages of Jacob Nagle*, ed. John C. Dann (New York: Widened & Nicholson, 1988), 48–50.
2. *Ibid.*, 55–61.

Chapter 7. Joseph Bates

1. Joseph Bates, *The Early Life and Later Experiences and Labors of Elder Joseph Bates*, ed. Elder James White (Battle Creek, MI: Steam Press, 1878), 36–45.
2. *Ibid.*, 46–73.

Chapter 8. Dartmoor Prison

1. James R. Durand, *The Life and Adventures of James R. Durand, During a Period of Fifteen Years from 1801 to 1816, in Which He Was Impressed on Board the British Fleet, and Held in Detestable Bondage for More Than Seven Years* (Rochester, NY: Massachusetts Historical Society Archives, 1820), 67.
2. John Melish, *A Description of Dartmoor Prison, with an Account of the Massacre of the Prisoners* (Philadelphia: Massachusetts Historical Society Archives, 1815), 1.
3. Joseph Bates, *Life of Bates*, 74, 75.
4. Nathaniel Pierce, *Journal of Nathaniel Pierce of Newburyport, Kept at Dartmoor Prison, 1814–1815*, vol. 73 (Essex Institute Historical Collections, Massachusetts Historical Society Archives), 25.
5. Bates, *Life of Bates*, 75.
6. *Ibid.*
7. *Ibid.*
8. *Ibid.*, 77–78.
9. *Ibid.*, 78–79.
10. Pierce, *Journal of Nathaniel Pierce*, 30–31.
11. *Ibid.*, 37.
12. Bates, *Life of Bates*, 80–81.
13. Pierce, *Journal of Nathaniel Pierce*, 39, 82.
14. Bates, *Life of Bates*, 81.
15. *Ibid.*
16. Melish, *Dartmoor Prison*, 6.
17. Bates, *Life of Bates*, 82.
18. *Ibid.*, 82–83.

19. Pierce *Journal of Nathaniel Pierce,* 41.
20. Melish, *Dartmoor Prison,* 6.
21. *Ibid.,* 12.
22. Bates, *Life of Bates,* 83–84.
23. *Ibid.,* 84.
24. Pierce, *Journal of Nathaniel Pierce,* 41.
25. Bates, *Life of Bates,* 85–86.
26. Pierce, *Journal of Nathaniel Pierce,* 43.
27. Bates, *Life of Bates,* 86.
28. There are also various reports concerning the massacre. Pierce says 50 were killed or wounded in the yard and then mentions others killed or wounded in the prisons. The Dartmoor Prison account states that 7 were killed and 31 wounded and the officer in charge ordered the troops to fire because he thought the prisoners were attempting to escape.
29. Pierce, *Journal of Nathaniel Pierce,* 59.

Chapter 9. Stephen Cabot

1. Stephen Cabot, *Diary of Stephen Cabot, 1814–1815,* Massachusetts Historical Society Archives.

Chapter 10. James R. Durand

1. See N.A.M. Roger, *The Wooden World* (New York: W.W. Norton, 1986), 82–87, for a discussion of food on a British naval ship.
2. James Durand, *James Durand an Able Seaman of 1812,* ed. George S. Brooks (New Haven, CT: Yale University Press, 1926), 1–52.
3. *Ibid.,* 51–85.
4. *Ibid.,* 86.

Chapter 11. Thomas Urquhart

1. Thomas Urquhart, *Letters on the Evils of Impressment, with the Outline of a Plan for Doing Them Away, on Which Depend the Wealth, Prosperity, and Consequences of Great Britain,* 2nd edition (London: W. Phillips, 1816), 49–53.
2. *Ibid.,* 56, 57.
3. *Ibid.,* 75–78.
4. *Ibid.,* 94–96.

Chapter 12. William Molyneux Afterward

1. Kermit Molyneux Bird, ed., *Quill of the Wild Goose: Civil War Letters and Diaries of Joel Molyneux* (Celecom, 1994), 9.

CHAPTER NOTES

Chapter 13. John Newton Afterward

1. John Newton, "Introductory Observations," 16.
2. John Newton, *Amazing Grace: The Worship Book, Services and Hymns* (Philadelphia: Westminster, 1972), 296.
3. Letter from John Newton to Wm. Wilberforce, London, Sept. 12, 1788.
4. *Ibid.*

Chapter 14. Joseph Bates Afterward

1. Bates, *The Early Life,* 87–98.

Chapter 15. Jacob Nagle Afterward

1. Jacob Nagle, *The Nagle Journal: A Diary of the Life of Jacob Nagle, Sailor, from the Year 1775 to 1841,* ed. John C. Dann (New York: Widened & Nicolson, 1988), 332–333.

Conclusion

1. Richard Dillon, *Shanghiing Days* (New York: Coward-McCann, 1961), 11.

Bibliography

Bates, Joseph. *The Early Life and Later Experiences and Labors of Elder Joseph Bates.* Edited by Elder James White. Battle Creek, MI: Steam Press, 1878.
Bird, Kermit Molyneux, ed. *Quill of the Wild Goose: Civil War Letters and Diaries of Joel Molyneux.* Celecom, 1994.
Boston Newsletter, Oct. 17, 1720. Massachusetts Historical Society Archives.
Boston Newsletter, June 8, 1721. Massachusetts Historical Archives.
Boston Newsletter, August 14, 1721. Massachusetts Historical Archives.
Boston Newsletter, October 10, 1723. Massachusetts Historical Archives.
Brooks, George S., ed. *Durand, an Able Seaman of 1812.* New Haven, CT: Yale University Press, 1926.
Cabot, Stephen. *Diary of Stephen Cabot, 1814–1815.* Massachusetts Historical Society Archives.
Campbell, John J. "The Havana Incident." *American Neptune* (October 22, 1962).
Cordingly, David. *Under the Black Flag: The Romance and Reality of Life Among the Pirates.* San Diego: Harcourt Brace, 1995.
Cray, Robert E. "Remembering the Chesapeake, the Politics of Maritime Death and Impressment." *Journal of the Early Republic* (Fall 2005).
Davis, Joshua. *A Narrative of Joshua Davis, an Impressed American Citizen Who Was Pressed and Served on Board Six Ships of the British Navy.* Boston: B. Trudo, 1811.
Dillon, Richard. *Shanghaiing Days.* New York: Coward-McCann, 1961.
Dow, George Francis, and John Henry Edmonds. *The Pirates of the New England Coast, 1630–1730.* Salem, MA: Marine Research Society, 1923.
Durand, James R. *The Life and Adventures of James R. Durand, During a Period of Fifteen Years from 1801 to 1816: In Which He Was Impressed on Board the British Fleet and Held in Detestable Bondage for More Than Seven Years.* Rochester, NY: Massachusetts Historical Society Archives, 1820.
Fraser, Walter J. *Charleston! Charleston!: The History of a Southern City.* Columbia: University of South Carolina Press, 1989.
Hutchinson, J.R. *The Press-Gang Afloat and Ashore.* New York: E.P. Dutton, 1914.
Jervey, Louis P. "Thomas Hall Jervey, Man of God and the Sea." *South Carolina Historical Magazine* (April 1995).
Kemp, P.K. *History of the Royal Navy.* New York: Putnam, 1969.
Lehman, John. *On Seas of Glory, Heroic Men, Great Ships and the Battles of the American Navy.* New York: Simon & Schuster, 1995.

Bibliography

Lloyd, Christopher. *The British Seaman, 1200–1860: A Social Survey.* London: Collins, 1968.

Lucie-Smith, Edward. *Outcasts of the Sea, Pirates and Piracy.* New York: Paddington, 1978.

McCullough, David. *John Adams.* New York: Simon & Schuster, 2001.

Melish, John. *A Description of Dartmoor Prison, with an Account of the Massacre of the Prisoners.* Philadelphia: The author, 1815.

Miller, Nathan. *Broadsides: The Age of Fighting Sail, 1775–1815.* New York: Wiley, 2000.

Morison, Samuel Eliot. *The Growth of the American Republic.* New York: Oxford University Press, 1953.

Nagle, Jacob. *Voyages of Jacob Nagle.* Edited by John C. Dann. New York: Weidenfeld & Nicholson, 1988.

Newton, John. *Amazing Grace: The Worship Book, Services and Hymns.* Philadelphia: Westminster, 1972.

———. *An Authentic Narrative of Some Remarkable and Interesting Particulars in the Life of W.J. Newton, Communicated in a Series of Letters to the Reverend Mr. Hawlis.* 3rd ed. London: S. Drapier, T. Hilsh and P. Hett, 1765.

Penny, Joshua. *Adventures of Joshua Penny, a Native of Southold, Long Island, Suffolk County, New York, Who Was Impressed into British Services.* Brooklyn, NY: Spooner, 1815.

Pierce, Nathaniel. *Journal of Nathaniel Pierce of Newburyport, Kept at Dartmoor Prison, 1814–1815.* Volume 73. Essex Institute Historical Collections, Massachusetts Historical Society Archives.

Rankin, Hugh R. *The Golden Age of Piracy.* New York: Holt, Rinehart and Winston, 1969.

Raphael, Ray. *A People's History of the American Revolution: How Common People Shaped the Fight for Independence.* New York: New Press, 2001.

Rediker, Marcus. *Between the Devil and the Deep Blue Sea: Merchant Seamen, Pirates, and the Anglo-American Maritime World.* Cambridge and New York: Cambridge University Press, 1987.

Roger, N.A.M. *The Wooden World: An Anatomy of the Georgian Navy.* London: W.W. Norton, 1986.

Steel, Anthony. "Impressment in the Monroe-Pinkney Negotiations." *The American Historical Review* 57, no. 2 (January 1952).

Stephens, John Richard, ed. *Captured by Pirates: 22 Firsthand Accounts of Murder and Mayhem on the High Seas.* Cambria Pines by the Sea, CA: Fern Canyon, 1966.

Stradley, John. *Memoirs of John Stradley, 1757–1825.* Greenwich and London: National Maritime Museum Archives.

The Trials of Major Steve Bonnet and Others for Piracy. South Carolina Historical Society Archives.

Urquhart, Thomas. *Letters on the Evils of Impressment, with the Outline of a Plan for Doing Them Away, on Which Depend the Wealth, Prosperity and Consequences of Great Britain.* 2nd edition. London: W. Phillips, 1816.

Woodhead, Louise E. *Molyneux and George Molyneux Pardoe: Genealogy of William Molyneux and His Descendants.* 1976.

Zimmerman, James F. *Impressment of American Seamen.* New York: Columbia University Press, 1925.

Index

Adams, John 4, 8
Adams, John Quincy 8, 136
Advertisements 80–82
"Amazing Grace" 171–172
American Revolution 4, 183
Annabone 35
Auckland 4

Baltimore, USS 4
Bate, Joseph 174–180
Beasley 128–132
Benanoes 23
Blackbeard 87–88
Bonaparte, Napoleon 3, 13, 18, 154, 158–160, 200
Bonnet, Steve 88
Boschmen 63
Boston 4
Bread Revolt 116–118, 131–132
British Lords of Admiralty 4
British Navy 3

Cabot, Stephen 139–147, 198
Caffree 64
Canning, Lord 8
Cape Lopez 34
Cape Town 58–60
Carr, Capt. 177–180
Chesapeake, USS 7
Church service 108–10
Constitution, USS 12
Cowper 13, 147

Dartmoor Prison 12, 125–138
Davis, Joshua 44–48

Decatur 185–188
Diggio, John 10
Durand, James 11, 12, 126

Embargo 10
Enlistment 57
Escape 48, 60–63, 71–78, 102–103, 105–106, 107, 118–124, 128–130
Euclid 28

Florida 146–147
Fox Chase 145–146
France 108, 113–115, 137–138, 148–150

Gambia 24, 32
Ganges, USS 4, 124
Guerriere, USS 12

Hall, James 67
Hardy, Sir Thomas 188–200
Harwich, HMS 17–18, 21
Holland, Lord 4
Hottentotts 60–62
Howick, Lord 4, 162

Impressment 3, 11, 65, 110, 150–152, 153, 200
Indian Chief 75
Ireland 54

Jason 44
Jefferson, T. 9
Jervey, Thomas 13

King 3, 108
Kittam 30

Index

Lark, HMS 4
Law, Lyman 157–158
Leopard, HMS 7
Little Belt 11
Long Island 50, 77, 184
Low, Capt. Edward 84–85

Madison, James 111
Marblehead 127
Massacre 133–135
Massacre, Court of Inquiry 136
Melville, Lord 163–164
Minerva 53
Mirage 38–40
Molyneux, William 1, 168–170
Monroe-Pinckney 4

Nagle, Jacob 7–103
Nelson, Admiral 3, 108
Newfoundland 85, 175–176
Newspaper 116
Newton, John 17–143
Non-Importation Act 10

Opossum 53

Peace 130–156
Penny, Joshua 13, 50–65
Perseverance 51
Phillips, Isaac 4
Pierce, Nathaniel 127, 135–136, 138
Pirate agreement 85
Pirates 80–88; trials 86–88
Plantanes 25
Portuguese 141–144
President, USS 11
Press Gang 3, 8, 55, 56, 93, 101, 160, 161
Prison 100, 126–138
Prisoners of War 113, 115

Privateer 88, 127
Prize money 68, 78
Prizes 86
Protections 3, 12, 55, 56, 104–110, 158
Punishments 45, 67–68

Ramilies, HMS 188–200
Revolutionary War 183
Rio Grande 24
Roberts, Bartholomew 82
Roberts, George 84
Rodney, HMS 10

Shanghaiing 201
Shortland, Capt. 130, 135–136
Sickness 47, 56, 57, 70
Sierra Leon 22
Singleton, Capt. 140–146
Slave ships 56, 162, 165, 171–172
Spain 107–108, 141–144
Spock, James 10
Stateley, HMS 57
Storm 35–38, 52, 110
Stradley, John 88–100

Table Mountain 58, 71–74
Tingley, Capt. 4
Torpedo 187–200

Urquhart, Thomas 161–165

Victory, HMS 3

War of 1812 13, 112, 154–156
Washington, D.C. 181
Wilberforce, William 161–172
Writing 161–172

Zephyr 82

www.ingramcontent.com/pod-product-compliance
Ingram Content Group UK Ltd.
Pitfield, Milton Keynes, MK11 3LW, UK
UKHW041959140426
5217IPUK00015B/880

9 780786 443741